*Also by Rod Madocks*

Ship of Fools

Our Tan

No Way To Say Goodbye

Babbicam

The Rising Flame: Remembering Sidney Keyes

*Muzungu, musungu, mzungu, marungu, pl. wazungu, warungu.* Noun and adjective. Term for white person used in many phonic variants throughout Central and Eastern Africa. My Bemba friends tell me that it is not pejorative but sometimes it feels like it. I have heard that the word is also sometimes applied to black people who put on airs above their perceived station. It has been around a long time; the word appears in the nineteenth century David Livingstone's *Journal* and in H.M. Stanley's *Dispatches* and I found it in my father's Lozi and Chinyanja dictionaries from the 1920s. Some etymologists say it comes from a Swahili word meaning 'spin around'. White people in the old days always seemed to be turning about, staring in wonderment at the strangeness of Africa. Others link it to a generic Bantu word meaning 'to wander about'. Black African eyes likely saw the *muzungu* as a disconnected being, a lost wanderer, aimlessly drifting here and there, but not belonging to any one place.

# MUZUNGU

## A Rhodesian Testament

Rod Madocks

# Dogberry Books

# All rights reserved

ISBN (eBook): 978-1-7398164-4-5

ISBN (Paperback): 978-1-7398164-2-1

ISBN (Hardback): 978-1-7398164-3-8

www.dogberrybooks.com

www.rodmadocks.com

Cover by Oksana Chuhaevska

https://www.instagram.com/djinka_takasana/

*In memory of Peta and John, my mother and father, who loved Africa and its people.*

# Contents

# PART ONE

# 1
# Lost

*I cannot tell what part of me deceives the other.*

– Georg Büchner

I am usually lost again whenever I dream of Africa, once more adrift in the *bundu* with no map or compass to guide me. Maybe we are always lost in dreams but there is a distinct sense of panic to my African ones. In them, I inevitably seem to be threshing through head-high elephant grass, reeling in circles under a sledgehammer sun until I wake in a sweaty tangle. These dreams feed off a real event in my case. It happened in 1964 when I was twelve years old near the small town of Fort Roseberry in the country now called Zambia, then still known as Northern Rhodesia. My parents used to let me go shooting with Mr. Kruger, the local game warden. They probably thought he was personally supervising me but the truth was that he'd simply fire up his Land Rover at dawn and we'd roll out over a sandy track through the thick bush a mile or so out from his camp, where he'd stop and hand me a .22 calibre rifle and ten rounds and tell me not to come back until I'd got him a guinea fowl for his pot. The aim was for me to find my way back to his base on foot. His only guidance was not to waste ammo and to keep the escarpment of the Mansa River always to my left while heading away from camp and the reverse on my return. My parents were also probably reassured that I took our bull terrier, Buster, with me. Buster was bow-legged and not much seemed to go on inside his massy head but he would unhesitatingly attack anything that might threaten me, be it man or beast.

We drove slowly along the red sand of the track in the slanting, gauzy light. It was the height of the dry season and the scrubby *miombo* woodland formed a leafless grey-stemmed wall on each side. The night creatures had slunk away, leaving their tracks all over the sandy verges. The big game had mostly gone from the area but there were still plenty of smaller animals. I leaned out the window as we jolted along avidly scanning the dusty roadside, looking for the drag marks of porcupines, the riddling clefts of duiker and other buck, or most exciting of all, the fresh pug marks of a night leopard. I was all keyed up in intense anticipation of the hunt although I tried not to show it too much as Kruger did not favour overt displays of emotion. When we came to a creaking halt, he cut the engine, padded around to the back of the Landy, unwrapped the gun from a burlap bag and handed it to me. We'd practised with the rifle a few weeks earlier. He'd stood behind me while I'd pumped a *mopane* tree full of holes until he was satisfied I was competent. It might have been more efficient if he'd given me a shotgun to pot the elusive guinea fowl but a rifle gave you more options against the unknown threats of the bush.

"I want you back by noon, chop, chop, OK?" he ordered.

"Ja, Mr. Kruger," I replied.

He scrutinised me for a second, then nodded. Was there a hint of a smile on his tanned thin face? Hard to say. I was in awe of him. He had a strong presence, a *bwana mkubwa*, with grey eyes like chips of smoked glass under the brim of his worn slouch hat. Dad had told me Kruger had won the Military Cross leading the black infantrymen of the Northern Rhodesia regiment against the Japanese in Burma. Now he was the local game warden, shooter of rogue animals and nemesis of poachers. Rumour was that he'd slotted a few. I had once heard a local farmer referring to him as "that *hardegat*", meaning 'hard-arsed'. He was a taciturn, self-contained man who handled weapons with an easy familiarity, and who could read the bush in all its moods. I was not sure what he thought of me. I had the impression he must have confidence in me as I'd already made a few of these hunting expeditions on my own, and had gone fishing with him. I felt I'd acquitted myself honourably on these expeditions. On the other hand, maybe he merely wanted to keep well in with my Dad, a senior figure in the late colonial administration of the area.

I wanted to believe that Kruger recognised me as a kindred spirit and it was certainly true that I wanted not only to be liked by him, but also to be like him. When asked by adults what I dreamed of doing in life I'd always say "a game ranger". It was his formidable apartness, the romance of his rejection of the settled ways of most men that had entranced me. He lived in a semi-permanent camp north of Fort Roseberry. I'd heard that the young *mfazi* who worked at his place was also his wife. That was fine by me. I didn't have much time for the colour-conscious townie world my parents inhabited. Kruger's wife was a local Bemba. She never spoke to me but that morning she filled my water bottle with tea made with condensed milk and smilingly handed me a couple of packages of wrapped banana leaves, containing home-cured, incredibly savoury *biltong*.

Once he was back in the driving seat, Kruger gave me a last glance over, as if I were one of his soldiers going into action. His chilly gaze swept across the slung rifle, a single action Remington, the bulges of *biltong* packed into my shirt pockets, a water bottle slung on a canvas strap and my sheath knife strapped to my Ruzawi belt. He seemed satisfied and raised a brown forearm in mock salute,

"Good hunting," he grunted, then reversed and drove away.

The brake lights winked briefly in the soapy light like old dogs' eyes. There was the sound of chinking tail board chains for a time, then nothing but the muted sizzling of bush crickets as they warmed to their day. The wide mouth of the bush had opened up and engulfed me and Buster.

I knew I was well and truly lost by about nine that morning. The trouble began when I spotted a flock of guinea fowl. They were running in the underbrush shifting through the shadowed scrub like flowing smoke. It was incredibly hard to make out their dappled shapes and their bubbling cries kept luring me on and on. Every now and then I'd get down on one knee and draw a bead on them but I could never find a clear shot. I suppose that if Buster had been a better gun dog he would've headed them off and driven them towards me. The best he could manage was to bundle along beside me on his stumpy legs, his great puzzled head constantly turning towards me to see what I was about. I followed the guinea fowl mirage for an age, always seeming to be on the point of success, forgetting to pay any attention to where we were actually going.

At some stage, the flock evaporated into the rising heat of the day, my hunting drive slackened and I began looking for my bearings. The sun appeared to be moving in an unexpected direction and I was unsure where we were in relation to our starting point. The snaky-branched *musamba* trees hemmed us in, each one with its attendant cluster of grey-brown termite nests like crumbling totem poles. The landscape seemed impervious to orientation, wherever you looked it was identical to the adjacent parts. Buster lay down in the yellow grass, his red-rag tongue lolling. He didn't seem worried but I was filled with squirmy thoughts. *O.K., don't panic, pick a direction and stick to it*. I headed south as best I could calculate. South was good. Kruger's camp was south. My pace quickened and I became scared that Buster might run off after some creature leaving me truly alone. I attached the length of rope that acted as his leash, occasionally letting him pull me along. There was comfort in surrendering to his powerful bustling progress. At other times, I let the rope trail in the dust knowing I could always tread on it in an emergency.

We came to an outcrop of black-domed, granitic rocks and I quickly climbed up to gain a better view of my surroundings. I kept the rifle ready in case of baboons or a leopard, but had to sling it across my back to scrabble thirty feet up the smooth rock while Buster whined and peered up at me with short-sighted, worried little eyes. It was no better up top, just an unending vista of *miombo* canopy that shimmered in the haze for as far as you could see. *Sis, man! Where was I?* I pulled down my shorts and pissed over the rock. I enjoyed being diverted from my predicament, letting go and watching the flow, now going straight, now dividing and dropping to the underside of the rock. All of a sudden, a monitor lizard three feet long scrabbled out from underneath and stared back at me with a look of savage reproof. I realised then I'd been peeing down his secret nest. Africans had warned me that monitor lizards were friends of the *tokoloshe*, primordial gremlins that lurked in the bush, waiting to do you harm. It thus seemed doubly frightening to have so disrespected the big lizard. Our gardener, Musondo, had given me a smooth round stone to hold in my mouth that could render you invisible to *tokoloshe*. I wondered if it worked for angry monitor lizards also.

It was well past noon by my little, mechanical Timex and the sun was burning through the crown of my hat. I wished I could blame the *tokoloshe* for making me lost, but knew it was own stupid inattention. It was a horrible shock as I had already formed the erroneous notion by that age that my inner compass was unfailing and I could always reliably locate the correct direction whatever the circumstances. *Calm down, man.* I kept on with what seemed a southerly track until the bush opened into a grassy area and I stopped to pick out the spiky blackjack seeds that had crept into my high-sided *veldschoen* and stung my ankles. It was as I knelt there that the moment of sickening clarity came. I made out in front of me the clear curving imprint of smooth-soled boots and a dog's tracks also. I knew at once these were my own tracks and those of Buster. We'd been going in circles for hours. Time passed. Splinters of light hurt my eyes, minatory hawks circled above, as if contemplating dinner and an unseen creature kept up a baleful skreaking sound.

The heat was like a nail being slowly driven into my head. I pulled out the old military, felt-covered water bottle and drank the remains of the sweet tea, giving Buster a splash of the last of it in a cupped hand. We slogged on but ever more slowly. Buster kept looking back at me in a puzzled way. *Home boy, home, find home. Eish!* I was holding firmly to his rope now, hoping he could pull me out of this mess. At one stage, I blundered into a camel thorn shrub. The twin-bladed barbs carved a hole in my bare ankle. It bled into my *vellie* and stung grievously. Now my bare foot began skidding around in the wetness inside the boot.

Was it then or later that I lay down and cuddled Buster? I stroked his blunt muzzle, touched the crenellated, cerise patches of skin by his jowls, watching as the sun lamped through one white ear turning it rose-pink. It felt a blessing for his varmint eyes to behold me and to rest my head on his broad muscled back, the same back that Dad had broken his stick over, beating Buster for killing our neighbour's dogs. All at peace now, he held a deep, solid comfort as I buried my nose in his fur and took in his yeasty dog-smell. Did I cry a bit then? I might have although I'd already learned by then that it got you nowhere. I do know that we curled up then and slept the sleep of the doomed, the two of us together.

The sun was beginning to lose its strength when I awoke. Buster was shifting about. I remembered the biltong and shared it with my companion, both of us chewing peaceably together in the red dust next to a rocky outcrop. I was overcome then with a strange tranquillity, the dusty soil warm and comfortable beneath me, the rifle across my knees. *I know this land. I'm at home here and understand its ways.* The gun gave me confidence. I loved the burr of the stock, the nutty smell of the oiled parts. I traced with my fingers the reassuring message: *Remington Target Master Made in the U.S.A.* etched on the breech block. I knew I could fire off some signal shots but it was a small calibre weapon and the sound would likely not travel far. We were truly alone in a way that is unimaginable to the young nowadays. No phones, no drones then, *kinders.* The sun was definitely dropping now. Thoughts bubbled up of my shameful failure, the likely wrath and disappointment of Mr. Kruger and worry over what my parents might be going through. Yet, while these revolved, I calmly accepted my fate and there arose within me a determination to face up to the prospect of staying out all night.

I began to eye the jumble of black rocks above me, caulked with seams of red silt, while my tongue searched out salty traces of biltong on my dry lips. Bituminous shadows were gathering under the thorn trees. *What would it take to hunker down amid the rocks all night?* It wasn't just the predators you needed to worry about as darkness came on. Local friends had told me about lesser demons that hung about houses, the *utumbuna* and the *utuyebele*. There must surely also be special spooks that haunted rocky outcrops. The whole of Luapula Province where we lived was a witchy place and I had no charms to ward off demons, apart from the stone that Musondo had given me and I was none too sure how efficacious that one was. A protective fire would have been a good thing but I had no matches or flints, and hadn't yet learned the friction method of starting a blaze. I began to think I needed some sort of barricade and thought I could cut some acacia thorn with my sheath knife to form a mini stockade around me, a *zareba* as Kruger called it.

A *zareba* wouldn't save me from Chienge Charlie, the man-eating, white lion that I knew had once roamed not far from where I stood although my more empirical self reckoned that a hungry leopard would likely be the biggest threat. I knew leopards loved the taste of dogs, even though Buster would be no push-over. I was mulling these matters over, resting on one of the granite boulders as the air cooled, and the cape doves began their evening cooing, when I heard the clear yelping, *nkoya, nkoya* cry of a fish eagle far off to my right. It took a while to sink in but then I hooked on to it. A fish eagle always stayed by water. The only water in the dry season was at the Mansa River. Kruger's advice came back to me: if I kept moving with the Mansa to my right then I had to be heading in the right direction. I needed no further prompting and took off at a limping jog, Buster gamely trotting in front, the sun a fast-dropping balloon, turning from beaten gold to orange to umber.

We'd gone not half a mile when Buster bellied down, ears forward and a ridge of fur raised along his back. His muzzle was pointing off to the left away from our line of route. I was scared that he'd sensed a nocturnal porcupine and was going to run off to chase it. I pulled mightily on his rope but he stubbornly held his ground and started up a low rumbling growl. *Hell, man, it's a leopard. Now we're really in it.* All sorts of fearful thoughts welled but Buster was insistent. I crouched down next to him, racked a round into the breech and tried to scan for whatever he'd picked up.

It was hard to see in the charcoal light but then I heard it... *tink, tonk, tink, tonk* ...the unmistakable sound of domestic animal bells. They grew louder until a flop-eared lead goat appeared outlined against the pale grass, followed by several more goats and a boy herder with raggedy shorts and holding a long stick. I ran forward out of the half-dark and called out to him, *"We!"* meaning, 'Hey there!' I babbled away at him, and could have hugged him on the spot but he backed away from me. I must have scared him, a wild-eyed, rifle-toting *muzungu* kid erupting out from the dark. He was also probably worried since he wasn't supposed to be grazing his flock in a game conservancy area. Buster must have looked none too reassuring either, and was taking an unhealthy interest in the goats. I wrapped his leash more tightly around my hand and hauled him back, while also asking the kid where Bwana Kruger's camp was. He only said, *"Pepi"*, meaning 'near', and pointed with his chin.

I immediately set off in the direction the goatherd indicated, calling back thanks to him until he and his goats were swallowed up by the dark. Not long after, Buster and I came upon a pale ribbon of a dirt road that I could just make out was covered with fresh tyre tracks. It had to be the same one we'd driven up that morning. I started scurrying along it just as the sun dropped down behind the tree line and everything was consumed by the intense, velvety black of

African twilight. The sound of three evenly spaced rifle shots told me Kruger was not far off and I popped off three in return. It was the only time I'd fired all day.

A madly bucking Landy, headlights blazing through billowing dust clouds came charging up the track to meet me. Kruger jumped out and held me by the shoulders shouting, "Are you alright, boy? Where the hell have you been?" I affected nonchalance and when questioned about what had happened, attempted to explain casually that I'd travelled a bit farther than I'd thought, giving him some nonsense about how I'd shot a duiker, wounded it and spent all day tracking it. When he asked me what I'd done with the animal I hesitated and said I thought some jackals had taken it. This was probably a lie too far but I expect he was too relieved to have found me to question me much. I heard him tell his woman in Bemba that the boy claimed he'd spent all day chasing a wounded buck. At that, there came the sound of high-pitched giggling laughter in the African manner, "Ki, ki, ki." This wasn't the first of many improbable lies I told in childhood to shield myself from the wrath of adults.

Kruger drove me straight home after he'd got some supper and sweet tea down me at his camp and Buster had been given a deep drink of water. My Dad was standing in our driveway with a paraffin lantern awaiting us. He told Kruger he had been on the point of ordering up the Boma Land

Rover with a squad of rifle-toting District Messengers to go out to look for me. Kruger offered laconic apologies and I could tell he was annoyed with me for getting him into trouble. I felt I'd let him down but mainly I was thankful to have got away with so disrespecting the bush as to get myself lost. I was soon in bed with a purple daubing of permanganate on my ankle wound. Buster had to be woken from an exhausted slumber to eat his dinner. Next day, I went to the market and spent my pocket money on some fly-blown bones of a cow culled from the Boma herd to reward him for helping me to make my way home.

*Buster on his rope leash, Fort Roseberry, 1964*

Nothing more was said about the incident but I was never allowed out shooting with Mr. Kruger again. Looking back now, maybe all of life is a process of becoming lost and finding your way again by luck or calculation. Often since boyhood, I have felt I was going in circles once more. The question that gets louder and more insistent as I age is: how to find my way home when I am lost in the shipwreck of the years? I know that to find yourself you need to walk on the waters of your uncertain past. May this book chart that process. Only by writing and rewriting it will the hand live up to the heart's knowledge. Too many times, the incessant turmoil of the world has dragged me round in mistaken circles to half-baked approximations of the truth. I think I'm going to try and find Buster's leash again, that ribbon, the thread that I can grasp like Theseus to lead me out from the mazy bushlands of the past.

# 2
# Muzungu Chronicles

*It takes time to ruin a world but time is all it takes.*

– Le Bouvier de Fontenelle

Back then, you could leave Lusaka at first light, the dawn an apricot smudge behind the garden flame trees, and the first cape doves beginning their *kwerr kwok kwok* sound, and you'd take the Great East Road to Fort Jameson. Seventy five miles out, it would be a relief at first to leave the endless, sun-shimmering tarmac strip, with the brutal hammering of its corrugated sections and take a dirt turnoff to the left. There used to be an old Game and Fisheries sign to mark the turning but most of those that came already knew the place deep in their bones. This side road was soon a narrow track. The Land Rover would begin to slew in the sandy berm and red dust plumed in its wake. An hour or so of drubbing and the mopane and mwena trees began to crowd the way and the track would give out so even a Landy would have to stop.

From then on you were on foot on the rocky escarpment of the Northern Luano.

Nowadays, I'm told that motocross bikes buzz around the slopes, charcoal burners have nearly stripped the once limitless trees and most of the animals have been snared for bushmeat. In those days though, it was good hunting. It would take you all day to descend the precipitous bluffs into valleys filled with game and you could fish for giant *vundu* catfish in the slow brown rivers. You felt you were in the remote old heart of the continent and pushing through the thickety scrub at the confluence of the Lukasashi and Lunsemfwa rivers, you might find mysterious columns of stone and fallen embrasures, seemingly as ancient as the centuries old ruins of Great Zimbabwe. When asked, the local Soli people would tell you this was all that remained of Changa-Changa's house.

Forgotten now, Chief Changa-Changa of the Senga was once a titan ruling most of what is now southern Zambia. His real name was John Harrison Clark. He came to the Luano on the run from a killing in South Africa in the 1880s, before the region was colonised. In a fashion evocative of Kipling's contemporaneous tale, *The Man Who Would Be King*, Clark single-handedly came to dominate the local tribes and ended up commanding eight thousand spears. His word was law by the time he built his fort-like house in the Luano and flew the Red Ensign over it. He achieved his power by beating off rival tribes and expelling the Arab slavers and their African allies, as well as by marrying into the Chikunda paramountcy. From his fort, he reigned for two decades, until he was driven away by a new generation of empire builders and mining companies who outmanoeuvred and outgunned him. Cecil Rhodes' British South Africa Company built forts in his territory, finally forcing him from his house so that by the early years of the new century it was abandoned to termites and bush.

Clark ended up in the nearest large town, Broken Hill. Hard-handed and fierce, he remained a legendary presence who lived by wheeling and dealing. Amongst many other activities, he ran a brewery and owned the first motor car in Northern Rhodesia. He proudly carried his *Mashukulumbwe* tribal title, 'Changa-Changa' until the end of his life. It apparently meant 'it all belongs to me', though I've also heard it translated as 'clever-clever'. His name reflected Clark's immense drive and self-belief. Maybe there was a hint of mockery in it. Africans like to make sly fun of their rulers. Ambition so often comes to nothing amid the will-sapping realities of the continent, much as things don't end well in the far-off Hindu Kush for Kipling's 'King of Kafiristan'.

Clark died in Broken Hill in late middle age, officially of heart disease, though perhaps it would be better to say of heartbreak. Hundreds of tribesmen came to his funeral. I was to be born in the same place some twenty years after he'd gone. Once, in the early 1960s, I overheard our Lamba gardener refer to my dad as a 'Changa-Changa'. The title had persisted and spread, having come to mean 'local leader' or 'big boss' in modern Zambian usage. There are even schools and hotels called Changa-Changa, local people having now lost all memory of its legendary origin.

The Chinyanja-speaking folk where we lived in Fort Jameson also used the word *changa* for the bush-baby, that soft-furred, goggle-eyed, nocturnal creature. These people were somewhat scared of *changas* and warily relayed to me they were the ghosts of witches who screamed in the night. I kept one as a pet and named him — Changa-Changa, of course. He crawled about my bedroom after lights out and peed down my curtains. I fed him on grasshoppers and loved him dearly but my parents complained about his occult nightly squeaks and shrieks and I was commanded to free him one evening, which I did by placing him in the lower branches of a cassia tree in our garden. I trained my torch on him as he rapidly skittered upwards, then turned and took a last haunted look back at me with his glowing eyes.

"Goodbye, Changa-Changa," I whispered, a moment later, he'd gone.

The rains have washed through for fifty seasons and more since my family were last in Africa. My father was among those in charge of planning for our own removal in the form of the Zambian independence arrangements. The whites have long since disappeared, like most of the big game. They have been replaced by the Chinese who are the new Changa-Changas, so they say. Broken Hill, where I was born and where Clark is buried, is now called Kabwe. It is one of the most polluted places in Africa these days, thanks to the residues from unregulated lead mining.

Displacement is nothing new there. It is the African rhythm. Clark's Senga army was a temporary bulwark against Mpizeni's militant Ngoni who swept north in the 1880s in response to Zulu and Matabele migrations. The Senga and Chewa were pushed into the Eastern Luano shortly before Clark's time, having been displaced from their original homes in Malawi. Prior to this, the Lamba originally came down from the Congo to occupy what is now Kabwe, while long before all that, the Lunda Kingdom held sway over the area for two centuries from the 1600s. The Lunda subjugated, tithed and, in effect, colonised large reaches of northern Zambia and Angola before they, in turn, were forced to give way to fierce Chokwe invaders, armed with European weapons. Former vassals of the Lunda, the Chokwe in turn made slaves of their previous overlords. It is a myth that any one people are the original owners of the ground they stand on across all of the African continent. I certainly understood from early on that we, the *wazungu,* occupied only a brief moment, a wink of light amidst all the sun-dazed aeons of Africa.

As far as I can tell there now exist only three entities that can legitimately be called Rhodesian: a disease called 'Trypanosoma rhodesiense', which causes a particularly nasty form of sleeping sickness; the large, russet dog known as the 'Rhodesian Ridgeback', bred by the early settlers for hunting in the veldt, a faithful guard and lion-chaser but not really suited to urban life; and 'Homo rhodesiensis', a thick-browed hominid ancestor who lurked around the rock shelters along the Mulungushi river, some 300,000 years ago. Known only from a single find, usually referred to now as 'Kabwe Skull' in order to avoid mentioning the politically-suspect 'R' word.

Change the name, change the past; that's today's progressive mantra. We are besieged by erstwhile intellectuals in the humanities and social sciences with blindingly simplified and intolerant views. It does amuse me how much they unwittingly copy the imperialists of yore, whom they so detest, by inventing new myths about history, failing, like their similarly sanitising predecessors, to heed the contending voices that are still trying to reach us from out of the contradictory past. Listen to the ghosts, I say. They come from a landscape of savage, ever-changing light and shadow. The dead Lunda will tell you. Or their children, rescued from the slaver, Tippoo-Tip and his ilk. The menace of the Arabs and the Chikunda warriors with chains who came from the East was still a folk memory among the Bemba when I was a boy. Although few know it, and no one dares admit it nowadays, it was actually that current day arch-villain, Cecil Rhodes, who funded the forts and soldiers that ultimately crushed the East African slave traders after ten years of bloody struggle.

At boarding school in Marandellas, in Southern Rhodesia, a place designed for educating the male children of white farmers and soldiers, and run along military lines, I used to lie on rough blue dormitory blankets for the obligatory one hour siesta held in the early afternoon. While most of the others slept through the heat, I would sit up reading Kipling, particularly *The Jungle Book*. His stories made so much more sense to me than the anodyne English serial books for boys that my parents sent to me. I wonder now if I read Kipling so avidly because his stories were a reflection of my own future memories. I particularly enjoyed the tale of *The King's Ankus*, about an old king cobra who guarded the treasures of an ancient Indian kingdom in a hidden cavern, killing any tomb robbers who crossed his path. Then as now, I was enamoured of this image and, in a sense, I've ended up like that old king cobra, the last of my kind, brooding over the relics of a lost civilisation. Most of all though, I thrilled to Mowgli's song of threat to the city people:

*I will let loose against you the fleet-footed vines.*
*I will call in the Jungle to stamp out your lines!*
*The roofs will fade before it, the house-beams shall fall.*
*And the Karela, the bitter Karela, shall cover you all!*

I've often found myself reciting those favourite childhood lines when I ponder over how all that was good about the world I grew up in has been heedlessly besmirched and erased along with the bad in the crass name of 'historical re-evaluation'.

Browsing in the local markets around Fort Roseberry, you'd sometimes find heaps of the horned Momordica fruit, the bitter gourd or *karela* of Mowgli's song. The healers that were called *sangomas* or *siamas* and the wise women used the plant for purges and to cure all manner of afflictions. I find it incredible to think that this rampaging creeper that loves to inhabit ruins began life in Africa, then passed, over occult trade routes, through deep reaches of human time until it arrived in South Asia and many other places at least six thousand years ago, where it was domesticated and incorporated into Ayurvedic medicine, only to escape thereafter and run wild again all over the tropical world.

Maybe in Europe and the Americas a frost-resistant variant is, even now, mutating itself into being.

During the Second World War, Rhodesia sent more men, black and white, relative to its size than any other Commonwealth country to aid Britain in those perilous years. It never ceases to amaze me how much those of us former Rhodesians who were white came to be hated by the establishment intelligentsia of the country to whose aid we had so willingly come. It shouldn't do but, even after half a century, it still comes as a shock to me whenever I encounter that ingratitude and loathing. Only recently, an English friend of mine who has known me and my history for forty years told me that whenever he heard a Rhodesian or South African accent it made his skin crawl, as if all African whites were, and would ever remain, Apartheid supporters.

Well, if it's to be such a despised identity then let me get closer to it. That's the contrarian in me, the exile and the writer — Changa-Changa's legatee, who dreams of the day when the big game can safely return to wander the far-off, desolated Luano.

# 3
# My Inheritance

*Once bitten by a snake, he fears a rope.*

– African proverb

Voices, now clear, now murmuring and mumbling like bad reception on the radio, the clinking of ice in cocktail glasses, Doris Day singing, *Sugarbush, I love you so,* the lisp of bare feet on hardwood parquet flooring, Jonas intoning, "Yes, medem". Memories from within the womb when Mum and I were interfused and living off the same nourishments. Images too of my becoming: Dad standing in the portico of Broken Hill Hospital in a midnight thunderstorm; the obliterating roar of the rains on the flat roofs, the cicadas silenced; smell of wet earth wrapping around him as he paces; an unlit pipe clenched in his teeth, hands fisted deep into his khaki drill pockets; waiting, waiting, for mine was a long difficult birth; the wiry red-gold of the Scots doctor's moustache as he sought to reassure. A Caesarean was going to be necessary.

"This bairn does not want to come out and see the world. We will have to help him," Doctor Todd had said. All the hopes and wishes Dad must have had for me, all his fears for his wife. I was, even then, at once a hope for the foundation of a family and a hazard to the well-being of the mother. I've always liked the Buddhist idea that when a baby is born, it falls asleep and dreams its life, waking only when the end is reached. What a dream mine has been, oftentimes a nightmare.

My family moved every two years during the African years, shifting from one remote posting to another, so I can date my early memories quite accurately if I know their location.

My earliest distinct recollection is from 1956, of our garden in Fort Jameson, which now bears the decolonized name of Chipata. My mother and I had gone for a walk in the high grass beyond the msasa trees that marked our garden boundary. In the middle of our stroll, the cicadas ceased stridulating all at once, plunging us into sinister silence that signalled trouble. We were accompanied by Buster's predecessors, our rugged bull terrier dogs and the quiet was torn open by their furious barking at something in the thick grass. Then came the unmistakable coughing snarl of an angry leopard.

Mum was visibly frightened and began to run for home, dragging me after her by the wrist while the dogs battled the unseen enemy following us. It seemed to take an age to toil through the thick bush, trying to gain the safety of our compound as the vegetation around us vibrated to the nearby sounds of frenzied animal combat between our dogs and the big cat. We got back to our place and ran across the grass trying to shout for help to Dad who at first did not hear us. So, my first memory was also my first nightmare, one of struggling to escape great danger.

Actually, the leopard would probably not have attacked us so we were likely not in much danger. Still, the whole event seemed unutterably frightening at the time and forever set in my mind the notion that nature was both intensely beautiful and potentially lethal. When our dogs came trotting back later with bloody muzzles, they seemed none the worse for the altercation.

Although Mum rescued me from the ravaging leopard, she was also a source of fear to me. She tried to show love by tending to me, providing food and shelter but if you went too close to her, she couldn't help pinching, grabbing by the ear, or flicking painfully with a damp tea towel. Things could occasionally escalate into something much worse, explosions of fury when she'd lash out far more harshly. I got cigarette burns and dodged glass ashtrays flung at me in sudden rages.

Once she pounded me on the head with a stiletto-heeled shoe while I begged her to stop. At other times, she upended hot meals over me and administered stinging slaps. While it didn't happen constantly, it occurred with enough frequency to make me wary. I usually had done something to launch the attack, some naughtiness or clumsiness, but once I grew older, I came to understand that other mothers were not like mine, and that her reactions were off the scale.

Mum seemed to have a problem with maleness, or maybe couldn't handle an impulsive boy. It always seemed to be me who bore the brunt of her explosive fury, rather than my younger sister, Susan. Mum craved control and treated minor disruptions as disasters, slapping me down for the slightest infractions. It was as if she carried a molten terror within her that could erupt at any moment, like the time when I was about eight and went out fishing in a rowboat on a lake where I promptly fell into the water. She rushed me home and thrust me into a bath filled with kerosene in an effort to kill off any bilharzia parasites that might have been lurking in the water waiting to burrow into my innards. The reeking bath was bad enough but Mum's slapping and punching me at the same time cancelled out any good intentions. It was if her fears for me ineluctably transformed into wrath that I had caused her to be frightened in the first place.

Following her losses of control, Mum would bring me offerings of food, which I intuitively understood were her way of trying to make amends, even though she never said she was sorry at the time. It's a truism of clinical psychology that aggression may be an inverted way of showing love in humans, and can be especially prominent in a troubled mother's love for a child. But the child has no idea about such things. Mum's rage came from a secret place that we could only guess at. We knew nothing about her life before she met Dad yet somehow, even as children, Susan and I realised that our mother had been shaped by hurtful forces and could not help herself. I believe it was the philosopher, Nietzsche, who said that one should live dangerously and "build on the slopes of Vesuvius". Well, we didn't need the shadow of a volcano over us, we had Mum instead.

While it was obvious that Mum was beleaguered by an ever-present host of possible threats, I realised in adulthood that my otherwise robust and resilient Dad was also subject to disproportionate fears for us derived from his wartime experiences. Whenever we went out for walks in Africa, he'd warn against letting ourselves be silhouetted against the skyline. Passing through open grasslands with the dogs, he'd gesture with his stick and call out to us, "No bunching up!" as if recalling all the soldiers he'd lost to machine gun and artillery fire.

When I was sent off, aged seven, to my tough Southern Rhodesian boarding school, Dad gave me a photo of himself to take with me and I looked at it countless times during those early scary years of my schooling. The photo, taken in May of 1945 at Wismar on the Elbe, shows him on a horseback. He was, at that time, a major in the elite Sixth Airborne Division, the first mission of which was to secure the left flank of the Allied forces at the Normandy landings. He was only twenty-one when the photo was taken but he looked much older. The war had given him a premature, battle-hardened solidity. His unit had fought its way across northern France, Belgium and Germany during the previous year and a third of his men had been lost as casualties. That May, his unit was the first to meet Admiral von Friedeberg's deputation to offer the surrender of all German Forces in the West. Dad told me that his hard-bitten paratroopers had roughed up the German officers, taking their hats and decorations as souvenirs, but Dad had made them return these, and sent the delegation on to Divisional headquarters at Luneburg Heath for their subsequent newsreel appearances all over the world.

The photo, which I still have, shows Dad in his best battledress. You can see the Pegasus emblem of the Airborne Forces on his left shoulder. He is packing a 9mm Browning officer's pistol, the butt of which is sticking out from the holster flap. They needed to be vigilant as there were still threats, even though the war had ended. He told me how his men killed several holdouts from the Werewolf organisation after the surrender. Dad didn't really like horses and this is my only picture of him on one. Someone has tacked up the beast incorrectly and the neck strap is placed far too high. Perhaps an unwilling German prisoner had been dragooned into the work. Dad once explained that there were German military stables at his headquarters, and that he and his brother officers had commandeered the horses for a lark, which makes it essentially his victory photo.

*Major J.E. Madocks, Wismar, 1945*

So, that was the picture which accompanied me to boarding school. I struggle to imagine what I made of it at the time. As a child living in late-colonial Africa, I was used to seeing Dad in khaki shorts and bushshirt, or lightweight

Italian-style suits. He usually looked suntanned and Clark Gable-ish, with his pencilled moustache and wavy hair so this military equestrian pose must have seemed strange to me. I think he chose it for what it represented to him — a celebration of triumph over suffering and fear. It implied that you– that I – could survive anything and come out stronger. I think that I understood it similarly. It was an image of my Dad as the hero he then was to me, a man who dispatched all obstacles with the same aplomb, like the time he got our stuck Land Rover out of a muddy ditch in the Luangwa, while a pride of lions hunkered nearby. He turned his back on the lions and calmly instructed Mum how to steer the vehicle while he pushed. I kept glancing back through the rear hatch window at the tawny, menacing shapes creeping closer and closer, while Dad coolly ignored the danger and got the job done.

*My Mother, Peta Madocks, in 1964*

Mum, on the other hand, chose a quite different sort of photo to accompany me to school. Hers was a more familiar image than Dad's though, like his, it was a posed shot. It must have been a studio picture taken in Lusaka. I remember that blouse with its green and mustard floral decorations from that time. At first, Mum's image seems to be gazing straight at you but on closer examination she's actually looking above the camera. I used to hold the photo in my small hand during those early homesick years of schooling in an attempt to take some comfort there. She sent me loving letters every week but I already knew it was almost impossible to hold onto her. She often used to say that she wished I was still a baby.

"You were a perfect baby," she liked to say, "So quiet in your cot."

I suspect she found it easier to give love to an infant that had not yet formed a distinct identity. Maturation brought too many troubling demands. I have a vivid memory of myself at five years old in our house in Fort Jameson. She'd invited some women friends for a social gathering and, for some reason feeling needy, I approached her and moved toward her as if to nestle at her breast and suckle.

"That's not for you anymore," she said, pushing me away while the other women laughed uproariously and I ran off burning with shame.

A combination of the neuroses of my parents and the realities of life in late-stage colonial Africa imbued me early with the notion that bad stuff could, and most likely would, imminently happen. Aged five, I witnessed a village dog being bitten by a puff adder. It ran for a while in diminishing circles until it dropped, sides heaving as it lay in the dust until, all of a sudden, its panting stopped. Or there was the time my game warden mentor, Mr. Kruger, shot a marauding leopard in Fort Roseberry and brought the body to the Government headquarters Boma in the back of a Landy. A thick, black column of fleas, abandoning their felled host, streamed across the vehicle's corrugated aluminium floor. Or there was the car crash at Kabulonga. A Zephyr Zodiac had smashed into a street lamp and its pole had fallen onto the car. All you could see was a pair of bloody hands still grasping the wheel, with the pole where the head should have been. The public works men sang a work chant as they lifted it off the dead man.

Then there was the village headman killed by the African nationalist party, U.N.I.P., at Fort Roseberry during the sectarian battles in the run-up to independence. The Messengers brought the corpse for Dad to view, using a ladder as a bier. The dead old man had a grey furzed chin tuft, no shirt, threadbare shorts and bare feet with wisps of dried grass still caught between the toes. His eyes were open and sunk into his head like two prunes. He had a wide red hole in the dusty black skin of his chest. They'd used a muzzle-loader on him, with a heap of rusty nails for ammo, one of the policemen said.

Lastly, there was the time I was riding my bike through the shambas when I ran into an African nationalist political meeting of labourers. When the first few rocks came crashing down around me, one smashed into the wheel of my bike and wrenched it out of my hands. Next thing I knew, an angry tumult broke out and a hail of stones came flying my way. A moment later, dozens of Africans were running towards me shouting, *"Bulala muzungu!"* I knew that meant, 'Burn the whitey!' They made a humming sound like a swarm of angry bees as they advanced rapidly towards me waving axes and hoes. I fled as fast as I could, certain in the knowledge they'd kill me if they caught me.

# 4
# Ek Se

*You who never arrived*

*In my embrace.*

*You who were lost from the start.*

– Rainier Maria Rilke

In my boarding school days, I liked to copy my Rhodie chums by saying *ek se* all the time. The words were borrowed from Afrikaans and meant 'So I say' or 'I tell you'. It was pronounced something like "akhshai" and was used exclusively when males spoke to one another. The female form was *stekkie*. The phrase really didn't mean anything. It was simply an emphatic interjection that identified you as a tough guy so we added it to every sentence. It drove most of our parents mad. If, for example, I said, "Agh, ja, Pa, I'll drag my katundu out of here, now-now, ek se!" that really meant something more like, "Yeah sure, Dad, I'll take my stuff out of here sometime, maybe never, know what I mean." It used to irk my folks no end whenever I came out with clipped Afrikaans-inflected slang. They kept on trying to correct my speech to 'proper' English.

Only decades later did I realise that it must have worried them a great deal to realise that their son had formed an unambiguously African identity. It was already becoming clear to them by then that white Rhodesians had no future on the continent of their birth. I suppose that's part of the reason much of my adult life has been spent looking for my *Gummadoolahs*, another word we Rhodesian kids used. It meant your special place, your Never-Neverland, someplace to dream about that was known only to yourself and your god, a lush greensward in the dried-out bushlands that maybe existed out beyond the Limpopo, a paradise you could never reach, however hard you tried. We used it mainly as a jokey expression but sometimes in a wistful sense. We knew that it was a delusion yet we kept on dreaming of finding it one day. I think now that the *Gummadoolahs* makes an apt name for our unled lives, the African lives we missed out on after being forced down different roads. We white Rhodesians became *disjecta membra*, a shameful diaspora from Africa, banished to all the corners of the world and not to be spoken of in polite society.

In the contemporary common mind, the land where I grew up has become incontrovertibly associated with the futile obduracy of the Ian Smith Rhodesian regime, which ruled the nation that is now Zimbabwe from 1964 to 1979, so that nowadays British university students, in the grip of chiliastic fervour, like to seek out statues of Cecil Rhodes in order to topple and deface them. In reality, however, there were two Rhodesias. The other one, which is now Zambia, was the northern part where my home was, largely peaceful and rich in copper, timber and agriculture. Democracy might have been lacking there but the country was managed with humane efficiency by a small band of administrators, of whom my father was one. Northern Rhodesia was not officially a colony, but rather a 'Protectorate', where in contrast to the South, everything remained regulated by the British Government.

The whites I knew at home seemed mainly to be favourably disposed toward the black majority, although both groups led largely separate lives and, even as a small boy, I could sense that tensions simmered beneath the surface. I noticed early on, and often wondered why, black Africans tended to step aside from us on the street, as if obeying some unwritten rule and it was clear even to my child's eyes that black Africans were desperately poor in comparison to us whites. As such, I came to feel a keen sense of embarrassment, even shame, when I looked into the eyes of the black people.

By the time I entered my second decade, I grasped that while officials like my father were earnestly working to build up organisational capacity among the educated African elite, black people still had little or no voice in the running of their country. In contrast to other parts of Africa, however, there was virtually no corruption and far fewer cruelties were inflicted upon the black population compared to South Africa, or so I gradually gleaned, to regions ruled by the French, Belgians or Portuguese.

Life in the countryside, where we lived, tended, in the main, to be well-regulated and harmonious. The remote areas also seemed to abound with eccentrics like the French priest from the order known as the White Fathers who came to visit us now and then. He wore a sun helmet and a long, white, grubby soutane, and chain-smoked Springbok cigarettes while telling us tales of his adventures as an officer in the Spahi Light Cavalry. I can still see his capacious sleeves whirling as he made slashing movements to demonstrate sabre strokes.

Or there was Sir Stewart Gore-Brown, a friend of my parents, who fervently supported African liberationist politics yet built a stately home in the bush, or an Afrikaaner farmer whose Morris Vanette was permanently stuck in reverse gear so that he drove everywhere backwards at tremendous speed. As the small European community of Northern Rhodesia began to diminish in the 1960s, its white population dwindling away in the wake of massacres of settlers in the Congo, or the Mau Mau blood-letting in Kenya, many of these eccentrics held out, generally retreating further into the bush as independence approached, until in October of 1964, Northern Rhodesia finally became Zambia.

*Serenje, Northern Rhodesia, 1959. Dad jests with tribal leaders as he tries out a wooden club. Mum (in hat and floral dress) examines a garden rake.*

Given how social relations stood at home, it came as quite a shock when, at the age of eight, I was sent off to boarding school in Southern Rhodesia. All our countries were nominally united under 'The Federation of Rhodesia and Nyasaland' yet Southern Rhodesia gave off a distinct heady, testosterone-touched scent of biltong, boerewors and cordite.

Our classrooms tended to feature idealised illustrations of events like the Shangani Patrol, a famous last stand by a group of thirty-odd white soldiers against thousands of Matabele warriors in 1894. It is said that Lobengula, the Matabele chief, sought peace terms after the battle because his warriors had lost their stomach to fight against larger numbers of Rhodesians, a handful of hard men had thinned their ranks too grievously on the Shangani.

Southern Rhodesia was, of course, cast in the image of its southern neighbour, South Africa. White South Rhodesians were more numerous and cohesive, and liked to refer to the part of Rhodesia I came from as 'The Black North', maintaining that Africans there had got the better of the British and would soon hold "the whip hand". I immediately observed the greater apartness of white and black there, and could hear how white people used sharp, impatient tones when they ordered their servants about in Chilapalapa, a pidgin first developed in the mines that blended many African languages. I remember uneasily watching from the sidelines on a rare occasion when a black school played us at football and my fellow pupils deliberately stamped with their metal-studded boots on the black boys' bare feet. The black team bore it silently, while I pondered what they must have thought of us.

If my schoolmates were worried as nations all over Africa became independent, they didn't show it. I couldn't help but admire their sang-froid and the way their roots went deep into the rich, red, Rhodie soil. The signs of trouble were there though. In July of 1964, Piet Oberholzer, a foreman at a lumber plant was killed by ZANU guerrillas at a roadblock and petrol was poured over his family as they cowered in a VW Combi. That happened at Melsetter, just east of my school on the Umtali road. Oberholzer is now recognised as the first white casualty of the Bush War. The eventual destruction of white society was years off but after that incident, the school stopped us sleeping out on verandas under the African night sky for fear of grenades.

One day, some of us were taken to watch the Rhodesian African Rifles parading out of their Bulawayo barracks. The R.A.R. were the senior black regiment in the Rhodesian Army, Karanga tribesmen and Shangaans mainly. When they sang their famous regimental song in Shona, *Who Will Buy Me a Sweet Banana*, I was bewitched by the spectacle of the ranks of those hundreds of black soldiers in their tasselled fezzes singing in unison in resonant baritone. I can recall thinking then that I would not want to live anywhere else in the world but bitter events were already stirring and, within a handful of years, my family would fly away to England, while many of those peerless soldiers were to fight and die in the name of Rhodesia, and few were to survive the nationalist victors' later revenges on them.

When I was about twelve, I bought an African grey parrot. The bird was imprisoned in a homemade wire basket attached to the back of a dilapidated bicycle being wheeled along under the Flamboyant Trees on Cairo Road in Lusaka. After some haggling, the villager with the bike sold me the orphaned bird for 'a tickey coin', our term for a silver threepenny bit. The creature didn't thank me for this rescue. It was miserable and unpredictable. I once caught our cook, Jonas, holding a meat cleaver over its head because it had savaged his thumb. He told me it was *chitipu,* meaning it carried a curse or bane. "Best to get rid," Jonas opined. Eventually, I let the poor thing go in our Lusaka garden but it seemed frightened of the city, so different from its forest home. It spent weeks haunting the garden, fluttering above our heads. emitting loud reproachful shrieks until, at last, it disappeared.

I bought the parrot during our last year in Africa. Local kids used to run after our colonial official's car and wave as we passed through their villages but, in 1964, they started yelling out the word *Kwacha!* It was a new, nationalist political slogan, meaning 'Dawn', intended to imply that a new day was coming for Africans. Jonas instructed me not to go out cycling any longer in the *shambas,* the market gardens that surrounded the city, after I narrowly escaped a man out collecting firewood, who loped after me waving an axe and screaming with fury while I pedalled frantically to get away. I could hardly make out what he was shouting but the word 'muzungu' featured prominently. I sensed strongly that he would have chopped me up if only he could have.

The old order was passing and the dissolution of our corner of the Empire sent us back to the country of my ancestors shortly after. My parents called England 'Home' but when we settled back there I felt like that lost African Grey, hemmed in by claustrophobic English suburbia, while I cried out, albeit inwardly, for my lost home and all the future African friends and lovers whom I would never clasp to me now.

# 5
# Scars

*A scar nobly got, or a noble scar, is a good livery of honour*

*So belike is that.*

– Shakespeare

As a child, I was fascinated by the whorls of ridged, putty-like scars on the faces of Tonga tribesmen. Jonas told me that they used an acacia thorn to prise the skin open, then inserted soot, ash, dung and grit to form a bead of scar tissue. Those scars showed that they were *echt* people. They had proven their authenticity on their bodies. You would often see tattoos and burn marks on the skin to ward off witches and spells. There were many scarred faces among the District Messengers, the gendarmerie who enacted my father's orders. These marks came from either tribal decoration or from smallpox. Some of the men had stretched and pierced ear-lobes and the clerks in the Messenger depot sometimes used these as handy places to keep their government blue pencils!

Sergeant Limbani was the N.C.O. in charge of the Fort Jameson District Messengers. He was a Chewa, I think and his name meant 'strong'. His face was marked by both smallpox and battle scars from his service fighting the Italians in Somalia during the war. Everyone was a bit scared of Sergeant Limbani, including my father. He radiated complete authority, although his face always seemed to be totally impassive. He snapped "Leka!" meaning 'Desist!' when he caught me bribing his men with sweets to let me hold their .303 rifles and I never dared do it again. Dad told me that on parade during a dignitary's visit one of his young, white officer cadets, crazed by an overnight drinking session, had stripped all his clothes off and lined up totally naked alongside the ranks of Messengers. Sergeant Limbani had promptly dealt with the deranged man by whisking him away to the guardroom before marching up to Dad, saluting and barking out, "All men ready for inspection, but no Bwana Humphreys."

"Where is Bwana Humphreys, Sergeant?" asked Dad, trying to interpret Limbani's blank countenance.

"*Malisece*, very *malisece*, Sah!" replied the unflappable sergeant. This meant 'nude, very nude, Sir'.

"I see, carry on, Sergeant."

Dad knew better than to interrogate that scarred mask-like face any further. He would find out from the other men what had really happened and grasped that Limbani saw it as beneath his dignity to explain further. Needless to say, Cadet Humphreys was never seen by us again.

*Sergeant Limbani, almost front and centre, at inspection with his men. He stands next to Governor Benson in a hat, with my father left, Fort Jameson, 1959.*

I vaguely aspired to scars along the lines of Sergeant Limbani's and at boarding school in Southern Rhodesia I was to be granted the opportunity to acquire some. Up until the age of eight, I'd been left to run wild in the bush and I received little or no education as there were no actual schools to attend. I went to some classes run by missionaries, and had a few spells of formal schooling when we lived in the city briefly but most of my learning came from Mum. She taught me how to read and write using a book called *Bambi's Children*. This was followed by the more sophisticated *Heidi* and *Babar the Elephant*. Mum was an effective teacher, possibly because I wanted to learn quickly in order not to try her patience too much.

My free life came to a sudden end when I was sent a thousand miles south to Ruzawi School. There, I soon learned the proper meaning of fear under a regime of pointless rules enforced by regular beatings from 'the masters', although the chief terror came from the insane cruelties that the boys meted out to each other.

I received some vicious canings at Ruzawi. Often, they were so hard that my backside bled afterwards and crusted into my underwear. I could tell that the men who dealt these thrashings out enjoyed the experience by the grunting sound they emitted as they whipped me and by their flushed faces afterwards. My first and worst beating was from Mr. Curtis, the headmaster. I still remember with a shudder the red fuzz that covered Curtis's sinewy arms. His victims were usually summoned by Freddy, the school's African porter. Freddy called for me within my first fortnight at the school. I walked behind him down the elegant colonnade of the Dutch colonial-style building, staring all the while at the stiff pleats in the back of his starched khaki shirt and concomitantly filling with a growing premonition that something horrible was about to happen.

The Rhodesian boys in my class who'd seen it all dozens of times before whispered to me at the sight of Freddie,

"Watch out, man, you're going to get the *stok*." That was the Afrikaans word for the cane. My crime had been failure to memorise the catechism — it was a High Church Anglican school and laid great store in such things. Curtis explained in a calm tone that he intended to beat me and instructed me that I was to shake his hand afterwards and thank him, otherwise he'd beat me again. He then took off his jacket, rolled up his sleeves and washed his hands. I watched as he reached up to the glass-fronted cabinet that contained rows of canes. His strong fingers ran over the rounded handles until they stopped on one and drew the stick out.

The six ruthless lashes jolted through me like fiery electric shocks and the leather armchair over which I was bent juddered forward a few inches with each heavy whop. My backside felt as if it were crumpling under relentless blows and my face filled with scalding tears of rage and self-pity. I shook his hand afterwards and limped away to the door-less school lavatories where one boy advised me to sit in a basin to cool my flaming hind parts. Blood drooled through my shorts. I showed my stained garments to my school buddies like a virgin displaying the wedding sheets. I had my first scars.

Many more beatings followed. I grew hardened to them and, in turn, took pleasure in capturing new boys and whipping them with belts or straps of sisal. It somehow relieved me a little to pass on cruelty in turn. Thinking it over now, Curtis was probably not a vicious man as such but he was hard, and likely believed he was doing me a favour by hardening me in turn. I learned later that he had won the Distinguished Flying Cross in the war so he must have been brave. He had played international rugby for Ireland and I've read an old newspaper account which detailed how a New Zealand side had deliberately stomped him in an effort to remove him from the pitch but he didn't flinch or complain.

Later, once or twice in my school career, Curtis tried to be nice to me, calling me "Madockee" and offering to coach me at cricket but the harm was already done and I shied away from him. He'd given me a damaging lesson in life and ever afterwards I could never allow much softness between me and other men. I still carry a pleated transverse scar on my lower back where his cane once struck high and zipped open the skin.

*My class at Ruzawi School, 1963. Many of these little 'skellums' were later to be eaten up by the Rhodesian Civil War. I can't see myself among them. Maybe I was wisely hiding that day.*

My education in cruelty went up several notches a few years later when I met Spear. He was one of the prisoners who came each day to till our garden in Fort Roseberry. They wore uniforms made of coarse, white canvas cloth, and were guarded by one or two listless guards with half-century old rifles. Spear kept himself apart from the other prisoners, or maybe they kept themselves apart from him. They called him *ukoboko kumo* in Chi-Bemba, meaning 'one arm'. Strictly speaking he had two arms, it was just that only one functioned well. He seemed huge to me — a muscular, straight-backed man whose left hand was malformed and lay withered by his side like a flipper. His good arm was powerfully muscled and immensely strong in compensation. He started winking at me and making bird calls by which he enticed me until I came over to talk to him, even though I was wary.

He told me his name, that he was a Matabele from the south, and that he despised the other prisoners around him. Ordinary 'kaffirs' he called them, using white man's terminology, and even worse he sometimes called them *botsha,* the Ndebele for 'shit'. The Matabele were a tribe of Zulu origin who'd given the British plenty of trouble the previous century. Spear identified with his tribe's martial tradition. I saw him kick at the other convicts if they went near him or spoke to him in the wrong tone. He spoke with strong click consonants and said his Matabele name was Gwasa, with a click for the 's'. I believe that, strictly speaking, *gwasa* meant 'stab', despite his being known in English as Spear. I'm unsure now as to how we actually communicated. I knew a few Ndebele words from school so we muddled along with that and broken Shona, but also through sign language and by a weird, sub-linguistic vibration that existed between us.

We knew each other only for the six weeks of my first summer holiday from Ruzawi. He usually had something horribly fascinating to show me. He'd look around to check if the *capitaus* were safely off smoking *dagga* behind a tree, then he'd gesture to me to follow him to the shelter of a bush, where he might show, for instance, a bird he'd caught and placed under an inverted jam jar. We would both watch closely as it began to gasp and die slowly from suffocation. His eyes would gleam and he'd give out bass grunts of delight. If I tried to save any creature, his strong good hand would grab mine and he'd say it was *nani* — a Shona word meaning something like 'exquisite' or 'perfection'.

Many were Spear's cruelties. He spent one morning crucifying dozens of frogs he called *xoxo*, pronouncing the 'x' as a back of the throat clack. He impaled the frogs on pieces of straw stuck into the sides of a stream and together we watched them kick and dry out in the hot sun. Several times I netted tiny, iridescent fish in the irrigation ditches and gave them to Spear to do the same crucifixion business to them. I was more squeamish when he noosed birds and vervet monkeys for more sophisticated tortures. Spear enjoyed his role as my instructor in sadism, seeming not to want anything from me beyond my complicity. Whenever my Mum came out into the garden calling, "Rodney, Rodney!" to summon me back indoors at the end of the day, he'd push me to obey her.

Still, I used to sneak him food and sweets I'd swiped from our kitchen and once I gave him a red blanket. He, in turn, brought me intricate knives he assembled from bamboo and miniature arrows he'd whittled. Sometimes Spear's brutality could be useful, like when the water bowser came up from the river to replenish our water tanks, drawn by two plodding oxen. The beasts were slow and stubborn and refused to move off despite whacks from their *sjambok*-wielding driver. Spear grinned at me, trimmed a stick to a sharp end using a garden panga and jabbed it up the backsides of the oxen. At that, the beasts gave an indignant snort and made off hastily down our dusty drive.

One afternoon, Spear made a small fire on the beaten ground near a goat *kraal* and took my sheath knife and heated the blade until it glowed violet. He used his good hand to take my right hand and then pinned it under one of his horny bare feet. He then brought up the hot blade and touched it lightly several times on the pad of fat beneath my thumb. I squirmed about a good deal in the process and the air was thick with the charcoal and sulphur smell of burnt skin but I had little fear despite the pain. Spear spat on the wounds and scrubbed them vigorously with his strong hard fingers, then reheated the blade and asked me to do the same to him. The sign we gave one another was two parallel lines and a dot. It was our secret cicatrice, the mark of our amity.

I looked forward to my days with Spear, trapping helpless creatures and listening to his long lectures and gibbering rants, which I barely understood. Lord knows the actual nature of his psychopathology. Looking back through Eurocentric eyes, a professional might label him a psychopathic sadist but I think he was simply at one with the pitiless energies of the African bush. He was also likely interested in millenarian Christianity leavened by animistic beliefs, as so many remote tribespeople were and, maybe still are. Once, he showed me a picture torn from a missionary book of Bible stories, depicting tormented souls in hell being prodded by demons with pitchforks. That was also declared, "Nani, nani!"

It all came to a head in the dry season, when we burned the tall elephant grass to create a cleared zone to protect our house from the fierce bush fires of the season. The convicts

ran about firing the bush in a systematic way and pretty soon
the ground was covered with creatures fleeing the flames.
*"Umulilo ukulu"*, a big fire, muttered the Bemba prisoners.
They managed to set a hut ablaze by mistake and I watched as
a feral cat kept running back into the inferno rescuing her
kittens one by one. Further off, snakes, tortoises, lizards and
dozens of chameleons tried to make their escape from a wall
of flame. Spear drew me to a burning *donga,* a ravine
brimming with orange flames, where snakes writhed in
twisting black ribbons in the burning scrub. The sight of the
roasting creatures made Spear's eyes bulge and moans and
cries burst from his foam-flecked lips.

All of a sudden, Spear grabbed me with his good arm and
held me above the blazing *donga.* He seemed to be making
ready to throw me in to join the snakes. I was certain I was a
goner and that he was going to enjoy watching me sizzling
among the other creatures. I kicked and thrashed but it was
no good and he hefted me even higher up, like a javelin athlete
about to throw. A stentorian shout broke through
commanding Spear to put me down. I wobbled around in the
air as Spear hesitated, then slowly lowered me and stood
looking shame-faced. The tough police superintendent who
ran the prison had fortuitously turned up to watch the
burning and was, evidently, one of the few people who could
control Spear.

A strip was torn off the slack guards for not supervising him properly and the police superintendent told my father, "In heaven's name, don't let anyone go near Spear. He murdered his wife with an axe, you know." Spear was taken off the garden work party after that. I never saw him among the other convicts again though I looked out for him and missed our strange and toxic bond.

A year later I was in Dad's work car, a metallic, blue-green, Chevrolet Impala with huge tail fins and a fluttering Union Jack on the hood. We had an armed police escort in a Land Rover behind and slowed at roadworks on the corrugated, dirt road to Mpika. I was hanging my head out the window when we passed a line of prisoners working along the side of the road. All of a sudden, one dust-shrouded figure gave a wild yell and bounded along after us waving one arm. It was Spear. "Rodoney, Rodoney!" he called. I waved back with a lump in my throat until he was lost from sight in the dust-spume. Spear, my first real friend, who played his part in twisting my heart out of shape and inculcating in me a grim view of the world I still cannot shake. The scar he gave me lasted for years. I used to press on the raised lines whenever I needed courage, a touch of Spear in the night.

Ruzawi School, and maybe Spear too, taught me that if you did not fight back then somebody was going to stomp all over you. There was a boy there called Viljoen who began picking on me because I was from the erstwhile kaffir-loving north, and because I was a *soutie,* someone of English ancestry. We scuffled on the gravelled yard outside the school and he fell over and grazed his knee. He told me he was going to *donner me sterek,* which meant he was going to hammer me good. He was a heavy lad and soon got the better of me. He was kneeling on my chest as I struggled on the ground, trying to punch him on the chin like cowboys did in films but my blows simply bounced off him. Mr Lace, our woodwork teacher, separated us and made us stand up and finish the fight properly. Viljoen swiftly and expertly battered my face until I could hardly see for swollen, streaming eyes. Only then did the master stop the grisly business.

"That will teach you to give and to receive," he announced. I wept for real later, my mind full of hot, fearful thoughts. I felt I was not strong enough, not adequate, that I lacked the insouciance and inner toughness of my Rhodie peers. Sometimes I feel that way still.

# 6
# Secrets

*Three might keep a secret if two of them are dead*

– Benjamin Franklin.

As I write this, it will soon be sixty years since the Kennedy assassination. It is well known that there is a reverse echo in great world events that pins you back to the moment you first heard the news in your own little slice of the world. Another schoolboy told me about the killing of the American president as I was pulling off my rugby boots in the changing rooms at Ruzawi. We might have been thousands of miles from the places in which great political events unfolded in our Rhodesian backwater but external events did touch us. I knew at that moment that it was a world-altering thing that had happened in Dallas. I had somehow sensed already that we had entered a frenzied decade when drastic changes were taking place that felt propelled by powerful and mysterious forces that few could comprehend. It seemed to me that no part of the earth or heavens was going to remain unchanged when one of the masters pointed out Yuri Gagarin's Vostok spacecraft as a silvery dot gliding above us in the measureless vault of the African night sky.

In 1961, my father had been involved in the international outcry that followed the death of the Secretary General of the U.N. in a plane crash near Ndola. It was rumoured that Dag Hammarskjold had been assassinated by the British and Americans who were unhappy with his liberal policies. Dad later told me that he had been on duty in the Secretariat, the administrative heart of the colonial government, on the night the plane came down. Only years later did it ever occur to me to wonder why he was asked to be on duty that particular night. Perhaps they already knew in far-off London that something was going to happen.

Indeed, Dad seemed to me to have had a secret hand in a number of key events in 1960s Africa. At the beginning of the decade, the British Prime Minister, Harold Macmillan, made a then world-shaking speech in Cape Town in which he proclaimed that "a wind of change is blowing through this continent, and whether we like it or not, this change of national consciousness is a political fact." This speech is widely seen as the announcement of the end of British colonialism in Africa and the beginning of explicit criticism of the apartheid regime in South Africa. Two score years later,

Dad showed me an official memo he'd written that predated the speech, the diction of which was nearly identical to Macmillan's text. Dad surmised that a speech writer in the Foreign Office had read his briefing notes when Macmillan toured Northern Rhodesia, and had incorporated them into the milestone speech that was delivered not long afterward in South Africa.

Mum brought her own enigmatic history to Africa. My sister and I realised early on that Mum never talked about her origins or childhood. Sometimes, the curiosity born of this baffling secrecy couldn't help from bursting out. When I was perhaps ten, we drove up to the border post on the Katanga crossing point into the Congo. It was a dangerous place during the Congolese Civil War and the roadside was littered with bullet-holed abandoned cars. Mum and Dad were visibly tense. Katanga was like a finger that projected into Northern Rhodesia and we had to cross this risky strip of Congolese territory in order to reach our home in Fort Roseberry as this was the only road home. It was called 'the pedicle road', an eight hour crossing at top speed on a rutted laterite strip bordered by thick, scary bush.

At the border post east of Mufulira, Dad made me hide my cap gun and we children were warned to be silent while a drunk and belligerent Congolese soldier searched our car. Dad produced our passports and I distinctly remember defying his warnings by grabbing at the documents and calling out, "Now we can find out about Mum". I then began to riffle through Mum's passport, which she snatched back before giving me a vicious slap across the face. I felt the echo of that slap over the years and learned from it never to question Mum about her life. She came from nowhere. Her family origins were a blank that she filled with fear and rage that leaped out at you when you least expected it. Her secrets formed a defensive, prickly and fearful *zareba* around her. I, in turn, felt bound to her by the awareness that I mustn't let on to anyone that I knew nothing about my own mother's past.

It was the same with Dad but different. Whereas Mum concealed her life before the war from us, Dad's childhood was an open book. It was his experiences during and after the war that he hid from us. A case in point was his service in British Mandate Palestine, where he was posted with the rest of his division in 1946. Only once when I was well into middle age did he guardedly relate to me that in the officers' mess in Gaza he'd overheard his comrade, Roy Farran, discussing 'eliminating' Zionist terrorists. Farran was a war hero, a founder member of the S.A.S. and one of the most decorated soldiers of World War Two. He was insanely brave and ruthless and had dispatched numberless Germans during the war. He'd been recruited to the Palestine Police in 1946, along with some other Special Forces types, to form a unit to 'deal with' the nationalist Jewish terror gangs of the time.

According to Dad, Farran kept repeating, "Just get bloody rid of them!" Shortly after this, Farran was court martialled for allegedly murdering a sixteen-year-old activist from the Jewish resistance group, Lehi, who had vanished after one of Farran's patrols had apprehended him. Controversially acquitted by the court martial, Farran fled back to England. A year later almost to the day, the Lehi sent a letter bomb to his family home in Staffordshire that wound up killing his brother by mistake. Having survived the revenge attempt by the Lehi, Farran went on to have a high-profile political career in Canada. Dad had clearly known the truth about what had happened in the Farran case all along, but had never said a thing.

Maybe, having been shaped by the war, including the liberation of Bergen-Belsen concentration camp, Dad had internalised the dictum that truth is the first casualty of conflict. He was close-mouthed about what really went on in the war, the same as he was about what had happened behind the scenes in African colonial power politics. He once revealed to me that his unit commander in the Second World War, a man whose name features prominently in respected military histories of the period, used to hide in a hole or pretend to be captured every time they went into action. Dad said that no one ever mentioned it and the officer was always allowed to resume command once the shooting had stopped. Everyone in the unit knew that it was really my father who gave the combat orders and ran things in battle.

*Dad in action in the bundu, Serenje, 1955*

What was truth in Africa anyway? Since I left it has often seemed to me that the continent was too vast and mysterious to be embraced by such a limiting notion as truth. Adults were always giving me explanations about things when I was a child there but I never knew which ones were true, like when Kalulu, my pet hare, disappeared while I was away at school and I was told by various people that the creature had been bewitched, bitten by a snake, taken by a caracal, or had merely hopped away to find a lovely new life of freedom. I never did find out what really happened to my little friend and comforter. A few years later, it was the same with the story of what happened to Buster. When we left for England,

Mum and Dad told me the old tale that he'd "gone to live on a farm" near Lusaka. They kept this ruse up for years with imaginary updates on his happy progress. Only in adulthood did it dawn on me that they'd had him shot the day we left.

Years after their deaths, decades after my childhood, I still feel as if I'm disobeying my parents' lifelong precepts by having spoken openly about them like this. You should never trust those who tell you other people's secrets; that was what they believed and maybe I do too. As a family, we never said what we were thinking, much less what we were feeling. Such was the way of their generation. It's as if I'm freeing myself now by looking back at their world in a clear-sighted way and speaking of it with candour. Every writer makes that betrayal in the end. I want to maintain that cool gaze, like an assassin leopard in a tree, watching and waiting. As for my own secrets, I want to tell you about them, reader, but I can't do it just yet. My own dark abandonments and shrouded revenges, my base acts of betrayal and murderous desires, must stay hidden a little longer until I'm ready to let them go.

# 7

# Jonas

*As the heavens for height and the earth for depth,*

*So the hearts of kings are unsearchable.*

— Proverbs 25:3

The sibilance of calloused skin on parquet heralded the arrival of Jonas, our cook. Everyone who worked for my Dad was provided with shoes but most preferred the freedom of bare feet. I'd often watch fascinated as Jonas bent down with a grunt of annoyance to draw out a massive thorn from the thick skin around his big toe and then flick away the offending spike like a gnat. I learned in childhood to distinguish the distinctive sound of his scaly feet on the flooring and dreaded his disapproving stare if he discovered me about some mischief. His was an imperturbable protective presence through all my young years in Africa. Trusted by my parents to look after me while they were away, he was both disciplinarian and confidante. Our bull terriers were petrified of him although they made other Africans' lives a misery by constantly pursuing and nipping at them. He had a similar power over me.

Jonas was a Bemba tribesman. He told me he came from the same royal clan as the tribal Chief Chitimukulu, and taught me Chi-Bemba words and the ornate protocols of his people, like how to greet people formally by making a clapping gesture and saying the greeting, *Mwapoleni mukwai*, followed by an enquiry about how well they were eating. The Bemba liked to know where you were from so they could place you and your ancestors in context but I was never sure as to where I originated. Born and raised in Africa, my kin were merely visitors to the continent. Jonas therefore advised me to say, *Nafuma ku Londone* — I'm from London — when meeting tribesmen, though I was never comfortable with this half-truth. Whenever my parents were away, Jonas let me stay in his servant's quarters at the bottom of our garden, where we'd eat local food cooked by one of his several wives — skillets of delicious fried grasshoppers and smoked fish, chased down with mealy handfuls of *sadza*, a thick porridge of white cornmeal.

Lord knows how old Jonas was; he seemed as ancient and everlasting as a baobab tree to my young self. He told me that as a child he had seen a contingent of what must have been von Lettow-Vorbeck's German army crossing Lake

Tanganyika on a steamer. That would have been at the outset of the First World War. Jonas often gave me biscuits and cakes he'd made but he was also strict and scary and woe betide if he caught you in his food cupboards. My parents sometimes asked me to call him from the servants' quarters and he'd emerge slowly, after a long pause, straightening his white cook's hat and tunic as if roused from sleep. At these times, I used to sense annoyance in his inscrutable steady gaze and I felt ashamed that I, a *muzungu* kid, had the impudence to summon such a lordly man. It was in those moments that I first began to understand the abyss that lay between white and black in Africa and between master and servant, coloniser and colonised.

In 1965, Jonas put me up on his shoulders among the crowds in Cairo Road, Lusaka to see the Ethiopian emperor, Haile Selassie, on a state visit to the new nation of Zambia. Jonas was tall and I caught a clear sight of that haughty, Amharic face as the Emperor passed in a speeding, open car, surrounded by the red and white pennons of a mounted escort of lancers. The crowd ululated with joy to see an African king, though his own people were to murder him fifteen years later in a frenzy of vengeance at the unbounded corruption of his reign and he ended up buried under a lavatory.

Independence did not bring freedom to all Zambians. Tribal enmities and fears boiled up at the dawn of change. Jonas also took me to watch the army come out from their Lusaka barracks to quell the Alice Lenshina Revolt. Like Jonas, Lenshina was a Bemba, a prophetess who'd created a new religion called the Lumpa Church that mixed tribal customs with millenarian Christian beliefs. The Lumpa became violently hostile to non-members and the colonial authorities battled to control them during the handover of power to the new Zambian government. The African nationalists of the U.N.I.P. party hated the Lenshinists because they, like the Jehovah's Witnesses, rejected U.N.I.P.'s secular political creed. The shadow cabinet and president-in-waiting, Kenneth Kaunda, a good friend of my father's, urged forceful action and police mobile units were sent to control the Lumpa. A young police inspector whom we knew, Derek Smith, was speared to death in a Lumpa village. I overheard Dad say to Mum at the time, "He looked like a hedgehog, dear, with those spears in him." That killing led to the army being sent in. Jonas and I watched them march out and load up onto lorries going north. I'll never forget the look of those men going into action, row upon row of resolute black faces under floppy bush hats, lugging their F.N. rifles and Bren guns.

Those guns were to make short work of the Lumpa a few days later. Lenshina told her followers that they couldn't be killed by earthly powers. They rushed at the troops and were mowed down in their hundreds. The newspapers reported that only seventy Lenshinists had been killed but it later came out that more than a thousand were left to rot in the bush. Thus was the new republic born in blood and the surviving Lenshinists escaped to hide in the Congo. Who cares, or even knows, about it now? The government of Zambia has shut down all memory of those events. Similarly, we former 'colonists' are now given a cartoon caricature appearance in African history that does not mirror the complexities of what actually took place between peoples. I wish now that I'd asked my parents more about the Lumpa and so many other many things. If I cannot record their lives, then who will?

*My only photo of Jonas, here cooking in the open during one of my parents' journeys. 1955, Serenje.*

Mum had a Siamese cat called Ming in Africa. He was a fine creature and Mum doted on him. He used to sleep curled up inside the inverted dome of Dad's colonial uniform sun-hat, known as a 'solar topi'. My parents, like many senior colonial staff, returned to England for six months leave every few years. On one such occasion, they left Ming in the charge of a Provincial Commissioner, a senior officer whom they trusted. While they were away, they got a letter from the Provincial Commissioner, stating that he regretted to inform them that their cat had died of tick fever. This was sad enough but a month later they received a clarification from Jonas, written by a letter-writer as Jonas was illiterate. This meant that he had gone to the immense trouble of somehow getting an English contact address for my parents from the colonial administration and then paying the letter-writer to communicate the following message, which I have to this day:

*dear bwana mkubwa and dona mkubwa. I am sorry to say the cat ming was not sick. the true thing I say – he was killed by the pc's dogs. sincerely yours, jonas chimfuntu.*

My parents could rely on Jonas to tell them the truth. A rare thing in Africa between black and white. There was a decided change in their treatment of him after they received that painstaking letter, more respect and more affection.

# 8
# Nights

*You, darkness*

*from whom I came.*

– Rainier Maria Rilke

I've been thinking about my Vesta Spacelite, a heavy metal torch with ribbed metal sides, which I got for Christmas in 1961. I used to load it with chunky Ray-O-Vac batteries bought from the Daya Stores at Fort Jameson. In fact, I got Mum and Dad to buy so many batteries for it that I was able to send away for, and eventually receive, a Ray-O-Vac baseball hat as a complimentary gift. It was the first time I ever saw this, now ubiquitous, style of headgear. The American cap had a rusty umber colour, the same as that of the battery boxes. The fabulous torch had red and green filters as well as a conventional main beam light. It also had a Morse code button, in addition to the on-off slide switch, and I'd often stick the torch through the bars of my bedroom windows and send messages out into the teeming African night sky.

All the windows of our isolated house had heavy iron bars to keep out marauding animals or persons and my main use of the torch was to wait in darkness until I heard a faint noise on the garden paths outside, at which I'd flick on the beam to catch a glimpse of nocturnal wildlife. Usually, it would be the hunched shape of a porcupine shuffling along in the dust. They were very common and our dogs used to try and have a go at them, after which Dad had to pull snapped-off spines out of their foreheads and muzzles with a pair of pliers. One time, I caught a caracal, a wild cat with tufted ears, in my Ray-O-Vac beam. In its mouth was the limp, fresh corpse of one of my pet chickens. What I really lusted after, however, was seeing a leopard and I kept long night vigils hoping to catch a glimpse of one. But they were elusive, chimeric beasts although you'd find their pug marks all over Mum's flower and vegetable beds. Finally though, I caught one in my torch beam, a lithe, spectral shadow as if out of a dream-scape, its head turned towards me and its eyes reflecting cold green fire.

What I know I didn't dream was the moment a few years later when I was eleven. We were living in Lusaka city. I went to the kitchen in the night to get a drink and heard a sighing sound. I switched my light on to see a shape pressed against the zinc wire mosquito mesh of the outside window. It was a black African, his face pressed against the wire, the eyes wide open and glaring at me. We stared at each other in silence. That sighing sound was his breath puffing through the mesh. Weirdly, I didn't wake my parents even though we all knew what happened to Lilian Burton in Ndola in 1960, set afire while still alive.

In the wake of those events, Dad had started keeping a pistol in the car, a Luger he'd captured in the war, with a tiny eagle clutching a wreathed swastika etched under the breech slide, and a house weapon, a Greener shotgun with trapdoor Martini action. I retreated from our nocturnal visitor, went back to my bedroom, placed my .177 calibre Webley air rifle and sheath knife on the pillow and proceeded to stay awake all night. Maybe I'd developed the belief that the whole continent was hostile so there was no point in waking my parents.

As a kid, I was told about a girl, the same age as me, who was taken by a lion from her school dormitory at Mpika and eaten. I used to gaze up at the milky shroud of the mosquito net that surrounded my bed in Africa and imagine the lion's great head pressing in on the fabric. My parents told me about nights camping out in the bush. They used to leave their bicycles leaning against their tent to give some protection from nocturnal beasts. Once, they felt the walls of a tent shuddering in the darkness and, in the morning, found that a lion, likely sharpening its teeth, had chewed their rubber bike tyres off their wheel rims.

*My sister, Susan, and I, armed against the world, 1965. I've got my air rifle and sheath knife, while she carries a spear and knobkerrie taken from Lenshinist rebels.*

The many mysterious sounds that I heard by night in the first decades of my life are still fresh, a tuning fork invisibly vibrating within me. When, stalked by fears and worries, I struggle to go to sleep at night, sometimes I still think I can catch the eerie call of the red-chested cuckoo that used to turn up in our garden during the rainy season. We'd hear it calling day and night with an insistent sound that, according to Afrikaaners, was like *Piet my vrou, Piet my vrou* — Peter my wife, Peter my wife. The *piet-my-vrou bird* could drive you mad. Dad would sometimes get up in the night and shine his torch all over the garden in a fruitless search for it in order to scare it off and shut it up. To me in boyhood, the cuckoo's insistent calling in the night somehow came to echo all the loss in the world. More than sixty years on, it still does.

# 9

# Come back, Shane!

*Anybody who has survived his childhood has enough information about life to last him the rest of his days.*

– Flannery O' Connor

I was often dogged by fear as a child that something wicked I'd done would be found out. I seemed always to be testing the boundaries of the adults around me by committing acts of unpleasantness that, if discovered, were usually deserving of punishment. My earliest little atrocities were perpetrated against my sweet sister. I once cut a V in her fringe with nail scissors while she lay helpless in her pram. Later, I decapitated her dolls and dangled their severed heads on fishing wire outside her bedroom window.

As I grew older and the testosterone levels ramped up, I became even more extreme in my pranks. I knew, for example, that many tribal people had a dread and terror of chameleons. To them, the chameleon was a deceitful shapeshifter, the frightening familiar of wizards and witch doctors. Some imp of the perverse in me made me gather up chameleons from our garden bushes, especially big, feisty ones that turned black with fury and gaped their mimosa-yellow mouths and hissed when riled. I'd bundle these slow-moving lizards into my shirt then wander into a village, nonchalantly feigning a typical *muzungu* child's innocence. Then all of a sudden, I'd drop the enraged chameleons into the dust next to a group of seated villagers. The gratifying result was usually panic flight, screams and upended cooking pots and stools, followed by a volley of imprecations shouted from a distance. If my father wasn't around, sometimes a District Messenger was called to give me a sound telling-off.

*A District Messenger delivering a reproof, 1955, Serenje*

My crimes continued to mount as I got older. I seemed to have an internal mechanism that cloaked my ill-doings from both grown-ups and myself. I lied all the time to adults and distracted myself by constructing a fantasy world derived from the Hollywood films I occasionally saw when we visited Lusaka. Yet in these fantasies, I was not a villain but a wounded hero. Looking back, I think that I harboured barely-formed notions of artistic self-transcendence through imagination ever since reading Kipling and a children's edition of Homer's *Odyssey*. This included the intuition that such transcendence came only at a cost, that insight could only be gained by some horrible shock, a profound *bouleversement*.

Quite often, when I shut my eyes, I'm eight years old again in our garden at Fort Roseberry. I've climbed a gum tree after first scanning its loose bark for any *boomslangs*, highly venomous tree snakes, that might be up there. I've shinned up the tree, its papery bark abrading my bare knees, and wedged myself into a forked branch. I'm wearing a cowboy outfit that makes me feel omnipotent: a black Stetson, a toggled neckerchief and a leatherette gun belt holster for my Colt .45 cap gun with chased filigree barrel. I imagine I'm 'Joey', the boy in George Stevens' western classic, *Shane*, which I saw on the huge screen of the Lusaka drive-in. In the film, Joey is in awe of the taciturn gunman, Shane, as I hero-worship the keen-eyed, rifle-toting game wardens and hard-bitten, pistol-wearing policemen who report to Dad when he's on duty in the bush.

There's a movement down below and I swivel in the tree and level my gun at our house servant, Hosanna, an easy target in his *kansu* white blouse and white skull cap. He's finished ironing our washing, which he does in order to kill the *pootsi* flies that like to hide in the fabric of shirts then burrow into your skin. Now he is flapping the polishing cloths he uses for buffing our parquet floors. He usually ties these to his bare feet, one foot for spreading Cobra Polish and one for shining. To me, he's a 'Red Indian' and I've drawn a bead on him. I'm immune and invulnerable. Now he's in my sights. I tighten my finger on the trigger and mouth, *"Kapow!"*

At that moment, there comes a bass droning sound, I flip round to see a dangly-legged African hornet, its belly tipped with a poison dart. It hovers and its armoured mask face tilts. It has seen me and registered a threat. The drone rises to a frantic pitch. My gun is no good against this whizzing adversary. Shane would've reacted instantly and thrown his sheath knife at it but it's too close for me to use mine now. The hornet has come from the land of grownups and it's going to get me. There's a blinding electric jab to the side of my neck. I convulse and the cap gun rattles to the ground, there's a burning nail stuck in me, "Shane, Come back! Come back, Shane! I'm falling ."

I feel my bare legs sticking to the red leather seat of our Vauxhall Velox, the *umami* taste of Mazoe Orange Crush in my mouth, parked up at the Lusaka drive-in flix, Joey's voice calling for Shane sounds from the loudspeaker attached to the car window, echoed by scores of other loudspeakers in the ranks of parked cars, this above a tremendous shrilling of crickets in the dusty grass all around. Perhaps that was the first time I fully shed my childhood self to briefly become another boy, tow-haired Joey, who revered the enigmatic gunfighter, Shane. In the beginning, the writer's imagination is a reimagining, copying thing, rehearsing and recapitulating other people's stories until it is ready to create its own.

I also took enormous pleasure in re-enacting scenes from 'Shane' with my friends, the Van der Ruit brothers, on their farm in Marandellas. I think now those sessions of make-believe were the birth-moment of my writer's mission to impregnate the imaginations of others with my own fantasies. To launch our pretending, we'd catch the farm horses that grazed in the bush, slip bridles on them and ride them bareback through the long grass, cradling our .410s and pellet guns. We'd decide in advance who was a tyrannical cattle rancher, who a courageous homesteader, and who a gunfighter without a past. Then we'd ride out against each other and fight our mock battles. I caught a pellet in the face in one of our engagements and still have a neat round scar there. Mr. Van der Ruit had to dig out the lead nub with a pair of long-nosed pliers. He swabbed the wound with purple permanganate solution, muttering that we were turning into wild bush skellums.

In the course of one such fantasy fight, we got caught in a real battle. Having left our horses to graze, we'd stumbled onto a territorial troop of aggressive baboons. They began to drive us through the long yellow grass. I could see the big dog baboons as they hopped up onto the tops of the tall termite nests to see where we were and bark out calls to the other warrior males to encircle and attack us. Their hoarse, squealing cries and relentless pursuit of us started up an icy turmoil in my guts. Eventually, they pinned us against the smooth rock walls of a *kopje*. We counted out our remaining air rifle slugs and filled our shorts pockets with stones. I tried to stop my friends seeing that my hands were shaking while I put forward an untenable plan as to how we might climb the rock wall and escape. But one of the brothers said, "*Chongo*, man! We've got to stand and fight the *babijahn*; that's our only chance." Howling and lobbing stones, we charged the baboon skirmish line and scattered our simian foe before us. Both sides left the field with honour that day.

# 10
# What Ndewenu Taught Me

*To be men not destroyers...*

– Ezra Pound

The villagers in Fort Roseberry seemed willing to forgive my evil doings. I think they appreciated that I took the trouble to learn their language and tribespeople in general seemed to have an acculturated fondness for children so they enjoyed taking up a tutelary role, explaining the real ways of the world to me on the assumption that *muzungu* parents could not. I spent months following around an elderly man called Ndewenu who tended our kitchen garden. He was a member of the Watchtower movement, which combined millennial beliefs and Christianity, and which predicted that the time was coming for the rise of the black man. Ndewenu delivered long lectures to me about the beliefs of his movement, which he called '*wa-chi-tawala*'. His name 'Ndewenu' meant 'I am yours, God'. I was never sure whether this was his tribal name or a Watchtower *nom de guerre.*

Ndwenu lived nearby in a hut with a conical thatched roof, the interior walls of his hut were papered with sheets taken from *The Watchtower* magazine. He often drew me in there to point to illustrations of biblical scenes while he gave me long lectures on religious matters. He needed to watch his step as Jehovah's Witnesses in general, and Watchtower members in particular, were persecuted by the dominant African liberationist parties of the time because of their refusal to vote or otherwise take part in the democratic process. Also, the colonial authorities occasionally cracked down on the more militant streams of the movement.

A haughty and fierce old chap, Ndwenu would likely have seen off any U.N.I.P. supporter who tried to railroad him. He was one of those Africans, like Jonas or Limbani, who had managed to rise above the internalised self-contempt that colonialism sometimes inculcated. He had an independent, even aristocratic air about him, despite wearing one of Dad's old tattered safari jackets, and notwithstanding the seeds that lodged in his beard or the constant streaming of his rheumy eyes from crouching over his hearth fire. He waged endless battles with the *babijahns* and vervet monkeys which were forever attempting to raid his patch and in periods of rest he eased out the long hot afternoons by playing on the *kalimba*, a homemade instrument of flexible metal prongs mounted over a dried-out gourd sound box.

I'd often ask him what song he was playing as he made his rapid rhythmic plinking music accompanied by a low chanting. He'd put the *kalimba* down, glare at me, wipe his face with a flat-handed African gesture and reply sharply that the song was called "Don't listen to the European." He'd often laugh wheezily after that and I'd join in the merriment. He spoke to me quite rudely, addressing me as "Eh-we"which in Chi-Bemba meant, 'Hey, you'. He also threw stones at Buster whenever the dog tried to follow me down to the vegetable garden. Despite his gruff ways, I liked to hang out with him and he reciprocated after his own fashion.

Ndewenu was an excellent gardener and under his care our garden yielded bountiful crops of gooseberries, guavas, pawpaws, mangos, granadillas, melon and cucumbers. He had a special method for planting tomatoes whereby he'd get me to take some seeds from a ripe tomato from Mum's kitchen; he'd then dry them in the sun for a while. Next, he'd sow the seeds straight into the bare earth before dancing and hopping about to flatten down the soil above them with his bare feet, while chanting out a repeated incantation. If plants didn't do well, he'd complain darkly that it was *ubuloshi*, or witchcraft, that had blighted them. He also grew zinnias, marigolds and morning glories for Mum's flower arrangements.

I couldn't wait to go down to his plot for the day, sometimes secretly taking him a present of a bit of honeycomb, or some breakfast rolls freshly baked by Jonas. Ndwenu accepted these gifts as his due, like tithes brought to an emperor. I followed him around as he tilled the soil with a *badza,* a kind of hoe, while discoursing upon God, mixed with stories about his ancestors' hunting prowess. Sometimes he'd load a heap of snuff onto an antique brass implement that looked like a flattened tea spoon that he'd bring up to his nose and inhale mightily from the mound of brown dust. After much snorting and throat-clearing, he'd clamp one of his nostrils shut with a horny finger and jet out a stream of matter from the other nostril.

Ndewenu had a lot to say to me but I couldn't follow it all. Generally, I'd agree with him, repeating the assent word, *Eh-he,* sometimes to encourage him. At other times, he'd become more directly didactic, getting me to repeat Bemba words after him to learn their tone and pronunciation right. It was a tonal language for example a cat was *icona* but it also meant 'big nose' depending how you pronounced the tone. My favourite Bemba double meaning was *mumpuue,* which meant both 'a thief' and 'a person who eats alone'.

Village women would come each day to bring food and check on Ndewenu's welfare. I was never sure whether they were kin or locals who revered him as a *mzee*, a wise elder. The women were a jolly bunch, wrapped in *chitenge* body cloths that only just covered their breasts. Their racy talk went over my head. They teased me a lot, sometimes leading me around by the hand to raucous laughter, calling out they were now '*muka ka-bwana*', wife of the little bwana. They brought Ndewenu *nsima*, a porridge of mealie meal, or crushed cassava leavened with bits of anything else going — snippets of bush-meat, mopane grubs, green caterpillars, whatever the bush supplied. He'd reheat this, stirring mightily, with the sticky mixture going *bleb-bleb* in an iron cauldron over a fire. Then he'd serve us both a dollop on a banana leaf with some gravy or a relish and a handful of coriander from the garden. We'd eat silently together, sitting on our haunches. We were in amity at these moments.

I was accepted and it felt good to have earned my place with Ndewenu. Looking back, I like to think that my friendship with him may well have mirrored relationships between black and white that had existed centuries earlier, before colonialism and racial slavery got fully underway — a quiet wonder between disparate equals. It also taught me how to be with someone very different, yet to stay yourself. He gave me a lesson that I have carried with me all my life — that friendship could exist despite the divergence of another human being from anything else you have known. Yes, friendship, love even, can flourish despite the complete strangeness of another human being, or perhaps because of it.

# 11
# Gifts

*To fill a gap, insert the Thing*

*That caused it.*

−Emily Dickinson

I've mentioned that I ran into a crowd who stoned me on the outskirts of Lusaka, as well as the man who chased me with an axe, these incidents stand out in my memory partly because they were so atypical of relations between black and white folk in late-colonial Central Africa. The real picture was much more nuanced and by no means as extreme as in apartheid-era South Africa. In fact, many Africans of the time were concerned that independence would not necessarily bring a better quality of life for ordinary people. They rightly, quite rightly as it turned out, feared the return of violent tribal enmities and the rise of corrupt tyrants.

The British civil administration was, at least, not corrupt. All my father's colleagues foresaw the inevitability of independence and worked hard to build a sustainable social structure in the country. My father spent much of his time during those final two decades in the life of Northern Rhodesia organising the construction of roads, schools and health clinics and training up African administrators to run them. The white population of the country was about forty thousand at its height, less than two percent of the total and we spent our lives mixing amicably with the African majority. As a child, I spoke Chi-Bemba, the dominant tongue among dozens of languages in the region. I also had some Nyanja, which was spoken in the Lusaka area and some Shona, the main language in Southern Rhodesia.

Ordinary, rural tribespeople genially put up with my hanging around and asking them dumb questions all the time. I was not shown any special favour as a bwana's son, but rather was a regular source of amusement to locals, who frequently imitated me as well as my parents. Their sharp eyes were particularly good at picking out our more ridiculous personal mannerisms. I felt at home in earth-walled homes amid the comforting fug of wood smoke and loved squatting by a hearth fire as sizzling, fat, green caterpillars, or other morsels were grilled on a skillet and handed to me with a blob of *nsima*. You'd roll up a porridgy ball to the size of a small plum and, with a forefinger, drill a hole into the sticky mass into which the caterpillar fry-up, or other meaty gobbet, was stuffed, before dipping the lot into an accompanying dollop of gravy or relish and popping it into your mouth. All then sat around munching in silence.

In the rainy season, when roads and *dongas* filled with murky spate water, I'd join village kids swimming in torrents and skidding about in mud, even as the lightning was still cracking down. At Fort Roseberry, we often played with a vervet monkey, an ex-pet that had been banished from its former living quarters. One elder told me this was because, "It's very bad and stinks like the bowels of a mole!" The monkey had taken up residence in a nearby mango tree, but had gradually become deranged by loneliness. I sometimes used to try to feed it fruit but it attempted to seize my hand and bared its long yellow teeth at me. There were games of dare when all of us kids, black and white, lay down together in a row, arms entwined, the most fearless positioned closest to the vervet's mango tree. We waited, giggling and trembling, until the creature came dashing down to try and get us. We'd then spring up at the last moment to escape, screaming with a mixture of fear and delight although the game eventually turned sour when the sad little crazed thing ended up biting one of the girls on the backside.

My father's duties forced us to move on to new places every couple of years so I often had to say goodbye to my African friends. There was sincere sadness on both sides at these times. I'd usually give them knives bought with my pocket money or tins of English sweets filched from Mum's cupboard. They, in turn, gave me small gifts to remember them by: miniature weapons or toys made of wood or hammered out of tin cans. My good companion, Musondo, carved me a wooden tortoise. I've treasured this present ever since. It seems doubly significant as a parting gift since Kamba, the tortoise, is a foundation creature in regional tribal mythology. In stories told at night by the hearth fires, old men recounted how Kamba held up the primordial earth upon his shell at the dawn of cosmological time when all else swirled in chaos.

*The tortoise Musondo carved for me*

By the mid-Sixties, however, there was a new vibe in the air. There was a rising class of black politicians and activists, alongside whom Dad worked intensively as independence approached. They visited our house for dinner on several occasions but when they did so Jonas glared at them and told me they put on airs and were getting ready to steal from the people wholesale. Concomitantly, something scary was going on in the townships; most Africans remained friendly but outside beer halls drunk men would shout "Kwacha!" at us and make menacing gestures, or stones would thump onto our Vauxhall Velox if we travelled down the wrong streets. Lilian Burton, the woman I mentioned who was burned to death in her car in front of her children, began to seem emblematic of the fate that might well be meted out to any of us.

I longed for the return of the African heroes of my childhood, like Amos, a Muslim Yao from Malawi, with his square beard and round skullcap. He'd walked with me right through my early childhood wherever I went outdoors. He carried an axe on his shoulder and whenever I asked him why he always answered, "For the lion that will come." I am certain that he protected me so faithfully not because he was paid to, or because he feared my father's authority, but because he had given his word that he would and he believed in discharging that duty righteously, with honour and with care.

As a boy, I thought I'd live in Africa forever. I imagined that maybe I'd end up like 'Chiripula' Stephenson, a famous early figure in Northern Rhodesian history whom my parents had met in his old age. He'd been sent by Rhodes to fight off slavers in the wild lands in the Hook of the Kafue then became a mining prospector and many other things besides; he was another Changa-Changa, I suppose. He lived in style in a large house he built in the bush in a valley in the misty Irumi Mountains and wooed three wives from the Lala and Lamba tribes. He was a figure that commanded respect from both black and white. A chief not aligned with the colonial authorities, a scholar, an expert on Egyptology, a mage and a warrior. It was said he could look into your mind and see the truth, and always walked with a *chikoti*, a hippo-hide whip, dangling from his wrist. Mum had a copy of his biography, *Jungle Pathfinder*, signed by him and dated 1951. I often read the book as a boy and lingered over the photos of Chirapula's Lala wives and the house he built called 'Stonehenge', dreaming of the African life I'd in turn lead and of the adventures waiting for me.

# 12
# Sorry

*How hopeless underground*

*Falls the remorseful day*

– A.E. Housman

I'd noticed that the black African people who were used to hearing English spoken had an endearing habit of saying "Sorry, sorry" whenever you hurt yourself. Be it a thorn in the finger or a hornet sting, you'd get a "Sorry, sorry" as an expression of sympathy. At some point during our last few years in Africa, a young charcoal burner was carried into our compound at a remote outstation with an axe deeply buried in his foot. Dad drove him two hundred miles to the nearest mission doctor. He asked me to help keep the man still during the journey. The wounded fellow made scarcely a murmur, only compressing his lips as we rattled over the rutted dirt road while he lay on newspapers and an old blanket in the back of the Landy, the axe still in his foot. I tried to make him comfortable and gave him sips of water. I found myself saying "Sorry, sorry" to him and at times he echoed me, whispering "Sorry, sorry" in return. I suppose we both ended up saying "Sorry, sorry" together as a salve against his pain and maybe also for all the differences this harsh world puts between people.

Those were personal apologies we made each to each. I've little time for the formulaic rhetoric of universal victimhood and the contemporary trend toward collective apologies for selected misdeeds of the past. The wise know there is no end to unjust worlds. Current educational orthodoxy in the English-speaking world demands we approach modern western history in a rigid way as a Punch-and-Judy show with stock characters. The former heroes have become villains and yesterday's beneficiaries are today's victims. In truth, the present post-Imperialist narrative is as specious and simplified as its imperialist antecedent.

The ancient cave paintings we found in the *kopje* caves as kids often showed armies of stick figures fighting with each other with bow and arrows and spears. Conflict often seemed latent in the Africa of my childhood, it seethed below the surface and seemed to erupt with little warning. I'd often watch gangs of men beating and kicking at each other outside the beer halls and shebeens of the townships. I asked some locals why they were fighting but they usually shrugged and said there was no particular reason, the dislocated migrant workers often seemed to want to distract themselves in violent delights with violent ends.

Let me tell you about the only larger battle I ever went near personally. It must have been in 1964 as we were living in Fort Roseberry, now called Mansa, after the river that skirts the town. Dad was Provincial Commissioner, a senior post that meant he was effectively in charge of an area that covered thousands of square miles. He once had to travel to the far north, near Lake Mweru which borders the Congo, and took me with him. There was a white policeman in the front compartment of the Land Rover and I travelled in the open back, along with the policeman's red setter dog and two District Messengers in blue *barathea* tunics and large-brimmed bush hats and carrying Lee Enfield .303 rifles.

We sped down rutted red dirt roads, once passing through a bush fire blazing on each side of the route, while the Messengers stamped on the embers that rained down on the jerry cans of fuel stacked in the rear along with us. The bush became thicker and greener as we entered the wooded uplands near the lake. Many villages there grew guava and bananas and suicidal chickens, unused to motor traffic, ran wildly from the huts straight under the Landy. They made *bompa-bomp* sounds under our vehicle as we ran them over.

Dad gave a speech at the Nchelenge Fish Fair, while I spent time looking into the obligatory snake pit that was a central feature of all such agricultural fairs. It fascinated me to watch yellow, fluffy chicks stepping gingerly over the masses of inert snakes. The chicks seemed to know they were food and had an air of frozen terror, making not the slightest peep. Dad's speech was mainly about the coming Zambian independence. Here, near Kashikishi, the salt fish port to the Congo, it was militant U.N.I.P. territory and there were many Lumpa churches nearby that were fiercely anti-government. Dad spoke in Chi-Bemba and English about the rule of law and democratic process and I could hear the crowd muttering a drawn out "Eh-he" sound, the Bemba word for agreement.

*My father giving a speech at Nchelenge, 1964*

It was either going to or from Nchelenge that we halted somewhere on the Luapula River, which forms one of the headwaters of the Congo and drains into Lake Mweru. I already knew the river as we crossed its broad, slow, green back on a diesel ferry at Chembe whenever we passed along the pedicle road through Katanga that I've mentioned previously. We went through miles of thick scrub, punctuated by a few isolated and impoverished villages where the locals scraped a meagre living. The Messengers told me you could not track anything, not even an elephant, through that bush, the thickets were so entwined that they flicked back and covered the spoor.

We stopped by a large, sandy berm on the banks of the Luapula, where British officers were sitting in deck chairs on the bank gazing through binoculars across quarter of a mile of water dotted with small islands. The dark fringe of the opposing bank was Congolese territory. My main impression was of a constant succession of rolling thuds and booms interspersed with echoing rattles at a higher pitch. The greasy expanse of the river seemed to act as a sounding board and I was enthralled by the soundscape of battle. I'd been a devotee of war books since I was small and could identify most sorts of weapons. Dad told me that the sounds we could hear came from the Congolese army on the opposite bank, backed up by European mercenaries who were pushing the Simbas out of the area. The Simbas were Cuban-supported rebels renowned for their ferocity. I'd heard their speciality was ripping up Congolese nuns. They were in retreat all over the Congo, but massacring locals and Belgian settlers as they melted back into the bush.

The hot air quivered with the sounds of battle. The noises seemed to come from one area then another. Once or twice, I heard the unmistakable churning of machine gun fire but I couldn't really see anything apart from drifts of smoke over the far flat-topped trees on the other bank. Dad and his colleagues remained on their deckchairs like sightseers on an English holiday beach. Beside them, a couple of African soldiers with a Bren gun, the gun's bipod propped on sandbags. Dug-out boats were paddled across to our side containing terrified locals. Dad said the Simba were firing at the islands where fleeing people were hiding. There were fresh spurts of white smoke in the middle of the river and an odd ringing sound like rocks being poured into a metal bucket.

"Mortar!" I heard one of the imperturbable deckchair men say. A motorised dugout boat came up to our bank. It contained a stout middle-aged white Belgian man accompanying a group of weeping African women who were escorted away by police and soldiers. Dad seemed to be in charge. He came forward and slowly explained to the Belgian in schoolboy French that he needed to persuade the other refugees to come over to safety on the Rhodesian side of the river. I could see the Belgian's sweaty, scared-looking face as Dad kept repeating slowly and loudly, *"Il est nécessaire, monsieur."*

Eventually, the Belgian gave a shrug, puttered back midstream and disappeared into a patch of high reeds. Later, we heard a heavy burst of firing and we could see an empty boat twirling round and round in the current. When I asked Dad if that was the Belgian's boat he nodded. We were interrupted by a *'crack, donk'* sound right over us. Dad said that the snap was the air being forced apart by a bullet and the thump was the explosion of the round in the rifle. You could tell the distance of the firing position by measuring the time interval between the two noises.

"He's a mile away, the shooter," Dad said, "but you'd better get in there." He led me to a clay-walled *rondavel*, shrouded by a mound of sandbags. I spent the rest of the time inside the hut and remember being fascinated by a neat bullet hole that went right through the corrugated iron of its conical top. The Messengers took shelter inside there too. They seemed impassive and uninterested in the war as they leaned on their rifles and ate handfuls of musty-smelling *kapenta*, a concoction of tiny dried fishes that resembled whitebait. Dad must have eventually satisfied himself that everything was under control and called the Messengers to load back up. I tried to take one last look at the scene and went to investigate some sodden, shapes drifting to the river bank. Not human surely, lumps, glistening inert lumps and then a pulpy hand floated free at the end of a disjointed arm and I was pulled away before I could get a proper look. When the Landy roared up and it was time to leave, Dad said, "For Heaven's sake, don't tell your mother about any of this."

# 13
# Hondo

*All the things we have forgotten scream for help in dreams.*

– Elias Canetti

The news was full of the Congo Civil War in those days and it was odd to hear broadcasts relayed from Britain on the BBC World Service, in which the reporter could be heard saying, "I am speaking to you from Elizabethville", accompanied by a background sounds of heavy machine gun fire, which we knew was happening only a few hundred miles from us. Whenever I hear fireworks nowadays, their distant explosions still remind me of an African war. The sort of sounds Southern Rhodesians got used to during the Bush War, or the Hondo, as they called it, from the Shona word for war. We listened to these reports of the wars around us on our bulky, wood-encased Grundig radio, with a dial that pointed to mysterious locations like Hilversum and Zagreb. We gathered next to it each night and when Dad would switch it on, there'd be a humming sound and the display would glow a spectral green. First, there'd first be the announcement, "This is London", then the Purcell march tune, *Lilliburlero*, which somehow symbolised the faraway 'home' country to me. It seemed a haunting melody, floaty and distorted and sent over the airwaves across intercontinental immensities.

The Congo became independent from Belgium in 1960 and almost instantly the toxic legacy of the previous sixty years of the most ruthless oppression witnessed in colonial Africa exploded into raging, multi-sided civil war. The effects of this maelstrom were felt by the whole of Central Africa and it would not be far-fetched to say that war has continued there, hot or cold, ever since. It began with a mutiny of the Congolese Army, in the wake of which parts of the country hived off into warring factions along tribal lines and opposing political parties. Congolese of all ethnicities visited their long-simmering rage over seventy-five years of brutalisation onto the large Belgian population living in the country. Thousands of refugees, white and black, poured into Northern Rhodesia through Kasumbelesa and other crossing points. I remember passing through the Copperbelt and seeing hundreds of abandoned cars pocked with bullet holes and with shattered windscreens, all of them with CB (Congo Belge) number plates. There were so many families with silent men and bandaged, blank-eyed women holding terrified-looking children streaming through to sanctuary into Northern Rhodesia that major programmes had to be mobilised by the civil administration to help them. We rarely saw Dad as he became immersed in supervising the response to the crisis.

One day, Mum took me aside and told me that a Belgian family was coming to stay with us for a few days and I needed to treat them with sensitivity. It was all very awkward, the couple arrived with two children and no visible possessions. I heard crying at night and whispered conversations. During mealtimes, Dad struggled to speak to them in French. I had taken French lessons with a White Father missionary but few of the words I learned were much good apart from *désolée*. Mum told me to play with the Belgian kids. The younger boy took little interest in my things and sat rocking to and fro but I remember the girl vividly.

Her name was Nadine and she was about twelve years old. I showed her my die-cast toys: tanks, jeeps and the pride of my collection— a heavy, chunky, red fire-engine. Nadine stared down at the toys; there was no expression on her pretty, elfin features. She reached out and picked up the fire-engine. I summoned up the word, "Rouge" and, without warning, she slammed the heavy toy into the side of my head. Mum stanched the wound with Styptic and I had to throw away my blood-dabbled Aertex shirt. I left the silent Belgians to themselves for the rest of their stay. Who knows what horrors they'd seen and what they'd gone through. Whose fault was it? Not theirs anyway apart from being deluded enough to think it was going to be alright to remain in such a damaged country. It's the same for much of Africa's bitter history, people simply get eaten up. Those Belgian cars stayed abandoned and rusting for a long time along the Copperbelt roads, a warning of what might be coming.

The Congo emergency roiled on in the background while I continued to face my own small tests of courage. I was taken out fishing in Fort Roseberry by an older boy called Nicky who was about eighteen. Scarily tough, he later commanded a Royal Marines brigade in the Falklands War. It was the dry season and the water was low. We were using spinning lures to go for the striped tiger fish that lurked in the river's shallows. Nicky didn't talk much to me. I think I irritated him, and wonder now if my Dad paid him to go fishing with me. Nicky got even more annoyed when I snagged my line on something in an unfathomable black pool in a side branch of the river. He told me that he didn't want to lose the lure and line and ordered me to wade into the river and pull it out.

"What about the flatties?" I protested weakly; 'flatties' was Rhodesian slang for crocodiles. Officially, there were no flatties in the Mansa but I knew differently. I'd seen a spaniel get eaten by one when its owner, newly arrived from England, threw a rubber ball into the very same river and commanded it to fetch. In reply to my objection, Nicky unslung a .22 rifle and stood on a projecting broken tree trunk above the pool feigning watchfulness. I did not want to get into that water. I also knew that a .22 bullet might bounce right off a croc's head. Afraid to rile Nicky further, I advanced hesitantly. I can still see my naked legs shimmering in the inky water beneath me. My feet were clad in light rubbery plimsolls from Bata that we called *takkies*. I remember trying to sense objects on the sludgy bottom by prodding it with my *takkies*, fearing at any moment that a giant Nile saurian would come exploding upward. I inched out until the water reached the waistband on my khaki shorts, clinging anxiously to the fishing line as it disappeared into the black depths.

Nicky lit up a cig and seemed to be looking the other way. In reply to my whimpering call, he shouted at me to go further out but I came to a halt, too afraid to go deeper but too proud to come floundering out. Nicky kept barking out orders at me but I remained standing still trying to control my shivering. After what seemed like an age, Nicky said, "Look, no flatties!" and fired two shots into the water which fountained up next to me. Still, I couldn't move so he put down the gun and thrashed past me muttering, "For Heaven's sake!". He plunged into the water, swam a few strong strokes into the lagoon and ducked down.

There were bubblings and stirrings from the basaltic depths and he seemed to be gone a long while. I hurried back to the bank and picked up his gun. I was beginning to wonder what to do next when he burst to the surface waving the silvery lure. He looked furious and commanded me to hook up again and move further downstream – away from him. I was bitterly ashamed of having been too cowardly to go farther into the dark water, but tried to pull myself together and concentrate by studying the water to work out where the fish were. I knew it would irritate Nicky if I were successful, which made me desperate to be so. In the end, I caught three strong fish with rows of pointy teeth like cat fangs. I killed them by whacking them on their heads and then strung them through the gills with some sisal. Nicky caught nothing. I brandished the string of fish at Dad when he met him later. Dad asked Nicky, "How did he get on?" Nicky looked at me directly for the first time that day and answered, "He did alright. Caught some fish, didn't he?"

Then there was Seany, my mate from Mufulira, which he called 'Muf'. His dad did construction work for the Public Works Department in Fort Roseberry. His was a tough working class family from the Copperbelt, utterly unlike the genteel world of my parents who saw themselves as forming the top of the socio-economic tree. Yet due in part to where we were growing up, Seany and I shared a keen interest in war and weapons and compared notes about the military traffic we saw driving up north to the Congolese border. Seany taught me how to spew choice abuse in Rhodesian and how to fight dirty. We played knife-throwing games at each other's bare feet and he made each of us a wristlet out of the severed heads of white ant soldiers. He 'created' these by getting the big ants to bite at each other until their mandibles interlocked then he'd twist the heads off.

Seany and I had *kleilat* fights where we threw mud and sand-clumps and shot catapults at each other, as well as potting things with our air rifles together. The blue skop lizards that bobbed their heads in gardens took a terrible hammering. One of our favourite games was to play *tok-tokkie,* which involved knocking on doors then running away, or 'roof rattle' in which we'd chuck stones onto people's sloped, corrugated iron roofs and then scamper off before the annoyed inhabitants emerged. He also egged me on to go into the changing rooms during the Social Club Christmas panto of *Cinderella* to surprise in her 'skimpies' the well-built teenage girl playing the lead role.

In retrospect, I see Seany as the archetypal white Rhodesian, full of boundless confidence and aggression, the sort of guy who'd later become a 'troopie' in the Rhodesian Light Infantry during the Hondo War. We once took on some African boys in a catapult fight. The black lads responded with a willingness that came as a rude surprise and we soon began to get the worst of it as their 'catties' were made of car inner tubes and were much more powerful than our feeble store-bought things. The stones were really flying and even Seany began to look worried, "Sis man, let's get the hell out of here," he muttered. Looking back, it's hard not to see that skirmish as presaging the future battle for independence in the South.

When a young African man in neatly-pressed whites passing by on a bicycle saved our skins by ordering both us and the black boys to stop, Seany shouted back, "Ewe, muntu, voetsak!".

"That is very rude!" the African called, at which Seany took aim with his cattie and hit the Good Samaritan on the side of the head with a stone.

I stood down, shocked by Seany's belligerence, while the man rubbed his head and yelled, "You ah very bad boys. I will tell your faddas and I pray to God they will beat you."

Somebody must have called the police as, moments later, two white N.R.G. constables whizzed up in a blue Landy with metal-grilled windows. They questioned the man with the bike and he kept pointing at us saying, "Bubili bwabo!", meaning "The pair of them!". Despite his plainly being in the right, he was the one who ended up getting arrested, while we ran home laughing. No wonder we had a sense of entitlement and the notion that we could get away with anything... but the boot would be on the other foot in the fullness of African time.

# 14
# Vikounta

*Old and young, we are all on our last cruise.*

– Robert Louis Stevenson

The sound of planes in Africa usually meant good news, especially the characteristic drone of the four engine Vickers Viscount that came into Lusaka once a week bringing mail from Salisbury and the Cape. The locals used to catch that sound and convert it into enthusiasm. Jonas's children ran about excitedly when those turboprop Rolls Royce engines came pulsing over, and would call out, "Vikounta, Vikounta!" The weekly Viscount wasn't always lucky. The Rhodesians lost two civilian Viscounts to ground-to-air missiles and Hammarskjold came down in its Douglas opposite number, a DC-6. Dad told me that the police found pieces of that DC-6 being sold in African markets around Ndola within hours of its crashing. In fact, that was how they located the crash site.

Dad was an imperturbable flyer, despite unnerving experiences in the war, like the time German 20mm flak punched through the wooden fuselage of his glider over the Rhine in 1945 during 'Operation Varsity', the final invasion of the Reich. His two pilots were so frightened that they refused to descend for his troops to deploy. Dad told me that he'd had to slam his boot onto the pilot's control stick, forcing the glider to dive and escape the flak, which likely saved not only the pilots' lives, but also those of Dad and his men.

My parents made a point of never travelling together on planes without us when we were kids in case a plane went down and orphaned us. We had to use the infamous Comet to fly to England and, for a while, I flew to school there alone while we were still living in Africa. The Comet was the world's first commercial jet airliner, and was touted as the pinnacle of British aviation at the time. It didn't have a great reputation, being known for its instability on take-off, a flaw that caused a series of crashes. One Comet broke up over Elba *en route* to Africa, killing all passengers and crew aboard, including ten kids going home from school like I did. The air safety investigators found out later that the fuselage around the square windows was weak and had a tendency to crack at altitude. All jet planes were made with rounded windows after that crash.

The search and rescue people fished out the mailbags from the bottom of the Mediterranean after the destruction of Comet Flight 781 and delivered the water-damaged blue aerogrammes to their destinations in Northern and Southern Rhodesia. I remember being shown one of those recovered envelopes by a school master of mine. The blue onion-skin paper had puckered and faded to a pale lilac. I felt chilled holding it and have occasionally wondered whether I was magically infected by some nebulous pent-up terror of flying that passed from that ill-fated missive into the depths of my being.

Plane travel remains forever associated in my mind with lone journeys to various boarding schools. These began with my flights in a war-surplus Dakota to my preparatory school in Southern Rhodesia and continued with my despairing unaccompanied journeys from Lusaka to London. There was a terrible beauty looking down upon Africa by night from thirty-thousand feet. There'd usually be no lights visible at all but a few times Lake Victoria appeared, a vast, dimpled, silver mirror in the moonlight. Once I saw an orange circle in the blackness far below that seemed to flicker and morph, and realised that it must have been a huge bush fire, maybe twenty miles across, blazing unseen by anyone else in some remote wilderness.

Over Entebbe one time, the cabin filled with white vapour. The other passengers shrieked and screamed and one man leaped from his seat and shouted out, "We're going to die!" and began hammering on the door to the pilots' cabin until he was felled by an uppercut from a thickset mining engineer who'd been sitting next to me and drinking whiskey all through the flight. "That shut his bliksem row!" the grinning engineer said to me on returning to his seat. Shortly afterwards, the air cleared and our little interruption was blamed on 'technical difficulties'.

Then there was the time we landed in Khartoum for refuelling. Soldiers surrounded the plane and columns of black smoke could be seen rising up from the city beyond the airport. "They are burning the American embassy again," one passenger commented dryly and no one else seemed particularly surprised. In those days, Africa was going through such tumultuous times. Even my own tribe could be dangerous. On one trip from Lusaka to London, a wild-eyed, middle-aged Englishwoman announced to me that my parents had asked her to look after me and I was to do everything she said. I knew my parents had never spoken to her and employed all my boyish wiles to escape her lunatic clutches. She was still calling out to me as I scuttled away from her through customs on arrival in London.

*Our little family in Athens, 1965, the year of Rhodesian U.D.I.*

My last flight out of Africa was in an Alitalia Caravelle with my family. We stopped to see Athens *en route* and toured the Acropolis, birthplace of democratic government. The Greek newsagents had all the British papers and we read the shocking headlines: It was the 11th November 1965 and Ian Smith, the Rhodesian premier, had announced the Unilateral Declaration of Independence. He'd been a Spitfire pilot in the war and probably chose the day for its patriotic associations with wartime sacrifice. In our hotel room, Dad tuned his little transistor radio to the World Service and we listened to Smith declaring: "We Rhodesians have rejected the doctrinaire philosophy of appeasement and surrender. The decision we have taken today is a refusal to sell our birthright. We may be a small country but we are a determined people who have been called upon to play a role of worldwide significance." In long the silence that followed Dad shook his head and said sadly, "I think we've just heard announced an intention by a whole people to commit suicide."

The previous day, our last day in Africa, my sister and I went out into our Lusaka garden and collected things that would remind us of our birth continent. We stored what we found in red Bata shoe boxes, one for each of us. In my box, there's what looks like a piece of bamboo stem, a phial containing red earth, a twist of filmy shed snakeskin, an iridescent beetle's wing, some husked jacaranda pods and an envelope with my boyhood writing on it that reads 'seeds'. Maybe I'll sow them one day and see what comes up after sixty years.

There's one more object in my Africa box that I'd been carrying around like an amulet for weeks before that day when Susan and I stored away our last mementos of Africa. It's a severed hawk's foot, still with its ruff of brindled feathers. It came from a hawk I shot with my .22, a goshawk I think. I remember fixing her barred chest in my sights as she glided low over the yellow spear grass. I regretted my heedless shot the moment I found her on the ground staring at me with blazing golden eyes that held no pity for either herself or me as I advanced for the *coup-de-grace*. I kept her foot, the claws forever grasping in mid-clutch. I think I must've chosen to carry it with me, ever since, as a mute reminder of my severance from Africa and all that might have been for me.

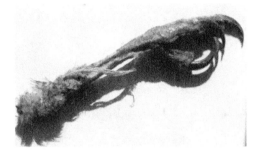

*The Goshawk's Claw*

# PART TWO

# 15
# Very Much a Rhodesian

*The blunt fact is that it is by no means certain we shall be in Northern Rhodesia much longer. Developments in the last few weeks have not given me confidence to look forward to a much longer period than that. I am faced, therefore, with the necessity of sending my son on to England. However, he is very much a Rhodesian and looks with disfavour on English schools.*

−Extract from a letter by my father to the headmaster of Ruzawi School, 1964

You can bet your *babijahn* arse that my Dad spoke true and I remained a Rhodesian even though I was flung into the dank corridors of a pair of provincial English boarding schools. When faced with a geography class, I'd always turn my atlas to Central Africa and pass my finger over the outline of my lost country, murmuring to myself the magic place names: "Mazabuka, Bangweulu..." If other boys encroached on me I'd spit out "Voetsak" to them and in my French oral language tests I would always commence with the prepared phrase, "Je suis né en Rhodésie".

Dad had lost his own mother and father by the age of twelve and had escaped straitened circumstances by means of a grammar school education. He truly believed that by sending me away to school in England he was giving me fabulous educational opportunities that had been denied to him. My orphaned Mum never spoke of her life before meeting Dad but used to weep whenever I went off to boarding school, perhaps because she knew herself what horrors such institutions held.

My first English school was Hawkhurst Court in Sussex. The place has now vanished, thankfully. I understand some of the buildings survive in the guise of bijou homes. There is little documentary evidence that the school ever existed but the fabric of the surviving buildings, the very dust, must groan with the accumulated distress of hundreds of miserable school boys who attended the place over the years. The mere sound of its name still gives me a shudder. I used to fly there from Lusaka and was brought to the school from London by one of my parents' friends. It was the first time I'd spent a lengthy period in England, one of many wild colonial boys sent to the hellish dump because the place was supposed to be a crammer for the educationally backward.

I'd been toughened by attending Ruzawi from the age of eight but Hawkhurst was no picnic in comparison. For one thing, the masters there were far more perverse than the hard but straight-laced Rhodesian ones. Sequestered deep in the Sussex woods, bitterly cold for lads from tropical zones, merely being there caused me to suffer from near-constant chest infections. The air around the main building, Old House, smelled perpetually of cabbage and we were taught in chilly Nissen huts that had formerly been occupied by doomed Canadian soldiers training for the 1942 Dieppe Raid disaster, famed for its seventy percent casualty rate. The soldiers had left their names and other inscriptions carved in the trunks of the beech trees that clustered thickly around the school and it seemed a haunted place.

The lost spirits were not only of soldiers. It was reputed among us that the spectre of the wife of the school's terrifying headmaster and founder, Mr Maunsell, walked the rose gardens at the back of Old House by night. Maunsell kept the garden as a memorial to her and any boy caught interloping there would get a vicious caning. I have a copy of a handwritten letter from Maunsell to my father extolling the virtues of the school. The writing is hard to read, the pen-strokes jaggedly awry, an indicator of the aberrant character of its author. I can just make out that Maunsell wrote of me, "*We will do our best to bring him on. He will come to us with a pretty low standard. They invariably do these days from Africa*. Maunsell was tall, elderly and stooped but still savage. I once watched him beat a boy with one hand while holding him by the ear with the other. The ear tore part way from the head and the school nurse had to suture it up.

But Maunsell was not the worst by a long shot. There were the almost uniformly creepy male staff, perpetually watching us queuing naked for showers as we held out our hands for a squirt of Vosene to wash our hair. Then there were the infernal Welches, Mr Welch, beefy, red-faced, flaxen-haired and forever demanding to know, "Have you been touching yourself, boy?" His allegedly once glamorous wife was now head-scarfed and harpy-like, pushing boys forward for Welch's post-luncheon public beatings in his classroom with a sawn-down cricket bat. There would always be a scrum of boys watching the spectacle, yelling and jostling like a crowd at some eighteenth century public execution, while the petrified, pallid victims were prodded forward by a smiling Mrs. Welch.

Most of the teachers were misfits who'd been ejected from other schools. Some were broken down and meek, others sadistic beaters. Many were war-damaged men like the naval officer, Commander Crook, an ex-POW, who shook with rage if you inadvertently mentioned Japan and who had pulpy fingers with no nails because the *Kempei-Tai* had pulled them out in Changi Gaol. Then again there were the outright perverts, including one – I seem to have buried his name, but vividly recall his feral body smell as he pressed too close to me – who marked my work in class with a pen in one hand while the other burrowed into my trousers. He also liked to grab boys' nipples with his pincer-like fingers and twist them, leering as he did so.

Unwary boys got 'the full treatment' if they foolishly allowed themselves to get caught in his rooms. I was strong and wily enough to elude him though, and compared notes on my evasions with the handful of other Rhodesian lads who attended the school. It made me laugh out loud to receive an email from Sussex Police a few years ago enquiring whether I'd experienced 'abuse of any kind' at the school. It was so funny, not only due to the irony of the suggestion that any boy there *hadn't* been abused in one way or another, but also because sex seemed to lurch out from a seething pit of repression in those days and grown-ups who secretly grasped and grabbed were everywhere so that we were hardly aware at the time that anything was out of line.

We seemed to have imbibed the notion that human, or at least male, sexuality was fundamentally a coercive business. It appeared to us to be about the ungovernable thrusting themselves upon the unwilling, much as I had witnessed among troops of *babijahns* back in Rhodesia. It never so much as occurred to me to tell my parents about any of it. There was no point; it was simply how school life was for the lot of us. Besides, had I thought to speak of what went on there, how would I be able to explain the horrors of Hawkhurst Court to them? Or maybe it was that I simply presumed they must've endured similar horrors in their own childhoods or in the war about which, nothing could be said.

*Boys arriving for summer term at Hawkhurst School in 1966, heading for their 'Lord of the Flies' experience. No uniforms but plenty of rules, of both the written and unwritten sort. (Photo courtesy of Kirby English).*

In the middle of the night, or on fuzzy autumnal afternoons, the feeling returns, there is an amorphous pressure on me, a shadow falling and my chest banging with terror but my legs cannot carry me away. The feeling stays with me for a few suffocating minutes, then departs as swiftly as it descended, like a raptor springing up into air and away. For years, I did not name it but in middle age I began to call it my 'black hawk time'. Where did it originate, that recurrent terror? Only by forcing to light events that time had long sought to dismember could I at last find a locus for it. It had been at Hawkhurst Court, of course; in Old English did not 'Hawkhurst' mean 'wooded hill of the hawk'?

Yes, when 'black hawk time' comes, it's always spring of 1966. I'm trapped in Mr Pelmore's rooms, high up in towering Old House. In Pelmore's rooms, there is the smell of pipe smoke, the metal-framed Crittal windows are misted up, no need for curtains. I've lost most of my clothes. My skin is cold, my entrails colder stilling, filled up with the icy slush of terror. Pelmore's domed mantel clock is ticking loudly. His meaty hands, with their ridged nails are rending my flesh. He mumbled commands to do this and do that. Liquid begins to seep from my wounded secret parts. I scurry away after pulling up my trousers, to an accompaniment of muttered threats mixed with specious gestures of kindness, an attempt to ruffle my hair.

Matron stops me in the corridor. My first instinct is to run. We were frightened of her pointy face and metallic voice and called her 'The Wicked Witch of the West" behind her back. She leads me to her treatment room and cleans off the mucus and blood trails that have run down the insides of my legs. She averts her face from me but her voice is full of seeming concern. She says, "You must call me if Mr. Pelmore asks you to go to his room again," but I know she will not really protect me. And besides the other boys have told me that she is the one who selects the victims and steers them to him. Fat, monocled Mr. Pelmore, was that really his name? I've summoned it from the depths. I am not sure but his name is writ in darkness, whatever it was.

It is Black Hawk time visiting me again, coming from nowhere. His hard, red eyes, the rustle of his wings. He presses his beak to my cheek. He is the king bird, come back for me. I recognise him now, no longer a sharp-clawed enemy, no, I see now he's trying to protect me. I'm going to welcome him from now onward. Black Hawk, take me in your wings, fly me away from the nightmares of childhood. I will not bother you further with tiresome complaints of victimhood. It's strange how fierce the voices of victims have become nowadays. At the time, I presumed Pelmore picked me out because he had divined some deficit in my character, some essential weakness or timidity. If so, then he inadvertently activated the emergence of a steely adult persona. Whoever expected that life would not be hard? How could it be any other way? Black Hawk has sharpened my senses, his eager talons drawing blood as he grips my wrist.

# 16
# An English Education

*If every day in the life of a school could be the last day but one, there would be little fault to find with it*

– Stephen Leacock.

Looking back, the few decent teachers at Hawkhurst seemed to form a cast of characters of an ebullient, tough-minded English type that's all but extinct now. I think mostly of Mr. Singleton, pug-faced and wheezing from having been gassed in the trenches of the First World War. He was kindly, wise and sad, always coming out with ironic Latin metonyms like "Celeriter", trying to get us to hurry along the corridors. He once showed us photos of his brother officers killed at Loos. Singleton was a bachelor teacher, quietly mourning his dead companions. He taught us Common Entrance, giving extra lessons in his poky cottage on the school grounds, even though he was manifestly ill.

We'd sit in his cramped sitting room while he doggedly gave us cramming sessions. His hands shook when he took my exercise book and he seemed to be in constant pain, forever mopping his face with a voluminous handkerchief and excusing himself to go, groaning, to the lavatory. When he came back there would be drops of blood on his tweed trousers. The last lesson he gave was agonising for all of us. He managed to last out the hour, told us he could do no more for us and bid us good luck and farewell. As he ushered us to the door, we timidly told him we hoped he'd be feeling better soon. He raised his hand in a gesture of dismissal, "Consummatum est," he muttered. We heard he'd died a month later.

Despite the terrors of Hawkhurst and the deficiencies of my African education, I managed to pass the Common Entrance Exam, the entrée to English public school. My godfather, the Reverend Sam Facey, had been a colonial officer in Northern Rhodesia before the war and had attended Blundell's. I think he suggested to my father that the school would amply suit a colonial boy like me. That was how I came to that Devonian public school in the autumn of 1966. The boys were divided up into 'houses', cavernous Victorian barns each with their own strange rituals. I was still in my civvies as I dragged my tuck box and trunk up through North Close's metal-sheathed front door. My new straw boater and brick-coloured school jacket lay packed within that trunk, along with sets of white shirts and bundles of stiff starched collars. Mum also included a surfeit of 'Chilprufe' thermal woollen vests out of fear that I'd be unused to English winter weather.

Also tucked into that trunk were two 45 r.p.m. single records. One was *Ag Pleez Deddy* by Jeremy Taylor, a best-selling, brutally amusing song about South African white working class teens. I knew and understood the context of every line. I also brought with me *My Generation* by The Who. I'd played the stuttering, snarling hit-record anthem to my parents before I left for school. They'd listened to it in shocked silence, maybe sensing from its clanging guitar riffs and shouted chorus the storm that was in store for them from their son. Oh, and hidden among my handkerchiefs was a brass knuckle duster I'd bought off a Rhodesian chum. I was brewing trouble, already scarred, suspicious, wary and disdainful of bourgeois English ways. The omens were not good for a stellar school career.

Past the towering limes fronting tall white rugby posts, rust-red stone buildings same colour as our jackets, arrowings of jackdaws from the school tower, sherry-coloured autumn light, glittering of dew on the chapel lawn, the walls of many of the school buildings close-matted by crimsoned Virginia creeper, the bells ringing for breakfast and boys from all the distant houses would come running. Our detachable collars were a devil to manage with cold fingers and many of the lads pounded along with their collars sprung free like small white wings to each side of their necks.

Most of the English boys had never left home before however I was a veteran of far tougher places. I knew you needed to establish your dominance early on and in the words of my Jeremy Taylor record I needed "*to moer all the outjies*". Accordingly, I selected the biggest boy in my group and without warning, after breakfast one morning, I bloodied his nose with my knuckle-duster. Very sportingly, he did not report me but word got around that it was unwise to mess with me.

Ah, those days in the winter of 1967, antecessor to the vaunted Summer of Love, of which we knew next to nothing. In the mornings the unheated dorms could be so cold our bath towels froze stiff on their runners. Monitors flicked laggards with wet flannels and slammed open the sash windows to dispel the frowsy night-reek of twenty adolescent boys penned together, Breakfast was a fried egg skidding in a puddle of grease, avidly gobbled, for we were always hungry, and washed down by an anthracitic cup of tea dispensed from giant metal pots. We'd file into chapel under the brass plaque inscribed '*In Pious Memory of Peter Blundell*', where we sang from *Hymns Ancient and Modern* and listened to the hypnotic prose rhythms of *The KJV* and the incantatory poetry of *The Book of Common Prayer*. Then out again we marched beneath the commemorative Toc H lamp and the gold-lettered lists of Blundell's war dead, accompanied by the rumbling and pealing of the chapel organ.

Bells rang incessantly as we speeded our way to classes lest we get 'six blue sides' for lateness. Masters followed behind us, wrapping their gowns around themselves to ward off the cold. Each day was bound about by arcane rules: First year boys may not have any jacket buttons undone; only seniors could walk on certain strips of grass; monitors alone are permitted to have hands in trouser pockets. We were also introduced to strange new words. If you were 'in a bate', for example, you were angry, while 'to gribble' meant to grasp the testes. This one had a passive and active sense. On the one hand, there was the leisurely, voluntary activity known as 'pocket gribbling'. On the other, were violent attacks when other boys tugged or twisted your genitalia. You had to mind out if you got caught fighting for then you were in danger of a 'swishing' (the cane).

The school introduced us to a Darwinian cosmos, where we younger ones were a lower order of life known as 'ticks', relentlessly preyed upon by senior boys called 'nobs'. The use of Latin gave us the sense that we were caught up in some atavistic *Tom Brown's School Days* existence. The masters called out '*aeger*?' when asking if anyone was absent due to sickness. *Exeats* were granted six times per term and comprised liberty to visit the nearby market town of Tiverton on a Saturday. An *absit* was for a longer period of time; I got one to go down to Exeter, the nearest city, for an x-ray after injuring myself falling from a bicycle. *Aegrotat* was a coveted sick pass that got you off 'games', which denoted our afternoon sessions of team sport. The words '*Benedictus benedicat*' resounded before each meal...'May the blessed one give a blessing'.

We treated each other with few blessings, however. No-one dared show weakness that would attract vicious taunting and could get you a dreaded nickname that could scar your school life forever like poor Rodgers who became 'Skunk' Rodgers due to the smell of his rotten socks or McGuffie who got the name 'McGurk' due to a slight stammer. If someone coughed in class others made noises in their throats in ironic salute. If you had a touch of teenage acne known as a 'shag spot', it was supposed to indicate self-abuse.

"Shag spot! You dirty bastard, you've got a shagger!" the nobs would yell, drawing out the word 'shagger' and rolling the final 'r' in an exaggerated way.

Other strange rituals: At the beginning of classes, boys lifted their desk lids with one finger and let them fall as we rose to attention when the master entered the classroom.

Thus, 'the beak's' entry would be marked by the sound of drumming thunder, the weaker the master, the louder the noise. On those same antique oak desk lids, our fingers traced the carved inscriptions and gougings of legions of boys gone by. Our olive-green Latin textbooks were similarly inscribed. Many were those who had their Latin Primer title amended to form that age-old schoolboy joke: 'Kennedy's Shortbread Eating Primer'.

There were so many ways for the bored pupil to misuse his tin of Oxford Mathematical Instruments, with its blue picture of Balliol College on the top. The tedious classroom hours were eased by using the compass point to bore holes in one's desktop, while the six inch wooden ruler was handy for flicking pellets of spit-hardened blotting paper. Sometimes, we were issued with wooden-handled dip pens with brass nibs like a bird's beak. You could dab these into your Quink bottle and then covertly flick droplets of ink onto the necks of boys in the next row.

Lunch was a godsend for roiling bellies although you had to avoid sitting next to a master or his wife, with their obligatory stifling conversation. *'Benedictus benedicat'* and you'd peer down at your plate to see what slops had been offered up. "What the dickens is it?" I heard one new boy exclaim. It might be Irish stew with stranded dumplings floating amid the greyish scum atop, or charred curlicues of liver and onions followed by a block of synthetic yellow ice cream, or stodgy pudding made of a length of dough speckled with raisins and known as 'matron's leg'. It never occurred to anyone to actually complain about the food. If someone had thought to, you can be sure they'd have been squashed quick-smart.

Individuals didn't matter; any nails that stood out were to be hammered down for we were being given new identities as Blundellians, after all. Each of us ticks was paired with a second year boy whose role was to tutor us in preparation for the school knowledge test. If you failed, you and your mentor would get a beasting from the monitors. Questions were fired at you such as, "Where do you find a school squirrel?" (Answer: 'In the chapel window and on the cadet corps badge'), or "Who was Peter Blundell?" (Answer: 'Of this town, sometime clothier, died 1604'). I failed my test intentionally and my mentor and I had to scrub floors as penance. I knew the answers well enough, but let myself fail out of contempt for the sneering monitors. It was an early intimation of my stubbornly rebellious nature. My Rhodesian accent had begun to fade yet I still spewed out Afrikaans insults under threat and a sullen antipathy to everything about my English school had already set in.

There was a brief respite after lunch when we went back to our houses. There, mail was laid out on a long table. Older boys sometimes received perfumed letters which they carried off with cries of triumph. We could also read from newspapers put out on the battered common room armchairs. This was the time to go to 'the tuck shop' and stock up on some Swizzells Lovehearts — each fizzy lozenge was imprinted with an amatory message to lift the heart of even the most hideous schoolboy — or purchase yellow and brown bags of Peanut Treets which you could eat quietly without detection in afternoon classes.

Those deathly endless afternoon periods — what a relief when I could sneak into Mr. Panther's empty biology classroom, where there was much to divert me in the form of African animals: mounted antelope horns on the wall, a stuffed crocodile and sundry other examples of Victorian imperial taxidermy. Even better were the giant Kilmer jars in a looming antique glass cabinet. These contained ghost-white salamanders and toads floating in preserving fluid and, most fascinating of all, the suspended, waxy form of a macrocephalic human foetus which resembled Dan Dare's insidious alien enemy, The Mekon, who featured in our weekly *Eagle* comic magazines.

Dinner, known as 'tea' started promptly at 5.50, often sausage and beans followed by bread and jam. Occasionally, you got cake or a bowl of greyish semolina into which you dropped a gobbet of jam and stirred mightily to turn the concoction mauve. Back in our houses, evening bells rang out the changes; 'fags', which is to say, informally enslaved younger boys, rushed about doing their elder masters' bidding, "Go and warm my bog seat, fag!"..."Burnt the toast again you, infernal tick!" Thud of a flung cadet corps boot and the scuffling retreat of a wretched fag.

Next came Quiet Hour — murmured conversations and radios played low. Juniors often wrote home at this time but you knew not to leave letters lying about because bullies liked to scrawl jocular comments on them such as, "Dear mater and pater, I'm ever so useless. All I can do is blub, blub, blub." At this hour, boys mooched about the great Victorian hulks of the boarding houses, which were often shrouded in chilly, Devonian evening mist. Come 7.15, the main doors of the houses were locked and we were sealed in for the night. First 'prep' began, the time when we were supposed to do homework. We juniors sat in our common room, one wall lined with shelved wooden tuck boxes, on the other a large map of the world to the reverse side of which we'd stuck a poster of the pneumatic film star, Raquel Welch, in an animal-skin bikini from the film *One Million Years B.C.* We'd flip the map around during prep and gaze upon that Amazonian form, although Argus-eyed Mr Park, the housemaster, eventually discovered and removed it.

Evening Prayers broke the monotony. We gathered together, the house master read prayers and we sang, *The Day Thou Gavest, Lord Has Ended*. Then, second prep until 10.00., followed by wash time and 'lights out' at 10.20. Darkness in the dorm released muted sobbing from the homesick huddled under blue blankets. Anyone caught with a teddy bear had its head ceremonially removed with a penknife. Monitors opened the dorm door from time to time and uttered dire warnings about no talking. I'd furtively click on my Pye transistor radio, insert the ear plug and try fruitlessly to get an African station.

Sometimes there were rougher dorm activities, like the ordeal called 'doing the rounds', where each boy in a new dorm had to obey the unwritten rule that you must complete a circuit of the dorm without touching the floor. I was an old hand at such rituals from my previous schools and knew that it was essential to succeed in this initiation rite. So, in the first nights at the school before the tougher boys had mobilised, I bounded across rows of beds in the dark, swung along coat hooks mounted into the back wall, traversed the monitor's creaking wooden partition, skipped back down the bed rows along the opposite side, fighting off anyone who tried to impede me, before clambering across the rattling sash windows and back into bed.

You hoped all the while that no monitors would be roused by the racket and beat you with a plimsoll, or make you do house runs across the frosted grass of a rugby pitch in bare feet. Worse could happen if the house master caught you. It was alright for the sporty and strong or wiry maniacs like me but a plump or unhandy boy would have to keep on trying to 'do the rounds' for weeks, getting caught time and again and taunted for being a weakling or 'a spazz'. We'd be midway through term and the poor bastards would still be hanging from the dorm coat hooks while someone wrenched their pyjama bottoms down.

Annoyance rather than pity would eventually prompted someone to grumble, "For fuck's sake, just let him get round. We need some sleep." Then the dorm would begin to settle although there could be other 'alarums' like dorm raids when another dorm would creep silently along the bitter cold corridors in pyjamas to burst in on their rivals and batter them with pillows and steal trophies like wash bags. Members of the defeated dorm would have to beg for their possessions back the next day.

Darkness pooled and weighed us down, gradually silencing even the most rambunctious ones. I'd press my Timex to my ear, listen to its faint ticking and imagine my life slipping away in English exile. Eleven pm: moans, furtive movements, a call of, "Madge! Stop whatever you are doing!"

One full moon midnight, we were roused by a terrible clang when a troubled boy suddenly rammed his head through the rungs of his iron bedstead. The school handyman had to be called to release him. Usually though, the dorm would eventually subside amidst whimpers and sighs as we drifted off into uneasy sleep and dreams of escape.

# 17
# My Generation

*Why don't you all f-fade away?*

– The Who

Blundells had always been a 'roaring' school, one that fitted well with my combative colonial African upbringing. R.D. Blackmore's John Ridd in the romance-adventure novel, *Lorna Doone*, learns at Blundell's that: "*the principle business of good Christians is, beyond all controversy, to fight with one another.*" It is said that the original seventeenth century school was made from timber recovered from the wrecked Spanish Armada, the detritus of war. The school hero was Parson Jack Russell, flogged during his time there for having put a ferret into the cage of a monitor's pet rabbits, I admired him for that although my favourite old Blundellian was Bamfylde Carew who fled the school in 1708 after grave misdemeanours and became a dedicated conman and adventurer, who eventually laid claim to the title 'King of the

Gypsies' and achieved nationwide fame for his dictated *Life and Adventures* in the subtitle of which he styled himself a *"rogue, vagabond and dog-stealer".*

The rise and fall of the turbulent River Lowman set the school pulse, not only at the Old School, which stands adjacent to its banks, and used to pack up all lessons and activities on flood days, but also, in an unconscious way, at the modern school in its new location a mile uphill at Horsdon. Most days, I liked to wander out the back of the school buildings and sneak off downslope to observe the changeful Lowman. I'd smoke minty Consulate cigarettes, usually sitting on a willow branch by the bank. Sometimes I'd fish its low pools for brown trout. When rain on Exmoor would make the river come *"foaming down like a great roan horse",* as described in *Lorna Doone,* I kept my distance. I remember seeing a farmer weeping after the irascible river had ripped through his chicken house, leaving his hens stuck to the wooden walls like white feathered patties.

We scrapped, brawled and mock-wrestled our way through the supposedly progressive and pacifistic late 1960s. Fighting, for real or in fun, was one of the few activities that linked me to my former African life. Even good friends tried to trip each other up unexpectedly and dealt out 'dead legs' by kneeing one another in the outer thigh, or giving numbing 'noogies' where you put your victim into an arm-lock and rubbed your knuckles on one of his pressure points. We were keen on knife-throwing games in bare feet on Milestones pitch. You had to place your naked foot wherever the knife stuck in the ground. The aim of the game was to get your opponent to stretch his legs out further and further until he toppled over. Occasionally, the knife hit flesh and it was off to matron for swabbing with permanganate.

We'd ride out in packs on our drop-handle bikes on cross-country jaunts, jinking and weaving, often trying to unseat each other. Our swift, silent approach and sudden bicycle bell-ringing on country lanes made the occasional surprised local leap for a hedge with alarm, and "You blasted Blundell's buggers!" would be yelled in our wake. My memories of the place carry a rusty tinge. The rows of rufous jackets bent over their school work as I daydreamed out the classroom window. Thick red mud dropped from our boot studs onto the changing room floors after rugby. Four to a bath, all at the same time, wallowing in chestnut water. Sanguinary snot trails from the bigger boy I hit in the face with a bike chain wrapped around my fist after he made the mistake of trying to bully me, not realising he was taking on a former Rhodie.

We also fought with outsiders and they with us. I was riding down Post Hill on my bike one afternoon when I was struck by a missile from a departing bus containing the sports team from another school. The projectile was an apple given extra velocity by our combined speed in opposing directions. It hit my head with the seeming force of a fast-pitched cricket ball, unseating me and necessitating a trip to Exeter Hospital. Our rivals' bus gave out a great cheer as I tumbled over.

Brawling with the local Tivvie lads carried the additional rancour of class war. There was the so-called 'neutral mile' of Blundell's Road leading into town but once you'd passed the stranded Great Western Railway steam locomotive mounted at the road junction with Fore Street at the edge of town, you were in their territory. After that point, it was best to go about in groups. During the annual parade from Old School to St. Peter's Church, a great column of us in straw boaters marched through town while a crowd of local lads jeered and made wanking gestures and we gave covert V-signs back. The old mill leats at Paradise Woods were our front line and we had many a stick fight there with the denim-jacketed Tivvy boys.

I think the fighting ebbed as we got older, or maybe it was that no-one fancied tangling with me in particular after I unintentionally broke a boy's arm in a scuffle outside the dining hall in my second year. He was a big lad who'd baited me many times. This time I surprised him by launching myself at him with all I had, causing him to fall backwards onto the point of his elbow. "Agh shame!", as the Rhodie saying goes. To his credit, he didn't squeal on me but despite his honourable conduct, it was still a great satisfaction to see his plaster cast in the opposite row at chapel each morning for the rest of the term.

Sergeant-Major Munday, late of the Army Physical Training Corps, once stopped me scrapping with a boy and ushered us to the gym where he made us put on boxing gloves. It was like with Viljoen at Ruzawi all over again. My opponent boxed far better than I and swiftly pounded my face to jelly. I could barely see out of watering eyes and stalactites of slime swayed down from my nostrils. Munday got us to shake hands afterwards but I bided my time and let my wrath grow. I later caught my opponent off-guard as we were returning from games and ground his head with my studded rugby boots until he squealed, "Pax!" Ruzawi had taught me that when it came to fighting only idiots respected the rules. I was given the nickname 'Herman', after the Frankenstinian paterfamilias in a black and white, American TV sitcom of the day called *The Munsters*. Like the character, I was a tall, ungainly fellow, with jutting ears and badger-brush hair and a high forehead. I also shared some of his awkward comic menace.

A hardened indifference settled upon me. As long as no one messed with me, then I looked on calmly as new boys were dragged past me to be 'bogged' by having their heads thrust down the lavatory. Although I did not participate in it myself, when ticks were tossed into the Lowman and *"the little boys, falling on their naked knees, blubbered upward piteously"*, as R.D. Blackmore had described the same business a hundred years earlier, I made no effort to rescue them. To me, suffering came from personal weakness and the rule of life was *sauve qui peut.* I've been told since that I'd fallen in with a tough crowd and this wasn't typical of the school at all. I don't know about that. What I did know at that time was that Vietnam and the Rhodesian Bush War were consuming thousands of young men only a couple of years older than me and I was preparing inwardly for things to get a whole lot worse.

Corporal punishment at Blundell's was on the way out. It had virtually vanished from the school by 1970 but our own cruel habits with one another did not change. In the fourth form, I developed a masochistic party trick of burning my initials onto my forearm using sunlight focussed by a magnifying glass. I think now that I must've been signalling that I couldn't be hurt by conventional means. I could be brutal to my own kind, especially to enemies, but I didn't share the taste for bullying that was so common among my English peers. Mostly I disliked the crowded nature of school life and simply wanted to be left alone. I'd spent much of my childhood and pre-teen years roaming the wild bush and was solitary by nature. I never really got used to the milling close quarters of school life: the communal showers and baths, the door-less lavatories (prevention of vice, you know), the literal pissing contests where boys vied with each other over how high they could get their stream and the termly school medical parades in the gym where we stood naked *en masse* to be examined by the school medical officer. As the Blundell's years rolled on, a sense of my stubbornly inhering African identity and a growing resentment of both institutional life and of my parents for inflicting it upon me began to distort my character so that a surly, mutinous dissonance began to dominate. Meanwhile, I kept on playing The Who's *My Generation*; it had become a personal anthem.

*1969, smoking by the Lowman, my ringed finger circling a Consulate Menthol.*

Dylan sang about how "your sons and your daughters were beyond your command and the old road was rapidly changing" and that was specific enough for me. I wasn't picky in my radicalism. I flirted with the National Front for a while and painted swastikas on my tuck box. Then I changed my mind, wrote off to the Chinese embassy and got a parcel of Little Red Books and Chairman Mao lapel buttons, which I distributed to select classmates. Sedulously scruffy and madly rebellious, I dug in for a long war against all institutions, apart from the military which I continued to revere. The oppositional times fed my native insurgency. In 1968, I failed my 'O' Levels, except for English and History. During my Geography 'O' Level exam, I wrote a jocular letter to the examiner instead of answering the exam questions. The young teacher, Malcolm Moss (later to become a Conservative M.P.), told me that the examiner had thoroughly enjoyed my piece but failed me anyway.

I also failed French even though I was becoming competent in the language and went to the library most days to read Paris Match back numbers. I'd been inspired by my paperback copy of Phillipe Labro's *Les Barricades de Mai*, an account of the 1968 Paris students' insurrection, and liked to write Situationist tags in my journals of the time, punchy French slogans like *'ni dieu ni maitre'* or *'soyons cruels'*. My extreme politics were wrapped around a conventionally morose adolescent romanticism and I liked to listen to Janis Joplin sobbing and wailing about having another piece of her heart taken, while watching from my junior study window as rain carried on westerlies from Exmoor cloaked the Lowman valley.

# 18
# No Cause At All

*How steep the stairs in stranger's houses, how bitter-salt the bread of exile.*

– Dante

Back home, things weren't much better. Dad told me I really ought to stop saying 'Ja' instead of 'Yes' in order to fit in better. We'd moved into an English house in the Midlands and had sat down together and watched the first screening of the Beatles' television film, *Magical Mystery Tour*. It struck me as surreal and amateurish, yet bustling with confidence as it ripped at the current social order. It held me spellbound. I'd had no inkling at Ruzawi or Hawkhurst as to what was going on in the western world.

Beatlemania had passed us by in Rhodesia. I stared at the eccentric haircuts and fantastical burlesque clothes the young wore. White African clothing was so strictly functional: khakis, sockless vellies and floppy hats to shield you from the sun. I wondered what my Rhodie mates would think of all this psychedelia. My parents certainly couldn't understand the cultural revolution to which they'd returned. Dad rustled his paper while Mum tutted and said the Beatles' film was "rubbish" but I could see they mainly looked puzzled and, yes, somewhat scared.

The thunder of desk lids at the start of class seemed to get louder as the turbulent '60s progressed. Once, in a chemistry lesson, the master made a mistake and a retort spat caustic soda into his face. He reeled back with a scream but most of the class laughed and made no effort to help him as he fumbled to get out the classroom door. Clearly, the generational conflict in wider society was manifesting in the school.

Blundell's prided itself on contributing to British meteorological reports using data from their weather station, which was situated within range of my study windows. I sniped the hell out of the anemometer and the white wooden casing holding the barometric instruments using a scoped .22 B.S.A. air rifle I'd smuggled into school. There were many attempts to find the phantom sniper but I was never caught, though my housemaster did find the rifle in the end. There were other clandestine revolutionaries, like the unknown hero who climbed the façade of the Big School and placed a jock strap around the neck of the statue of Peter Blundell, or the boys who sugared their house master's car and my chum, Tony C., who teamed up with me to make an I.E.D. out of fireworks to bomb some persecutory older boys.

My war against the school remained essentially a lone one though and gradually became more extreme. I left a cruel note on one master's desk stating that it did not matter what he said because in a few years he'd be dead but we'd still be alive. That one makes me shudder to confess. I'd also observed that the school seemed to depend on lists: Lists for punishments, sports activities, academic plaudits and all manner of other arrangements. These were posted on green baize notice boards in the main school buildings near to the head master's study. I used a bulb pipette filched from the science labs and filled with inky water to covertly spray those lists from time to time. This caused chaos and gave me immense satisfaction.

To my rebellious eyes, the school culture was nothing but one giant attempt to repress me through its tyrannical processes. As the Parisian Situationists would say, "*la culture, c'est l'inversion de la vie.*" The school never understood the ferocity of my revolt. Consequently, they sought to punish the rebellion out of me, at times switching over to attempts to cajole me out of my mind-set. In 1970, my housemaster, D.J. Park, writing in his termly assessment of me, remarked mildly: "He should think more before rejecting that which is of good report."

I see now that my discontent sprang principally from a sense of dislocation from my native place exacerbated by childhood traumas that had mutated into some sort of adolescent depression egged on by the drumbeat of the countercultural *zeitgeist*. Sodden with sullen rage and feeling as ugly as a grandpa's toenails, there seemed no end to my appetite for trouble. I was definitely heading for expulsion. I managed to semi-deliberately shoot an arrow into a cow during archery practice on Amory Field, and was interviewed by the transport police at Waterloo Station after I let off firecrackers in a carriage of the school train.

I began to conceive of myself as a stuntman, training myself by leaping from higher and higher branches of the giant cherry tree outside my boarding house. I also enjoyed climbing out onto the window ledge of my dorm after secretly attaching myself to the cable fire escape apparatus. I'd wait for some innocent passer-by on Blundell's Road, scream out that I was going to jump and leap from the window to the terror of the onlooker, only to be sedately lowered by the ratchet system on the cable. Once he discovered it, Park gated me for that crime and wrote to my long-suffering parents expressing concern. I ended up with a year's ban on leaving school grounds, and had to report at hourly intervals during all my free time. My sister has given me a letter I wrote to her during that period — a hectic scrawl on orange and pink paper:

*8ᵗʰ November 1970. Dear Sis, More of the Rake's Progress...*

*if I don't get out of here, I'll turn insane, or manic depressive, or a latent suicide. I'm planning to put a detonator and 15 lbs of TNT under the headmaster's seat in chapel and rocket him to glory. That's your lot from your loving and supremely bored brother.*

*love r... PS have bought a pair of groovy red velvet trousers.*

This letter denoted the high water mark of my active dissent. Something shifted in me quite suddenly at the end of 1970 and I turned from open mutineer to apathetic non-contributor.

I stopped trying to fight the system and instead poured my energy into masses of secretly-written poems inspired by reading Yeats, Hopkins and Auden. I've found evidence of this retreat in a folder of dismal school reports that my father kept in his files. Malcolm Moss wrote of me: "His general lethargy does not encourage one to predict success. Second from bottom of the class, he wastes his quite considerable abilities. In Geography and Current Affairs, he makes virtually no contribution. What are his priorities? The future has a great question mark suspended over it." Moss was a likeable master, youngish with a Northern accent, who sported sideboards and wore modish Hush Puppies. I sensed his concern about me but I had retreated too far away to respond.

Mr. Connor, another pleasant teacher unaligned with institutional orthodoxies, young and Byronically handsome, he liked to hang upside down from his classroom heating pipes, his gown hanging like bat's wings, while he called out to us to enumerate the chief reasons for the start of the Thirty Years War. He wrote about me: "I've been wondering if he will ever get round to doing some work. He has the best English style in the school yet he is bottom. Can't he just do a little bit of work? With him, apathy has become a way of life, a considerable pity."

Even the Headmaster, Reverend Stanton, pleaded with me, but I only despised him for it. He wrote to my father: "He needs to form a more mature judgement about things that matter most. Of course there is a good side to him but if he hides it then you cannot expect us to praise him. He has given a very convincing performance of one bent on academic suicide." How shameful now to contemplate my careless teenage self-destruction. Mr Patrick, my English teacher, seemed to sum up the school view on me, remarking once, "You are a world class nut, Madocks. Everyone knows it."

*School cadets: 1970, a scene mirroring Lindsay Anderson's film,
'If'. I'm on the far left preparing to shoot the new boys we called
'ticks', or maybe it's the masters I'm after.*

The only time I came alive was during any paramilitary
activities. I enjoyed several wonderful outings on night
exercise wearing my Dad's parachute regiment camo Denison
jacket. On one night patrol, we were creeping along a road
near Uplowman and arrived at a popular lover's lane area. We
crouched with our rifles next to a parked Ford Zephyr to find
the frightened moon faces of a courting couple peering back
at us from the steamed-up windows. It seemed a terrific
adventure to be driven out by night in the rattling, jolting
Cadet Corps Landy to visit local Devon units. I taught the
younger lads .303 S.M.L.E. rifle-stripping and naming of
parts, taking a purpose and pleasure in that which I found
nowhere else in my school years. By sixteen, my name was
down for Welbeck Infantry School and an army career
beckoned. My Dad was relieved as he considered it the best

place for a wayward son doing poorly at school. What he didn't know was that I planned to get training in the U.K. and transfer to the Rhodesian forces then battling against overwhelming odds in the Hondo.

I loved my excursions to Lympstone Barracks, the Royal Marines training base, on cadet intake days, crawling through flooded water pipes on the assault course, muscles screaming with the weight of wet equipment, combined with the dread of getting sucked under the black water. Running along the seashore with pack and rifle, white caps out on the Exe estuary, spume behind the fishing boats butting a March gale while gulls screamed overhead. Firing the S.L.R., *bap bap bap* into targets of a charging enemy soldier, yellow flicker of the ejected casings spilling over our boots, or letting rip with a tripod-mounted G.P.M.G., shredding targets at 750 rounds per minute. The buttoned-up faces of the marines instructing us, their fierce bright eyes. I admired them tremendously, their precision, their commitment, the tight nap and rake of their green berets, the way their uniforms moved with their compact bodies.

I wanted so much to be like them but, barely a year later, I threw it all away. Obeying the call of the hippie revolution, I took my name off the army lists and swerved into another way of being. Maybe it would've been better for me to be a soldier. I think that then I'd have really got to know who I was. Meanwhile, in 1970s Rhodesia, my old school chums were at war for real. I now think meanly of myself for not joining them. Better to fight for any cause than to have no cause at all.

# 19
# Toujours Rhodésien

*The true speakers are dead,*

*Cracked in the valley of hate.*

– Sidney Keyes

The Chimurenga was beginning to conflagrate in Rhodesia and most of the guys I'd known at Ruzawi had been conscripted. *Chimurenga* meant 'uprising' in Shona. The First Chimurenga referred to the Matabele revolt of 1896-97, which was put down by the British South Africa Company. The Second Chimurenga was the independence war against Ian Smith's regime. The new rebels spread the story that a powerful female spirit medium called Nehanda Nyakasikana, who had been hanged by Rhodes' men in 1897, had prophesied on the scaffold that a second Chimurenga would come in due course to sweep away the *Wazungu* forever.

I followed the news from Africa as best I could. The British press was becoming uniformly hostile to Rhodesia's quixotic battle to survive. I'd watched the 'shockumentary' mondo film, *Africa Addio*, about the meltdown going on in post-colonial Africa and was gripped by newsreel films of the Congo mercenaries, many of them older brothers of my Rhodesian school mates. During the Katanga secession, the mercs became known as *Les Affreux*, the frightful ones. I had a yen to be one of the *Affreux* in those polarised times. It's a shame that all young men with such aspirations these days are automatically cast and condemned as toxic extremists. While this might well be the case for many of them, for others it is not. Certainly, my unrealised ambitions in that direction were less the result of displaced aggression than of a need to fix upon an identity, the more extreme the better.

Meanwhile, most of our family friends had left Zambia, even those with deep roots in the country going back generations. Zambia had become ever more unfriendly to anyone who reminded them of the old order. Due in part to the Rhodesian Bush War, there was now a prevalent atmosphere of revolutionary fervour and racial paranoia. Africanisation policies had been introduced and many private businesses nationalised. By 1972, Zambia had declared itself a one party state where only U.N.I. P. candidates could stand in elections. A hundred and twenty prominent Zambian politicians were imprisoned for not toeing the party line, including Simon Kapwepwe, the former

Vice-President, whom my father thought to be among the best and brightest. Dad had, all this time, maintained a correspondence with President Kaunda, whom he'd known since Kaunda had been a young teacher in Chinsali in the 1950s. Once it became evident that the President was moving the country towards autocratic rule, this link petered out.

It was the summer of 1972. I'd left Blundell's with predictably dire exam results but one of the old, second tier, so-called red-brick universities said it would take me for its English and American Studies course on the strength of some poems I'd published. I decided I needed time to work out my direction in life and hitched down through Southern France. I had a half-baked idea of heading for Africa and, more crazily, the notion that I could turn up at the French Foreign Legion depot at Aubagne near Marseilles and enlist. The only thing I was really clear about was that I wanted an adventure, some paroxysm that would thrust me into an authentic way of life.

The further south I went, the more hostile the French locals became and the more the supply of lifts dried up. I got stranded near Chalon-sur-Saône and camped out in a dry gulch under a roadway. A group of Algerian 'illegals' arrived carrying suitcases balanced on their heads. They were skittish and fearful of the police but we all settled down, built a fire and shared what food we had. They sang and played on flute-like instruments and *darbuka* drums deep into the night. Our idyll ended as a golden dawn was heaping up in a violet sky. White-helmeted gendarmes came riding motorbikes through the sorghum fields and fell upon us. They pursued my companions of the previous night and I could tell from the screams when they found them that the beatings had commenced. I watched from a thicket as the Arabs were lined face-down in the dust and handcuffed, their suitcases emptied out and their meagre belongings burnt on our campfire.

I flitted away in dismay and headed for Marseilles where a thief cut a hole in my rucksack while I was walking along, stealing my money and papers. I took it as a sign that I wouldn't be getting into *La Legion* and moved on towards Nice. There, I joined other tangly-haired hippies who slept on the beach to the contempt of the bourgeois residents of the city who spat at us, threw bottles and dispatched the sanitary department each sparkling morning to turn their water hoses on our encampments. I still had shining thoughts of the person I could become but my days were spent on the sizzling beach shingle, begging from tourists and beating off stray dogs that came to forage among our bed-bundles.

I was rescued by a Christ-like figure clad in a woollen *djellaba* who appeared on the beach one day and asked us to join his commune on the outskirts of town. It turned out to be a monastic place run on Maoist lines where men and women lived in separate giant military-surplus tents. I spent my time stirring vast tubs of lentil stew and paid for my board by participating in the obligatory self-denunciation sessions convened each morning where we confessed all our anti-revolutionary thoughts and deeds. I passed the rest of summer there and quite enjoyed the austerity and discipline of the place.

*Sleeping rough on the beach at Nice, 1972. The hostile locals used to spit on us from the top of the sea wall. That wristwatch didn't last long.*

When whitecaps began to appear along the shoreline and streams of swallows were flickering south above our tents, I was rescued by a coincidental meeting with one of my Blundellian schoolfellows. I was sitting on the steps of the Russian Orthodox cathedral in Nice watching the crowds staring up at the blue onion domes when I spotted a lad who'd been a year below me at school standing with his mother while his father was getting ready to take a holiday snap.

I bounded up to my erstwhile fellow-pupil, told him I was in deep trouble and begged him for some cash. He looked horrified at my sunburnt, somewhat crazed appearance, made some excuses to his mother who kept trying to pull him away and slipped me all the money he had, along with a bag of peaches. Bless him, I never knew his full name and had never spoken to him while we were at school but he gave me enough to get a bus ticket up to Paris. It was to be the only time I ever relied on the old boys' network to help me. I wish I'd taken his address, I'd repay him a hundredfold now.

I met another footloose character on the way to Paris at a stopover in Grenoble, a South African who told me he'd treat me, as a fellow African, to a really 'lekker' meal. We sat down to a heavy Italian dinner at an upmarket restaurant. I was contemplating ordering a coffee at the close of the wonderful repast when my companion saw fit to tell me that he actually had no money to pay the bill. I had nothing either and almost instantly ran for it, my rucksack bumping on my back, while yelling waiters in long white aprons pursued me block after block until I hid under some laurel bushes in a public park. I never saw the South African again and can only assume the irate waiters caught him.

Things didn't get any better when I eventually made it to Paris. I lacked the funds to make my getaway back to the U.K. and spent weeks marooned on the hellish, eerie Parisian streets. I used to scratch about for small change lost in the dust under park benches and I'd use the small brass centimes I found to buy myself handfuls of gumballs that were sold out of coin dispenser boxes on the city streets. Those insipid sweets gave a taste of sugar and staved off the hunger pangs that used to cramp me at night while I curled up in the shrubberies. The cops beat the soles of my feet with their truncheons when they caught me sleeping on the park benches. Not that it was that easy to sleep on those boards as they were all fitted with sharp metal rivets to discourage tramps. Even then, Paris was overtly hostile to street people.

I evolved the risky strategy of getting free meals by allowing myself to be picked up by the desperate gay men who swarmed around the foreign hippies at the Gare du Nord. We sat on the pavement outside the station with our backs to a sunny wall. We called it 'the meat rack'. Hippiedom had moved from its idealistic to its nihilistic phase by then. Many of my companions were strung out on brown powder heroin and would beg for money and sell their bodies for the price of the next hit. We were known not to care about ourselves and were often hungry enough to try anything.

I'd let myself get approached by men then I'd manipulate them into buying me a baguette and glass of wine in exchange for doing the fell deed. I never encouraged them, but would usually simply lie on the pavement with my eyes closed until a pair of feet appeared next to me and a voice would say, "Viens, mon ami, pour passer un bon moment." I'd insist that I needed to eat straight away and they'd often reluctantly take me to a *bar tabac*. I'd usually bolt the food down, then feign illness, go to the reeking washrooms at the back and run like hell out the rear door. It was a risky lifestyle, given that I wasn't gay and disliked even being touched after my mauling at Hawkhurst.

Once, I was picked up by a middle-aged, Left Bank intellectual type, tall and thin with a scarf wound tightly around his narrow neck. He peered at me through rimless specs and I found it hard to reconcile his sallow, monkish features with his evident hunger for male flesh. I watched him with the eyes of a wolf regarding the hunter who, full of misplaced confidence, comes up to view the trapped beast in his snare, not realising his victim was getting ready to bite him. He asked me where I was from and I said I was from Rhodesia.

"Rhodésie!" he exclaimed, "C'est un pays de fascistes, pauvre garçon." He told me I must surely have left Rhodesia because I wanted to be free, to be liberated.

"Non, non. J'espère revenir," I mumbled, "Au fond, je serai toujours Rhodésien." At heart, I'll always be a Rhodesian. I said it to upset him; I wanted to give him a warning shot. Indeed, a troubled look came over his ascetic, intellectual features as he perhaps realised I was not your average peace-loving hippie. Perhaps he was a Foucaultian and believed that there could be no truth without its corresponding antithesis, because, despite his evident misgivings, he wanted to go through with our tryst. This he made clear by placing his hand on my inner thigh saying his apartment was nearby.

As soon as we were at a distance from other people in the street, I twisted his wrist and pushed him. He was stronger and heavier than he looked and kept his balance. His hands scrabbled at my arm and he tried to grab my shoulder but I slammed the point of my elbow into his face and down he went. As I clumped away in my worn-out cowboy boots, I paused and looked back for a moment. He'd got to his feet, one hand pressed to his wounded face the other making a spread-out gesture that tokened shock and dismay. I'm fairly sure that in a western European nation these days, an incident like this could very likely be treated as a homophobic attack, a small-time hate crime. Yet, I did not act out of hatred although it's true that at the time I had no concern at all about the fellow. My attitude was: if you play with fire don't squeal if you get burnt. He had clearly understood that he was trying to take advantage of someone who had fallen on unlucky times. He was fortunate to get away with a minor hurt. It all happened because my whole uneasy history, in both Rhodesia and England, had trained me to strike unhesitatingly at any man who laid his hands on me for whatever reason.

# 20
# Honey Badger Time

*There is nothing in this world that does not have a decisive moment*

– Henri Cartier-Bresson

A mysterious creature used to come down from the cleft hills above our house at Fort Jameson. No-one ever saw it but it often pushed over our heavy metal bins where we used to burn our rubbish. There'd be a rumble as the bins went over, usually around dawn, and the contents would be raked out by strong, invisible paws. Our family couldn't fix upon what was doing this bin-rolling. Surely neither the porcupines nor the leopards who'd only visit occasionally and were usually as silent as smoke in the night.

Whatever was emptying our bins clearly had no fear of interruption. I found some strange tracks by the bins and showed them to one of Dad's District Messengers. He pushed his hat back and squatted down to trace the spoor with a twig, then told me it was a *chibule*. I'd not heard of a *chibule* and questioned him about what manner of creature it was. He mimed a peculiar rolling gait and made a hissing noise. When I was still confused, he tried to explain further by saying, "*chikali*," which I knew meant 'angry' or 'fierce', a word that could be applied to either man or animal. I actually encountered the *chibule* shortly after that when I got up early one morning to spy on our rubbish-burning area.

The bin-roller was already at work. An untidy black and white creature about the size of Buster came shambling out of a pile of old tins. It stopped on seeing me and stood facing me square-on, its heavy front feet tipped by black bear-like claws. It slowly erected a battered pipe cleaner of a tail in a sinister signal of aggression and the meanest set of obsidian eyes I'd ever encountered bored into mine. Its heavy jaws slowly opened to show a purple tongue flanked by steel trap teeth and it made a hissing, grating sound that gave me chills. It looked completely unafraid despite its modest size. I felt it was saying, "Come on, try me and see what's going to happen to you." I backed off and it gave me a parting glare with its deep-set, peppercorn gaze. Then it seemed to decide I was insignificant and ambled away with a rapid, jerky motion, as if the ground was too hot for its feet.

I knew what it was then, I'd seen photos in a wildlife book and heard people speak about them. It was a honey badger. Honey badger might seem like an adorable name for a cute creature but what folks don't realise is that a honey badger makes a pit bull seem like a toy poodle in comparison. Its other Bantu name is *shanda*, which also means 'war'. Afrikaaners call the animal *ratels* for the hissing and rattling noise they make when annoyed. It is commonly understood in Africa that 'Ratels vat nie kak nie'; in other words 'Ratels take no shit from anybody.' You don't mess with the honey badger. A peaceful creature when left to go about its business, but incredibly aggressive when provoked, it is seemingly invulnerable to harm and just keeps on coming at you. It's far from being the biggest animal in the bush but even lions will avoid it because once it gets going, it has the will to do you harm, whatever the consequences to itself.

A real honey badger moment came for me during my mendicant hippie stint in France. I'd nowhere to sleep on yet another September night as the public parks were hard to break into and vigorously patrolled by *les flics*. I'd been ranging around central Paris that day on the hunt for spare change, and had sat up in a late café spending the few I'd found. At the same time, a hot wind began to blow down those unforgiving streets, a storm was coming up from the south. Evicted at midnight, I lingered by the café doors unsure of where to go next as the first fat raindrops began to wet my shirt. I'd left all my stuff at the Gare du Nord main train station and didn't even have a coat. *Now what?* I wondered. I had that peculiar young man's optimism that something would manifest. I'd been reading Kerouac's *The Dharma Bums,* and had committed myself to living within the holy void of the present moment.

Soon, something did turn up in the shape of a stocky, paunchy man in shirt sleeves flicking amber prayer beads to and fro in one hand and carrying a rolled newspaper in the other. He asked me in French if I had anywhere to go and offered to put me up for the night. I shrugged, scoping him for his threat level. He was short and unfit-looking, an Algerian or Moroccan I supposed. Something about him, perhaps his feigned casualness, put me off. I said, no, I was O.K., *tout va bien,* and he vanished into the wet night. I crouched in a shop entrance looking out at the unfriendly night streets and ranks of shuttered windows. I'd picked up the static of threat that night, sensing that something bad would happen. I was not sure where the danger lay, but was on my guard.

Sure enough, the prayer bead guy reappeared, his newspaper tented over his head to protect him from the violent downpour.

"*Toujours là?*" he said with a smile. I changed my mind about going with him. Maybe any contact with another being seemed better than remaining on those inhuman streets. I reckoned I could get the better of him whatever he had on his mind, although a warning did register that he must have been motivated enough to circle back to look for me a second time despite the storm. He gestured for me to follow and we scurried through a network of alleyways. We entered the hulk of a nineteenth century industrial building and pounded up some echoing worn steps. All the while my inner danger monitor was telling me to turn and run but I rationalised, *No, whatever comes, I'll handle it.*

We entered a large dormitory-like space with long lines of beds. That freaked me: the thought of gangs of men grabbing me. I drew back but he told me that everything was fine; these were the hostel beds of night shift workers. I still didn't like it, but still failed to flee. He unlocked a heavy wooden door and ushered me into a small room with circular walls. The door clonked shut behind us. A lock turned and a bolt rattled. Only then did he switch on the light. At first, I was relieved to be out of that dorm but I soon became worried about being trapped in there with him. I watched him in the gloom, but couldn't see where he'd put the key. He must have been a caretaker or supervisor and this was his bedsit cell, a turret room with a skylight window high up on the sloping roof.

Rain beat on the glass and the room lit up each time the lightning twitched and flickered outside. There were sounds beyond the door, the rumble of metal frame beds being moved and guttural voices calling out. Gut-stabbing thoughts jumped out and horrible scenarios played in my mind. I got my back to one wall and looked for a possible weapon in the squalid little dungeon. My nameless host must have picked up my unease,

"Calme toi," he said. He gestured to me to relax and told me the noise was simply some workers returning. He lit a dim lamp, made more soothing gestures and gave me a sickly sweet drink, then said, "Vas faire dodo" and made a sleep gesture. He led me to an old mattress on the floor. My adrenaline seeped away leaving a headachy exhaustion. I perched on the edge of the bedding, still careful to keep him in front of me. I'd learned in fights to direct the first blow centrally. There was only one lesson in combat, to get in the first strike and to make it count. Still, it didn't seem necessary that night. This guy seemed chilled. He showed me a heap of torn, old porno mags featuring naked white women and turned on a radio playing Arab music.

"Rai, rai," he said. I supposed it must be the name for that type of music. He shuffled around in a circle doing a shimmy dance, using a piece of cloth as a mock veil. I laughed uneasily. At least the music drowned out the unsettling sounds of the re-populating hostel dorm. The storm continued to beat against the roof glass. I was glad to be under cover at least. It began to feel quite cosy in the turret room and I felt oddly peaceful, dreamy even. My host appeared to subside. He turned the music down low and began to drowse in a home-made chair made out of a packing case with string and bits of old elastic. I watched him in the dim light. He'd taken off his damp shirt and his white vest rose and fell with his steady breathing. My new friend seemed to be asleep. I wondered what he wanted from me. I found it hard to believe in generosity of spirit alone. Maybe he was simply lonely. My eyes ached with weariness. All the long sleepless nights in parks and cemeteries began to catch up. I struggled to remain awake but my head sunk to the sour-smelling pillows and I was asleep.

I woke to find him squatting on my chest, buck-naked, his sweaty torso filled my vision and his blood-filled, raw sex prodded at my belly.

Now it began.

I pushed him off and we rolled and wrestled on the floor. His flesh was all over me. The heat of him as we battled skin to skin. I realised at some stage that he must have removed most of my clothes while I was asleep. I felt groggy, maybe he'd put something into that sweet drink. Still, I bucked and wriggled out from under his suffocating weight. I managed to get into a kneeling position beside him and elbowed him in the ribs. He reared back rubbing at himself then burst into tears. He started blabbering about me being his *môme*, his *copine,* his sweet-heart. I noted that he had allotted me a female role.

His grotesque pleading was interspersed with convulsive leaps at me which I would counter with a judo throw and he would roll away. All the while, his music wailed and rain thundered on the skylight. From time to time a lightning jag jumped the room into vivid spectral light. The man's lust was incredible. He seemed so determined to triumph over me and was a lot stronger than I'd anticipated. I could barely keep him restrained in mute wrestling bouts that seemed to go on forever. The strength was sucked out of me as we roiled about. At times I saw double from whatever he'd slipped me in the drink and filthy bits of cloth and old rags wound themselves round us as we battled on the floor of his grubby den.

That's when I got more violent. Sapped of the strength to restrain him, I switched to the more energy-efficient strategy of hurting him. I began driving him back with punches and elbow jabs to the body and strikes to the head and neck with the edge of my hand.

"Museeada!" he began to yell over and over. I didn't know what it meant but it sounded like trouble. I clamped my hand over his mouth. There were voices at the door and knocking noises. The dormitory was rousing. I kept my hand over his mouth and we reeled about the room. Then he started biting my fingers and only stopped when I cracked his head against a wall. That ended his shouting. At one stage I went close to the door and growled, "Tout va bien. Bien," mimicking his tone. The knocking from the dormitory side stopped for the moment.

*Choke-hold him, knuckle him, drive all breath from him.* That's about as far as I got with thoughts. I accepted and embraced that I had to truly ride the moment. That's when the honey badger entered the room, though whether its implacable spirit had possessed only me or him too is a tough call. My host reanimated and started shouting and grabbing at me. I felt sure that if I didn't incapacitate and silence him now, a mob of his mates was going to break in and it would be lights-out for me.

I elbowed him in the temple, then in the kidneys and whacked him in the collarbone like I'd been taught as a cadet. The trouble was I couldn't get in a really telling hit; it's harder when you're naked and he was a solid guy. What I'd thought was fat was really slabs of muscle. The only thing that finally worked was a palm heel strike to his phylum, the area just below the nose. When I did that he fell onto his back with a muffled shriek and rolled around holding his face, his bare legs flopping like those of a decapitated chicken.

Pretty soon though, he was back, hands outstretched, half-pleading, half-threatening. I saw his eyes in a lick of lightning. They looked zombified, crazed. I realised I needed to find the key and get the hell out of that room. Then I'd have to somehow fight my way through the guys in the dorm beyond. That was when I went for the chain. I'd noticed a mop basin in one corner. I ripped the chain and plug from its mooring on the ceramic, then got behind him and wrapped it round his neck. He made gurgling noises and fell to his knees with a crash then onto his belly. His hands came up to try and wrestle my grip off the chain but everything was slippery with blood. I released the pressure and put my face to his ear.

"Ou est la clef?" I hissed. He shook his head, his breath rasping out and mingling with mine. I put more pressure on his neck,

"Non, non," he mumbled in between chokings. Then his hand wavered out and pointed towards a cardboard box on the floor next to us. I heaved him closer to the box and let go of the chain to rummage in the container. But it was a ruse and the bastard lunged upward again. I had hold of the chain once more but my fingers were slipping in the blood slick. I managed to twist one finger into the loop to make a garrotte. His breath made a whooping groan when I did that. Then the chain broke and he reared back up carrying me with him on his back while he staggered around the room until he bucked me off.

*Stay fuckin down, you stubborn, old shithead.* That's all that was in my head as I blizzarded him with kicks and punches. Only then did he finally go quiet. Something I did — I knew not what — had finally stopped him cold. He fell to the floor and lay there curled up. Our hoarse breathing seemed to fill the room in the lull.

"Restez la," I told him. I could barely get the words out, my mouth was so dry.

"Mon ventre," he kept moaning as well as something in Arabic. The room had lightened a little and I could see him more clearly. He ended up kneeling facing me, black gore fanning down below his nose. He seemed defeated for the moment but my hand was on fire from where he'd bitten me and my body throbbed from various other hurts. I was sure he was still capable of harming me and he simply would not give up the key. Every time he made shuffling attempts to slither closer to me, I raised the broken chain as if to indicate I was willing to throttle him again and he would hunker back down.

The room went from ash-grey to yellowish. I got my jeans and boots back on once I'd found them under the mattress. I kicked at him from time to time in order to squash his minor attempts to move towards me. I don't know why but I let him dress. With dawn came the renewed thunder of feet outside as workers roused and left. Again, I gestured silence with a forefinger to the lips and raised the choke chain.

I was still not out of the woods. I had to get out of the turret room and through the dormitory. It was then that it occurred to me to change tack.

I said I was sorry, "Désolé, désolé, c'est ma première fois."

I told him I'd meet him that night at the same café. Everything would be different then. I'd do anything he liked. I cooed out all sorts of shit like that and even forced myself to stroke his bruised hairy forearms. The poor, mangled sap fell for it, even though he bore my chain mark etched on his neck and blood was still leaking out of his nose down into his stubbly beard. He blubbered over my hand, kissing it and laying his spiky cheek on it. He seemed willing to give his heart to the man who'd have killed him earlier. The fool even looked happy, or at least pretended it. He finally produced the key from the pocket of a filthy dressing gown and opened the door. I bid him adieu and rocketed through the dormitory, past a few men still sleeping in their narrow beds, and down the echoing stairs to freedom.

You might wonder, reading this, why I put myself into such dangerous situations in the first place; I know I have. I think it was that all the losses and hurts of my young life had built up a sort of Freudian 'death drive' within me, a compulsion to take things to the edge. I can see now that my aggression also gave me a kind of erotic thrill. Perhaps, in those days, it was the only way I had to connect intimately with people. I have a strange nostalgia for my honey badger self. That fight should have been solely a terrifying experience but the truth was I had, on some deep, dark level, enjoyed both the hurting and being hurt.

When I emerged onto the miraculous Hausmannian streets on that glittering Parisian autumn morning, the world seemed incredibly beautiful and full of possibility. My eyes drank in everything: the filigree shadows cast by the robinias in the Rue des Thermopyles, the stately blue-jacketed park keepers moving in unison as they dampened down the gravel with watering cans in the imperturbable daylight.

I was reminded of my night's troubles later though when I sat resting on a park bench under a canopy of pleached limes and noticed a street pigeon hobbling among its fellows. I caught the bird and found that someone had bound its feet tightly together with fishing line. I approached an elderly lady sitting near me, clad entirely in black, and asked her for help in freeing the bird. She was afraid of me at first, but then produced a pair of ornate silver sewing scissors from her black-beaded reticule. She nodded with approval when I cut the bird free,

"Comme ils sont barbares," she sighed, shaking her head.

I would always try to help an animal but I had less time for my own kind. As far as humans were concerned, I now knew that I too could become one of the barbarians. I hung onto that bloodied, broken rusty chain, with its plug still attached, for several years. It was my reminder that though the world might be full of myriad beauty, I had nearly been raped in a squalid, little room, and had been willing to kill my attacker to prevent it.

# 21
# La Golondrina

*It's a kindness that the mind can go where it wishes.*

– Ovid

All my life I've been looking for a certain sort of light, a seeping slow luminescence that lifts up the sinking heart, the kind you got on African afternoons just before the rains, lemon-rinsed and with a touch of copper-blue in there, a light that made you gasp at the wonder of it. I could never find anything close to that radiance in England, and thinking back now to my undergraduate years, they seem to have taken place in a sort of penumbral murk. The days were leaden and opaque but there were compensations. I became lit from within by ideas. I grew an unquenchable appetite for books, but lied about reading a hundred others for each one I actually had read. I found 'scholar of the liberal humanities' an easy fraud to perpetrate. I did well on my course but my anarchic soul awarded no more respect to the university than it had to school, in the same way that I had no reverence for the benign principles of the liberal establishment. Concomitantly, I could never be a true anarchist because I had no confidence in the essential goodness of humanity. My professors blithely identified me as a high flyer and I was awarded a top degree. They also wrongly assumed that we shared common values.

I remained, however, lonely as a stone and saw my university life as a form of charade, another one of many masks. Rhodesia was dying in the real world and my own sense of Africanness was bleeding away. I met no-one who shared my life experiences although one friend of mine did tell me that he could see me taking over a banana republic somewhere and running it like a benevolent dictator — or like Changa-Changa I might have added. There were some Zambian mining students living near me, isolated men wrapped in long woollen scarves, summer and winter. I'd say hello to them and we'd exchange jokes, my Bemba already rusty. One winter day, I found the Zambians kicking a football in the snow and called out greetings to them. None of us had words for the white stuff that we were standing in. Frost and ice didn't crop up much in Central Africa, even if I had learned as a child that there was a frozen leopard at the top of Mount Kilimanjaro. The mining students and I referred to it as *sinoo*, a Bemba version of the English word. It seemed to me that my life was becoming ever more dilute and second hand.

My parents were busy remaking themselves as British. Dad remained very ambitious. He was plainly disappointed that the Empire had gone, thus denying him an illustrious career, a governorship perhaps and a knighthood at the end of it. Still, he was an immensely resourceful man with an unquenchable drive to advance himself. He became influential in the worlds of commerce and finance, and served on numerous boards of directors including railway and television companies. He became High Sheriff and Deputy Lieutenant of Nottinghamshire. Decorations and honours followed and we watched as he received the C.B.E. from the Queen. He loved ornate British traditions and their regalia, and had his portrait done in the eighteenth century manner with knee breeches and a brocaded coat.

Mum supported Dad's social ambitions and created a home to mirror their success. She led the life expected of the wife of a prominent man, involving herself in charities, voluntary work and gardening. These activities brought her closer to her real self, I think. My sister studied Renaissance art and soon departed to live in Italy and work as an art historian, her own escape to an alternative world. There were still a few African things in the house: a clothes basket made out of Barotse reeds and carvings of elephants in black *mpingo* wood from the *miombo* forests. I liked to lay my hand on those objects, trying to draw out their deep memory of Africa.

My parents had been wounded by my horrendous school performance and remained fearful of my potential for disaster despite my academic success. I lived nearby in a succession of old, rented, terraced houses that I shared with other students. I pursued my first relationships with brave, hopeful young women who tried to humanise my deformed self. They never realised what they'd taken on although I was always the better for their ministrations. I was haunted by a pervasive sense of my own inadequacy and ugliness. I'd yearned for love as a teenager and wanted to lose myself in someone else. Along with that desire came the belief that I had to be more than myself to earn devotion. For me, love was a pretending game. That women could sincerely want me in return seemed an impossible notion. I thought I'd have to trick them into loving me, or somehow render them unaware to allow me to be close to them. I used to have fantasies that I was cast away on a desert island with a girl, and in that forced isolation she would gradually learn to care for me.

I soon realised, however, that the reality of relations between the sexes in 'my generation' were very different. There was a strange passivity about females in the 1970s. It was as if they were stunned by the extremity of the sexual revolution then taking place and felt they had to conform to its demands. I began to find that women strove to please me and I needed to make very little effort for them to accept me. I might have longed for a great romance that would take me away from everything, and become the transcendent force in my life, but too often I found a repeated sense of dissatisfaction and pity. The bitter pull from my inner core was always telling me to move on, to find my next Africa, to try someone or somewhere else. Thus it was that, embroiled though I was in young love's salty entanglements, I still wanted to escape and, in 1975, made arrangements to move to America.

I was awarded a Fulbright Grant to teach and study in Texas as a foundation for a doctorate. I came home for a while to box up my things as I wasn't sure whether I'd ever return. One of the objects I packed away was a leopard skin edged with green felt that had been my bedside mat when I was a kid. I suspect Kruger must have originally shot the creature because it was a goat-killer, or otherwise a menace. Back in Africa, I liked to lie on that leopard skin and finger the sewn-up hole where the bullet had passed through it and wonder about death and transfiguration, being and non-being. I'd lie spread-eagled, my boyish cheek to the cool, musky pelt, imagining the beast reanimated and carrying me through the

African night, a visionary animal scrying the future through its stitched eyes.

While travelling on those spectral journeys on the leopard's back, I used to sometimes encounter myself as a separate entity, a sort of mirror reflection, albeit one that moved and spoke independently from me. My alter ego spoke to me but I could catch no word of its utterance. Then the apparition would ebb away. Mum gave me a clue as to the possible identity of this spectre while I was folding away my telekinetic leopard skin. I think she was distressed by the thought that I was leaving for distant regions and might never return. Uncharacteristically, she confided to me that I'd had an older brother who'd miscarried. She told me he was in the old Protestant Colonial burying ground at Broken Hill, now called 'Kabwe Old Cemetery', near the Great North Road where Changa-Changa is also interred.

So, my shadowy double was really my ghost sibling, the first Rodney, who would not have disappointed my parents had he lived. The granite headstones are, so I'm told, still there: the older ones for the early settlers — Afrikaaner farmers, prospectors and Changa-Changa; the more recent ones for the sickly children of colonial administrators, now all lying forgotten together beneath the long yellow grass. Everything would have been so different had that brother lived. I think he would have fulfilled my father's expectations, instead of failing them so spectacularly as I did. I wondered whether his unheard message to me was an admonitory one: "Make them proud for once. Don't fuck up, like you usually do!"

I went to America looking for heat and light, a replacement Africa, but arrived in Houston to take up residence in a corroding apartment close to campus on Calhoun Boulevard. August thunderheads ramped up under a constant pall of dirty, yellow smog that stung the back of the throat when you stepped outdoors of a morning. One of the neighbours told me that the pollution was from the flare-off from the hundreds of oil wells dotted around the city. On my first night, a thunderous crash woke me in the early hours and I peered out my bedroom window at the 'Five and Dime' store across the street below. Two black guys had reversed their automobile into the windows of the shop and were looting goods from the shattered storefront. One looked up, noticed me watching and reached into his waist-band as if to draw out a pistol. I ducked down and wondered whether he'd come up the stairs and plug me, as might have happened in Rhodesia then. But they drove away soon after and everything was re-glazed and tidied up by that afternoon as if nothing had ever happened.

Being apparently English, I was accepted by everyone— white, black or latino — although no one had much interest in anybody who wasn't from Texas. All of us new faculty were given an invitation to meet the recently-widowed Lady Bird Johnson who came to visit the campus as part of her role on the Board of Regents. We were lined up to meet her in a reception room. I remember the high loaf of dark hair, the distinctive, lingering, aristocratic Southern intonation and her shy gaze. I was introduced by the senior professor as a Fulbright scholar.

"Ah, you're from England?" Lady Bird said.

"Well, actually, Madam, I was born far away from England in Central Africa, in Rhodesia, as a matter of fact."

"Why, how intuh-resting, from Africa? My, my. We must see how it all turns out the-ah. Hopefully, both black and white will rise."

"Hopefully, Madam," I replied, invoking ironic ambiguity.

*La Golondrina*, 'The Swallow', was a favourite of the *mariachi* bands that used to play for change outside Houston shopping malls and bars. I'd stop whenever I heard it and even sang along: "*A donde ira? Veloz y fatigada, la golondrina.*" I loved those words, written by a Mexican exile in the 1860s. The song throbbed with loss and yearning, and had such a haunting tune. It is still said to be a favourite of Mexicans who long to return to their native land. I took it as a signature tune for myself. It seemed to speak to me in particular : *Where are you going, fast-winged yet weary swallow? You are leaving, lost in the wind, looking for shelter, but not finding any.* For my first post-graduate assignment, I chose to write about the poetry of exile, opening my essay with an epigraph from Ovid's *Ex Ponto* about sailing in his frail bark on the harsh seas of exile. It was still an unconscious process but I was already choosing themes that struck a chord with me.

My academic title at the university was 'Assistant Professor of English'. It sounded grand but, in truth, I was merely a departmental dogsbody. I only later found out that my predecessor, also from England, had been shot through the buttocks and repatriated home after getting lost and unwisely asking for directions at a house in a rough neighbourhood. My supervisor was brash Professor Peabody and there were three other Fulbrights, Jane, a tough, cigar-smoking mature student from Bradford and two Italians, Ugo and Liana. We all became good friends and loved swapping stories about the eccentricities of our Texan hosts. Peabody showed us off to a faculty meeting and when one of his colleagues said, "Are these *your* Fulbrights then, professor?" He answered, "Yeah, no half-brights for Peabody!"

# 22
# The Comanche Trace

*The depth and dream of my desire,*

*The bitter paths wherein I stray...*

– Kipling

The university facilities were superb and the academic libraries were like air-conditioned temples but those Texas days seemed full of ever-present threats. The very landscape breathed out menace. East Texas was wrapped in stifling, humid heat most of the year, apart from the 'Northers', weeks in winter when the temperature would suddenly flip and empty lots and yards would be filled with hundreds of dead birds killed by the cold inversion. Visceral hatreds stalked the place. I kept clear of the rednecks who hated hippies and was repeatedly chased on the city streets by black dudes who wanted to stomp me for being a honky, a hippy, or both.

Peabody showed me a nickel-plated revolver he kept in his car and told me he carried it after his name, telephone number and address had appeared on a Klu Klux Klan hit list. His heinous crime had been "praising black literature". Numerous students at the University of Houston were also named. I made discreet enquiries about how I too could buy a pistol so that I could defend myself if the balloon went up. I was egged on in this by giant billboards that dominated the city showing the image of the business end of a pistol muzzle with the accompanying legend, *"The Magnum is Right for Houston Police'.*

*Klu Klux Klan Hit List containing the names and addresses of my colleagues. Houston 1975*

Once, on the way to teaching my classes, a sour patrolman caught me jaywalking and refused to listen to my legitimate excuse that the pedestrian lights were broken. He grabbed my hair and banged my head on the hood of his cruiser, "Repeat after me." *Clonk!* "Ah will not," *Clonk!* "Jaywalk evah again." Teaching was scarcely less stressful.

Embittered Vietnam vets glowered at me from the back rows, while girl students harassed or propositioned me for better grades. One day, the university football coach summoned me after I'd failed some of his players who could hardly write their own names. He put down his cigar as I entered his office, and growled, "You're the guy from England where they play pussy games like cricket, soccer and shit. You don't understand what goes here. Mah boys don't flunk! Geddit, prof?"

All the road signs around my apartment were bullet-riddled and it sometimes felt as if I were taking my life in my hands by walking to the local '7-11' store for groceries. Drivers seemed to hate to see anyone on foot, and would veer off the road towards me in a cloud of dust, trying to scare me. In the overgrown, spooky, deserted parks, the trees were laden with long tentacles of Spanish moss and groups of young gang members from the public housing projects would emerge from the subtropical vegetation calling out, "Hey, honky come here!" I knew that muggings were commonplace so I'd take off running. On a few occasions, they gave chase, leading me to throw my brown paper sack of groceries over my shoulder. That delayed them long enough for me to escape while they squabbled over the contents.

Buffalo Bayou, swept close to my apartment block. It was usually a chocolate torrent hemmed in by mighty earth banks.

When you walked close by, you'd hear a constant plopping and splashing. At first I imagined this was the local version of *tokoloshe* water sprites but it soon became evident that it was scores of wary, basking snapping turtles leaping into the water because they rightly feared any passing being on two legs. I enjoyed watching local birdlife along the bayou or in the nearby parks but the waist-high grass was also inhabited by packs of ferocious feral dogs and I had to carry a heavy stick to beat them off. One time, I found dozens of bloated, rotting canine corpses in the park. A Texan friend told me that the police periodically turned up and tested their new Magnum revolvers on the ferals. He begged me not to go into the parks anymore as it was too dangerous.

I took to reading the pocket Bible I'd carried ever since my Blundell's days and lingered over Psalm 23, repeating, "Yea though I walk in the valley of shadow of death" while on my way to or from the '7-11' and the 'U Totem' shop. It was at 'U Totem' that I saw a skinny Chicano teen shot dead by the storekeeper as he tried to escape out the revolving doors with his shirt stuffed with stolen groceries. I can still visualise his white canvas sneakers jammed in the door, slowly absorbing the spreading wings of his dark blood but it was not the worst thing I've seen. The shopkeeper was given a congratulatory handshake on his 'good work' by the cops. I accepted that this was how things rolled in East Texas. I had a frontier mentality myself and was hard-boiled enough to keep on shopping there. Not being one for moral outrage about this dirty world, I was mainly interested in not getting shot myself.

Despite the dangers, I'd often walk out at night around the university campus under the yellow Texas moon to the periodic, drawn-out hooting of night-time freight trains. That sound seemed to sum up all the longing and loss of America. Frequently, I'd stop to gaze into 'Shasta's Den', a small, hexagonal reinforced glass cage in which fluorescent lights blazed all night. Shasta was the university mascot for the football team, 'The Cougars'. The big cat would always be there pacing, snapping at flies with her black glistening lips. I felt as if she returned my gaze with a look of utter hatred. Her name was actually Shasta III, 'The Lady'. A notice explained that she'd been there since 1965, ten years a prisoner. Her number implied that there must've been at least two other captive cougars before her. Every now and then a team of heavy-set football jocks wrestled Shasta into a harness. Then, declawed, spitting and writhing, she was paraded before the crowd at half-time during university football matches.

I fantasised about smashing Shasta's cage one night and letting her go free to sneak through the campus live oaks and lap the waters of the nearby bayou. I decided against this act of animal liberation once it struck home that she wouldn't last long in a city that had three times as many firearms as people. Thinking about the captive big cat now, I realise that the loneliness that I saw in her eyes mirrored not only the forlorn bleakness of Texas, but also the dark, empty depths and down-dragging currents of my youth. I really had no idea what I was doing in that strange place, or where I would head if I left.

Walking along Buffalo Bayou after the periodic floods, I'd scan the churned-up foreshore looking for Karankawa and Akokisa arrow heads. Although I crossed their former lands every day, in Houston Native Americans had pretty much vanished. Texas settler history and a lingering belief in Manifest Destiny dominated the local mindset. Given my African upbringing, I found myself on the side of the original inhabitants. The university's library collection reflected little interest in the subject so I spent my spare salary on rare anthropological books sent from New York book dealers and my apartment was decorated with posters of Native American portraits by the great American frontier photographers, Edward Curtis and Frank Rinehart.

I also started going to American Indian Movement meetings held to raise money to cover the court costs of A.I.M. leaders. It was deemed a subversive organisation and operated on the edge of legality. They'd occupied Indian land on Alcatraz Island and at the Pine Ridge Sioux reservation over the previous few years. There had been a lot of shooting; government officials had been killed. The F.B.I. monitored everything and meetings were rife with informers. Still, I enjoyed the frisson of illegality about their gatherings and marvelled at the tens of thousands of dollars donated by affluent liberals to people who clearly hated them.

It was through A.I.M. that I met Jay, one of the few friends I made in America. He had wary, dark eyes above a droopy moustache and his bony fingers were heavy with Navajo turquoise rings. He lived mainly in Austin, taking some credits at the university there though he never seemed to actually study. I'm not sure how he lived but he was always rolling up blunts made up of vivid, green Mexican weed so maybe he did a bit of dealing on the side. He told me his grandmother was an Arikara and his family was still ranching in North Dakota.

I liked to talk to Jay about the natural world. He, unlike any of the urban Texans I met, could identify many of the birds and plants around us. He had a languid, relaxed air but was also driven by something I knew I could never really understand. He'd show up at my apartment from time to time and I went over to Austin to visit him on a few occasions. We swapped books and he told me he was researching

Quanah Parker, born of a captive Anglo woman, who rose to become the last chief of the Comancheria in North Texas.

One evening, Jay and I were out in his yard in Austin, with the first cool touch of fall in the air and a full moon throwing cold shadows over the grass. Jay said it was a Comanche moon and I asked him what that was. He explained that, at one time, the whole Southwestern frontier was afraid when a full moon rose in September. It meant the Comanche would come raiding south after a summer hunting buffalo in Kansas, Oklahoma and the Texas Panhandle. He said he'd show me if I liked. I asked him where we'd be going but his only reply was, "You'll see. All we need is a fistful of dollars for gas." We drove west all night by way of San Antonio. Dawn was a saffron bar at our backs when we reached Fort Stockton and turned south to Marathon on Route 385, heading toward Brewster County. It was as dry as the African bush there. The dun grass and swooping, speckled hills reminded me of the Matopos.

We stopped at a place called Persimmon Pass and walked up a long draw, boots crunching on the shaley soil that was gullied and seamed out, as if after an ancient flood. Morning was warming up the hillside, vibrating with an insistent grating bird call. Jay told me it was a cactus wren, and that they sounded like a '56 Chevy trying to start up. We clambered partway up some sandstone bluffs, avoiding the defending yucca spikes and sat on a flat rock, looking south down the pass towards blue mountains in the distance. Jay said these were the Rosillos and beyond them lay Mexico. He told me that the Comanche used to ford the Pecos River at Horsehead Pass further north, thousands of them on horseback. The Chisos and Apache who lived around here would let them pass as they poured through to go raiding in South Texas and across the Rio Bravo into Mexico. They'd come back laden with captives and livestock, all which were funnelled through this very pass.

"Do you see it?" Jay asked, pointing, his ringed forefinger glinting in the light. All I could see was bunched masses of *mesquite* and cholla clumps framed by frowning bluffs.

"There it is," he repeated, pointing again. I could see then that a pale line was visible, a perceptible thinning of the scrub that made a scar leading north and south like an enormous compass line. Once you got your eye on it, you could make out that it was, perhaps a quarter of a mile wide. Jay said that was the Comanche Trace, a trail worn into the land through decades of travel by the raiding parties and the warriors firing the scrub behind them to deter pursuers. He reckoned the tribal name, Comanche, probably came from the Spanish, *camino ancho*, meaning 'wide trail'. Apparently, in the last century, it formed a very obvious track across Brewster County and into The Big Bend but now that mark was almost gone, and will, no doubt, have vanished entirely today, nearly half a century later.

It was a marvellous and frightening thing to behold this last, faint evidence of a once great nation and their way of life. It seemed to stand for all the workings of history and the extinction of so many other peoples. It made me think of all the abandoned farmsteads in Rhodesia, and of what the remnants of my own family's life in Africa might look like. I knew then that all human turmoil and striving would become, in time, a dried-out river course, a barely discernible trace like this.

We stayed a long time walking up on the bluffs as the cactus wrens were joined by dawn choruses of mourning doves who kept up their lament of "*Where? Who? Who? Who?*"

"You should see it under a big moon like we had last night," said Jay, "Then the past really comes alive." He added that we should burn some prairie sage to please the ancestral spirits like his grandmother taught him. I tried to convey to him how strangely familiar that place was to me, how calming and reassuring and I thanked him for showing it to me.

"Guess it goes to show we're all just passing through," he replied. Did I thank him enough? He probably wouldn't have wanted that. His friendship was a sweet yeast in a dry time.

Laconic, generous Jay, one of my few guides in the arid, barren wastes of my youth.

# 23
# On The Other Shore

*We are given rivers so we know our hearts*

*can break but still keep us breathing.*

– Emily Walter

A second year of university teaching loomed but I'd lost any pleasure and purpose in living in Texas. The English introduction course I taught was an access level module that everyone had to pass to gain entry to other courses in the humanities. Many of the students failed early on. Either they couldn't keep up with the course while continuing to hold down jobs in order to afford to remain in college, or they'd come from appalling state schools where they'd never become fully literate or numerate, so that what was being asked of them was beyond their capability. It seemed a cruel system to so encourage hope and then just let the hopeful fail through little or no fault of their own. Peabody had also become difficult. One of my fellow Fulbrights discovered he was stealing his graduate students' work and publishing it as his own. The Italian Fulbrights jumped ship and found alternative places at a New York university. Peabody called me into his office and threatened that if I said anything he'd make sure I never worked in a university again. That did it. I resigned soon after.

I had a lingering desire to find something of the authentic aboriginal essence of the Americas and decided I should go south into the *fellaheen* lands of Mexico. I thought maybe I'd feel more at home there. I spent my last university paycheck on a Greyhound bus ticket and headed towards the border. The route crossed the rolling, open country of Central Texas, the boundless ranges dotted with the rufous smudges of Charolais cattle grazing amid the remnant prairie. Migrating pronghorn antelopes, much more numerous in those days, came rocketing out from the verges and bounded between lines of traffic before vanishing again down the clefts of rusty *arroyos*.

Everything looked weather-beaten and on the edge of failure in those barren lands. The giant billboards along Highway 290 for Buick (*Free as a Bird*) or Southwestern Bell (*We Care For You*) often had panels missing. Iridescent-feathered black grackles perched on the rusted struts in these gaps and through the breaches in those huge hoardings you could glimpse yet more endless grassy vistas, dotted here and there with abandoned clapboard farmhouses with sagging stoops down dirt roads that scrolled away to nowhere.

Flocks of redwings mobbed quiet streets in the empty-looking small towns. So many houses had photos in their windows of sons killed or missing in Vietnam. At a stopover in Bastrop, the diner manager came to my booth and stared at me for a long time with faded denim-coloured eyes and, without changing his stony expression, told me to finish my caw-fee and get my long-haired ass the hell outta his diner. I got to Austin in the rain and called in at Jay's place. A guy I didn't know came to the door and said Jay had moved out, gone, no forwarding address. My friend had simply vanished like the nations of his ancestors.

Dozing on the bus between Austin and San Antonio, I woke to find my thigh pressing against that of a young black woman who was absorbed in reading Jacob Riis's famous photographic essay, *How the Other Half Lives*, which documented the impoverished lives of immigrants in New York at the height of the Gilded Age. It struck me that only a score of years earlier this woman and I might have been required to sit in different sections of the bus. Ever since my days in Texas, I've always been amazed by the ambitious, hopeful determination of so many ordinary Americans to educate themselves.

We were held up near Brownsville while a large, yellow backhoe digger worked to create a berm to stem the rain-swollen Colorado River, which was threatening to drown the road. All traffic stopped and the bus disgorged its passengers. I took the opportunity to look down on the Colorado from the bridge embrasures. I love to haunt rivers. Perhaps it's a thing derived from having grown up in arid Central Africa and anyway, Jonas always told me that if you stood by a river long enough you'd see your enemy float past.

*My murky, rain-misted image of the Colorado in flood taken from the Greyhound bus. 1976.*

Back on board the bus, the landscape began to change. The buffalo grass gave way to mesquite; live oaks, with their beards of moss, were replaced by buckeye and Mexican sycamore. South of San Antonio came Dilly and Cotulla, towns where there were many more Mexican faces: labourers loading bags from feed stores, next to ranchers in Stetsons and long stockman's coats, salesgirls with white collars and ribboned pig-tails dreaming at soda stands and *borrachos* clutching beer bottles, leaning in phone booths and wailing out songs of suffering to themselves under the jackhammer Texas rain.

I arrived at the border in Laredo, off Highway 35, and crossed the long frontier bridge on foot. On the U.S. side, unsmiling officials went through all my meagre belongings. They found my copy of Kerouac's *Mexico City Blues* and carried it off to another office. I could see them tipping the book upside down and riffling through the pages. Were they checking for any illicit ideas that I might be smuggling out of America? I was waved through by a sleepy, indifferent customs officer on the Mexican side. Nuevo Laredo was obscured by a drizzled haze and the waters of the Rio Grande in spate boiled up against the pilings, carrying down uprooted clumps of mesquite and vivid green *carrizo* cane. Across the bank, I roamed the streets, hungry for experience and astonished by the complete change in atmosphere.

Back then, Mexico seemed free of the omnipresent cartel violence that plagues it now although there were often gunshots in the night. I loved its forgiving air after the edginess of Texas. I felt I could breathe there and my latent sense of misery and terror began to ebb away. Everything about it pleased me: the white-gloved traffic policemen blowing whistles and making marionette gestures, the smells of mud and beer, the bright yellow feet of the chickens in baskets at *El Mercado de Reforma*. Young boys tried to drag me into dodgy *cantinas*, "Pulque, señor?" I eventually succumbed and allowed myself to be guided to the veranda of a bar overlooking a square. Rain pocked on the awning above me.

I felt like a grandee as I drank beer and ate quesadillas looking out onto potted palm trees to which were tied thin ponies hunched under the deluge waiting to haul tourist carriages, and beyond them the curio shops selling giant earthenware replica Toltec heads. The square was full of the cries of children playing in the welcome rain. A little girl, maybe ten years old, in her mother's oversized, high-heeled red shoes came clacking towards me and stared with enormous brown eyes that seemed to look straight through me. I don't think she wanted anything from me, as such. She'd simply come to stare at the hippie *gringo*. I gave her a dollar, which she accepted as if it was her due.

I've still got my travel journal from that time, filled with bus tickets, bar receipts and dried pin oak leaves. For some reason, I carefully wrote down a quote from William Blake's

*The Marriage of Heaven and Hell* during those first days in Mexico:

*Those who restrain desire, do so because theirs is weak enough to be restrained; and the restrainer, or reason, usurps its place & governs the unwilling. And being restrain'd, it by degrees becomes passive till it is only the shadow of desire.*

I think I wanted the freedom of Mexico to fill me with a whole-hearted desire to make a life for myself that had evaded me up to that time. Sometime later, I got drunk under a yowling moon and tumbled down some cantina stairs. A concerned man picked me up and went through a pantomime of feeling my limbs. I slurred that I was, "todo bueno." He laughed and said, "Esta que ferro?" — are you made of iron? Iron maybe not but, for sure, I was toughening up and embracing my permanent sense of loss.

I was beginning to accept that nowhere would be my home, certainly not Mexico. There, I'd simply swapped being a spinning *muzungu* for becoming *un gringo perdido*. Several weeks later, I crept back to the States, past the now calm and limpid Colorado. I think it was then I admitted that I would find no replacement for Rhodesia. Henceforth, it was to be exile for me. I'd stay put in England and seek inner transcendence. After all, had not Ovid written in Book One of *Ex Ponto,* his epic of exile from Rome on the far-flung coast of the Black Sea that, "the griever who dies will die sooner than the grief"?

# 24
# The Years

*There's living and there's writing. Choose one. You can't do both.*

– Ascribed to Truman Capote.

The time before the November rains in Africa was known as 'suicide month' when the air felt like you were breathing hot gauze, the tar on the rough roads turned to soft liquorice and the air was smoke-haunted as bush fires scorched the earth and dust devils whipped up from nowhere, spinning and collapsing as if crushed by the relentless sun. All the while, the bush crickets shrilled their loudest, clamouring for relief. The culmination of the dry season wore on the soul and made tempers short. Your thoughts spun like trapped rats and people's moods were bleak. Everything was as dry as shed snake skin and all laboured under the heat and longed for the release that the rains would bring. Thunder would grumble on the horizon where sterile clouds massed but came to nothing. Nevertheless, the sapient trees seemed to sense something afoot, even though rain could be weeks away. The msasas would send up reddish, anticipatory leaflets while the jacarandas formed hopeful buds.

When, at last, it did come, the rain was the ultimate salvation. I can still evoke in memory an echo of the thrill that came when the first downpour pounded on our corrugated iron roofs, then boiled in the irrigation sluices and gushed in red rivulets into the dambos. I liked to join the black kids, larking in the wet and sliding in the mud. The storm water seemed to carry an electrical charge that made our skin tingle. And afterwards, the primal musk scent of wet earth, the essential perfume of Africa. There rose from that wet, ochreous soil a humming sense of the potency of the universe that percolated into our innermost being. It's no surprise that the rainy season was also the time for all sorts of witchery, spells and divinations. The return of the rains still seems a life-giving boon to me, a blood memory that stirs my imagination. Sometimes even humdrum English rain can provoke this feeling.

On my last night in Texas, I'd been staying at a friend's apartment waiting for my flight back to England. I was lying on a couch that acted as my bed with the patio doors open when a tropical storm came up from the Gulf and threshed the vegetation outside. At the time, I was reading Raymond Chandler's *The Simple Art of Murder*, a slim book I'd taken from my host's shelves. I was in the midst of a passage in which Chandler says that the best stories are about quests for hidden truth undertaken by lonely people. Those words provoked something in me. I leaped up, ruffling my hair, my mind full of tingling thoughts and, just at that moment, a sudden onrush of raindrops pattered off the red oak trees and tall palmettoes outside, battering onto the shutters and through the open doors in a drumming roar. It was a call from the past and I stepped out onto the veranda and let it soak me.

Jay had told me the Navajo held that there was 'male rain' or 'female rain'. Male rain came in the form of thunderstorms that crashed down but soon poured away, while female rain was the gentler, percolating seasonal rain that made the desert live again. This first storm onrush in Houston was definitely male rain and, as the storm water wrapped around me I first truly knew, in a strange *coup de foudre,* that I'd become a writer one day. My realisation strengthened through the night as I lay awake, the patio doors still open, while the milder, female rain fell for hours, soaking into my mind.

My study cupboards are stacked with the diaries of my years after returning from America. I formed the discipline of completing a page a day, whatever the circumstances: drunk, sober, work weary, or caught up in the deliriums of love. There are thirty or more of these volumes, which were my way of staying in touch with the discipline of writing. Day after day, over months and years, the pages piled up and formed a reef of stubborn purpose. I half-consciously made choices to explore all sorts of crazy avenues of living in order to nurture my writing vocation.

Journaling was my way of teaching myself to capture experience in words, and to look at the under-weave of my days although I was not yet ready to commit myself to any sustained writing project beyond that. Those stacks of journals captured a molten life and the spilling away of my youth. Ironically, I couldn't bear to open any of them right now to aid me in recalling that time. I'd compiled them not so much to aid a future memoir but rather they were my attempt to understand what my tumbling days actually meant to me. Often, I've not really known what I think about something until I've written about it and turned it this way and that in my mind. It's enough that the diaries exist, waiting for the day when I want to look at the many lives I've led. I have internalised the skills that they brought me and perhaps they also crystallised in memory many of the episodes I am recording here.

I realise now that those years after my return from America tell a story of my trying to come to terms with having been exiled from Africa. To the African healers, or *shiangas*, a successful life is all about finding equilibrium. They see our shadows as reflections of our souls which follow us everywhere, but which need to be re-anchored to us when we are out of balance. I definitely remained unsteady in those years after returning from Texas. I kept looking for the lover who would take me out of myself, which led me to ruin one romantic relationship after another, always in search of the next woman who'd rescue me. At the same time. I floundered through dozens of jobs including: oven cleaning at an industrial bakery, plasterer's mate, power station coal shoveller, furniture restorer and night petrol station attendant.

Rhodesia died in 1979 and with it went any thought of my returning to Africa. It was clear from the start that Robert Mugabe's ZANU-PF government in newly-renamed Zimbabwe would in time turn the racist tables on the remaining one percent of the white population, not to mention on non-Shona black minorities, or any other potential political opponents. Zambia, became sunk in deeply-corrupt one party rule and revolutionary turmoil seemed to grip the continent. Some of my old school-friends went to Kenya and set up fish-farms there. I could have joined them but a deepening pessimism convinced me that investing any part of yourself in Africa would bring inevitable heartbreak.

I somehow obtained a scholarship for a Doctorate at the end of the Seventies and studied Russian on the side, teaching myself and paying a gloomy, elderly Russian spinster for weekly conversation lessons. I squandered my two years of independent study tinkering with motorcycles all day and haunting rackety nightclubs into the early mornings. I was about to get kicked off my program by my tutor for failing to produce any written work when I locked myself in my rented flat, bought an ultra-violet lamp, a large supply of Pro-Plus tablets and maca powder and wrote day and night for six months. I submitted my thesis within days of my final deadline. I'd completed it as an act of revolt and saw no value in it although its subject was interesting enough to an exile like me. It was a study of the novels and ideas of Vladimir Nabokov and the literature of the diaspora of cultured Russians who'd been driven out by the Bolshevik Revolution.

I turned up to my *viva* examination in motorcycle leathers; I wasn't expecting to pass so I thought I might as well dress in a manner that would give my examiners something to talk about. I'd riddled the text of my thesis with fictitious references so that, looking back at it now, it was actually my first full-length literary work, a flagrant pastiche of what a Ph.D. thesis ought to be. I thought that should have been obvious to anyone in the know but it wasn't and I was solemnly awarded my doctorate. It was the days when it was easy for any plausible rogue to obtain an academic post and teaching opportunities soon came my way. I was offered a choice post as a Lecturer in Literature (As Nabokov himself had been!) at a Neo-Elizabethan manor house in Lincolnshire that had been taken over by an American university as its European base.

"Let me get this straight, Dr. Madocks. You're turning us down to be a gardener?" I can still hear the puzzled Mid-Western tones of the Faculty Head sounding when I told him I was junking my university teaching career in favour of life as a jobbing gardener. I hadn't lasted long as a lecturer. I never regretted that decision. The stifling cloisters of academe were not for me. I'd lost all respect for them the moment they accepted me.

My first short story was published in a little magazine in 1982 yet I could not seem to clear space or find focus for sustained creativity. I thought gardening would allow my mind to roam free and spent six years working in private gardens. It tortured my parents to see me spin away from any sort of profession they considered acceptable but gardening brought me discipline and tranquillity. After all, my earliest and most impressionable years had been spent living side by side with nature in Northern Rhodesia. I loved being outdoors in the changing seasons and burying my hands deep in soil. I could never get enough of that. I believed that working at one with the soil might heal me and I'd become my own *shianga*.

Time and space pre-dated me in the nineteenth country gardens where I usually worked. I enjoyed walking in the footsteps of the Victorian and Edwardian gardeners before me. I grew to be like the vundu catfish that can live on land or in the water. I showed I could thrive in a new element. The last vestiges of my Rhodesian accent disappeared although I retained an eye for African plants and grew the kaffir lilies the English called *schizostylis* and red-hot pokers, known as *vurpies* in Rhodesia. I also nurtured the flame lily, national flower of Rhodesia, planting its white tubers in hothouses where I worked. In the furnace of August days, the plants would put out quivering scarlet flowers, the secret badge of a lost country.

I liked to watch collared doves chirring and pattering about in the mottled English light. They could barely be made out, camouflaged amid the leaf litter as they pecked at the ground. Those doves had migrated from Africa during the previous fifty years. Before that, they'd only been rare visitors to Britain but, by the Eighties, were found in every garden. They were ideal British immigrants because they could scarcely be seen, yet among themselves they acted as if they owned the ground where their shadows fell.

So I lived from season to season as a gardener, making little money since I loved the work and often forgot to charge my well-heeled customers my full hours. To me, gardening was an artistic activity, a physical corollary to the mind's work. I still squatted on my haunches like an African while I weeded, and remained cautious when digging deeply into the ground as I remembered how, in Rhodesia, if you cracked open the hard, dry soil then, far down, you'd often find burrowing toads, seemingly dead and encased in a waxy sac biding their time in dry season dormancy. Those toads slept on for months, even years, hanging on for better times. I like to think I was mimicking them then, that I had a toad-self sleeping fathoms deep within me, waiting for its occult signal to break out into the light.

# 25
# In Search of My Kochanka

*Bold lover, never, never, canst thou kiss,*

*Though winning near the goal.*

– John Keats

I felt that my real life was not to be found among my jobs or pastimes, but that it lay instead in the pursuit of love. There were so many lovers and they were all wonderful to me but everything else was eclipsed by an affair with a married Polish woman which haunted me for decades after it ended. It was a relationship so gripping and overwhelming that I struggled to survive outside of it. She had such a vivid, electric presence that to be with her seemed to me to be the most perfect moments of life. I was a complete slave to her bidding and we were bound by a mutual pact to hide our love from the world. And though she left me in the end and went back to her husband, I've kept her secrets to this day. After a heady three years together, she told me in her usual, lucid and frank way, as if talking to a child, that we were not to meet again for a long, long time and I must be brave. The loss slowly sank into me. I wallowed in the grief of it and was filled with the yearning of an addict. I was tormented by the thought of her existing somewhere and believed that if only we could meet again for a few minutes, then everything would be rekindled.

Four years passed like that and, weary of walking in woe, I decided to try and find her in her home country. One spring, I applied for a visa and crossed Germany by train. It was still the days of the Iron Curtain and once you passed through the Berlin Wall, you were in bleak, communist lands. There was no tourism. Travel was difficult and you had to purchase coupons to eat at grim state restaurants. I wandered across Poland, the sick *pan doktor* in search of a love cure. I searched in vain for her in her home town of Bydgoszcz, then drifted southeast to the borderlands of the Soviet Union at Chelm. It was late April and warm and the women came out in flowered skirts and sandals with white ankle socks, just like the ones she used to wear.

There had been a terrorist outrage in the Garden of Gethsemane and England had chosen its team for the World Cup, that much I gleaned from the English tabloid I found in a railway carriage. I was sitting in the Stary Rynek, the market place where the town's Jews had been herded before being transported to the Sobibor Death Camp in 1942. I'd picked up that something peculiar was going on that morning when I watched a Russian military train, an old steamer with a red star on the front plate, go chuffing through the station. It was carrying great tanks of hazardous chemicals and the armed guards stationed on the chassis of the train cars all had gas masks hanging around their necks. My Polish was weak although I could speak Russian. Eventually, a friendly Pole said to me in Russian, "Are you crazy or do you really not care?"

I asked him what he meant and he told me that a monitoring station in northern Poland had reported that radiation in the area was five-hundred times higher than normal. The news had been suppressed at first but the Kremlin had announced on TV the previous night that there'd been an explosion at a nuclear power plant in Pripyat in the Ukraine, only a six-hundred kilometre drive past the Soviet border. The man said that a cloud of radiation was passing over Poland. He went on to tell me everyone was leaving, going as far west as they could, and that they were giving iodine to children to protect them from radiation sickness.

I soon found out that the name of the place where the explosion had occurred was Chernobyl. I had no idea what to do so I stayed put for another week. The days seemed muffled in saffron gauzy light. I felt hot and nauseous at night and thought it must be my imagination, or maybe food poisoning. The municipal daffodils and early tulips in the parks all seemed to suddenly wilt, while the pigeons that had cooed on the hotel window sills had vanished. We were warned not to drink milk, or eat salad or fresh mushrooms. There were queues at chemists' shops and everyone was asking for *jodina*. I became worse, fluids poured out of me, my mind moved slowly, my thoughts like numb houseflies.

I decided I'd better take myself to hospital and eventually located one in a brutalist edifice behind high fencing. On the way in, I spotted a surgical assistant in a soiled white coat with a tall white hat like a chef. He was carrying a pail and went round the side of the building and emptied it into a drain. A torrent of blood came out of the bucket. That decided it. I resolved then and there to get out and somehow made my way back to Warsaw. In those days, only one train a week went to the West from Warszawa Centralna. Seats were limited as there were only two carriages. I pushed through a jostling mass of desperate foreigners and got on the last carriage out by bribing the guard with a golden guinea I'd kept hidden in my sock for just such an occasion.

I continued vomiting and having gut pains all the way back to Berlin. The machine-pistol-toting East German *Grenzpolizei* seemed keen to get rid of me and asked me few questions. A young Palestinian man travelling with me who spoke Russian kept patting me on the back, giving me water and repeatedly murmuring, "Tyazhelo, tyazhelo," meaning 'Heavy, heavy'. The West Germans passed a Geiger counter over us when we arrived through The Berlin Wall. I didn't really care about the frenetic sputtering and clicking of the machine; I'd been taking a radiation cure for lost love.

Once I'd returned from that harrowing journey, I at last began to get down to some serious writing. I was strangely indifferent to the possible effects of the radiation but found solace in the creative process. Writing was a form of revenge on love's defeat. Maybe I hoped that by becoming a writer I'd transform myself into the sort of person my departed lover might take back. The ache of loss remained for years and the bittersweet memories never went completely quiescent. I sought out love in different places as the years rolled but still, every so often I'd dream of her, and wake gasping and reaching out. *Which arrow flies for ever? The arrow that has hit its mark.*

# 26
# All aboard for 'The Ship of Fools'

*It is only the wounded physician who heals completely.*

– Carl Jung

I had a foolish hope that my Polish lover might change her mind about me if only I had a salaried job. After all, her husband was a university professor, and security was important to a tough-minded Polish woman whose parents had survived deportation and total war on the Eastern Front. She often quoted a pragmatic Polish country saying: "Beauty does not season soup." So I gave up my free-and-easy gardening life and found a post teaching horticulture to disabled people. The project was temporary but I thought it might lead to other things and so it proved: I was taken on as a care worker in a day centre and soon progressed up the career ladder. It was yet another new identity and I didn't take it too seriously. I retained my African hard-headedness and lack of faith in institutions and authorities. All seemed well and I enjoyed the sociable side but my career very nearly ended prematurely. I'd become Deputy Manager of a residential home, after having been given a few weeks of training. No police checks were done on me, as was the way in those days. My responsibility was to do a twenty-four hour shift at the weekend. There were no other staff on duty at all at night and twenty or more residents to look after.

One evening, I accepted an emergency admission. I didn't like the look of him from the start. He was a stocky young man in his twenties, dumped on my unit because he was supposedly in crisis. I took one look at his pallid, feral features and weasley eyes, and knew he was trouble. I caught him late that night in Annabel's room. She was seventeen years old and non-verbal, with a scoliosed spine and a sweet rubbery face. She was permanently in a wheelchair and had a ladder of suture marks up her sparrow's chest from a heart operation. My new arrival had stripped her top off and was slapping and punching at her head and breasts. I pulled him off her by the back of his collar and dropped him on the floor. He hitched up his trousers, eyeballed me and advanced with truculent springy movements. I wrestled him out of the room and into the corridor while he continued to take round-armed swings at me. What made me really angry was the shamelessly calculating way he'd gone about getting at Annabel. He'd obviously got away with that sort of thing before.

I can still visualise his polecat face in that dim corridor. The bastard was smiling. I lost all pretence of professionalism and slammed him hard in the face, my fist batting into his chin with a crisp clopping sound. He fell instantly and silently and lay on his back in the corridor. I checked to see if he was still breathing. Mercifully, he seemed to be alright and began to stir. I dragged him down the corridor to his room, threw him on his bed in the recovery position and hurried back to see Annabelle. Except for some red marks on her face and chest, she appeared to be alright and babbled quietly to me. I really didn't know what the hell I was going to do and various wild options flared in my head. I went back to the miscreant's room. He was sitting up and rubbing his chin and shrank back when I appeared. I asked him if I was going to get any more trouble from him that night. He shook his head. In the morning, I gave him bus money and discharged him.

Of course, nowadays the police would be called and the whole ponderous, ineffective mechanism of a safeguarding investigation would be activated but that was not the culture then. In my Rhodie pessimism, I saw the nasty incident as simply being part of the ineluctable turmoil of life. I didn't think there was any point in risking an assault charge myself by warning the authorities about him. His file was already full of similar behaviour anyway. The risk I potentially posed to patients if I lost my temper was another thing. I'd come close to professional disaster and vowed never to let myself snap like that again — at work. Outside it was another matter.

I saw that same abusive ferret some ten years later at a conference about peer support for mental health sufferers. He'd become a patient advocate and even gave a little talk about how he supported people in mental health distress. I dreaded to think what he was actually doing with them. I was sure he recognised me. He directed a lingering varmint stare my way across the crowded room. I glared back but there was nothing I could do. I wrote a letter to the organisation he was with, suggesting that they look at him more closely, but knowing the British system of care for the vulnerable as I've come to do, I doubt anything ever came of it.

I'd read many alternative psychiatry books, authors like R.D. Laing and Thomas Szasz. I held that psychiatric illness was a myth, and that exposure to people with mental health difficulties could open my own doors of perception and help me to heal myself. I soon lost those ideas after retraining and taking on posts in community mental health. I think, at heart, I wanted to rescue my patients, even though I was too pessimistic to have much hope for them. While I was training to be a psychotherapist in the Nineties, I tried to comprehend my own psychopathology, a phenomenon typical among students of psychotherapy, most of whom are drawn to the field, like moths to streetlamps, by their own frequently egregious psychological problems.

My course was dominated by doctrinaire neo-Freudians as unwilling to question their masters' dogmas as Mediaeval Catholic seminarians, and about as interested as them in gathering objective empirical evidence for their magical beliefs. Naturally, this led me toward their great rivals, the relational psychologists, chief among whom for me was the rebel psychoanalyst, Ronald Fairbairn. What an enlightening shock it was to read Fairbairn's description of 'the schizoid position', in particular, how the schizoid was compelled by childhood trauma to sabotage love. Fairbairn described how the schizoid keeps his love within him. It is too precious to part with and too dangerous to release. The love of others must likewise be avoided because accepting it is too hazardous because it feels either too overwhelming or precarious.

That tragic 'schizoid position' described my experiences to a 'T'. My married Polish lover was perhaps the only person with whom I'd been able to break the mould. Did I come to fully exist thanks to the gaze of people who've loved me? There's no doubt I've grown by being loved. Women have healed me by their love though it's always been at great cost to them. But did any of them truly see me or I them?

In the end, I stopped my advanced psychotherapy training and retreated from working as a therapist although I think I helped my patients as, after all, it is the wounded physician who heals most skilfully. The reason I stopped, unlike too many practitioners in that field, was that I recognized that I had further to go to heal than most of my patients. It was then that I moved to my more natural environment — prisons and secure psychiatric facilities, where I specialised for twenty-two years in the management of highly risky patients who might harm other people. Now that was a subject I knew something about!

*Aged 40, 1992, by then a manager and clinician at a community mental health team. Photo taken by one of my patients during a home visit.*

# 27
# The Caul

*Cast a cold eye*

*On life, on death.*

*Horseman, pass by!*

– W.B. Yeats

The same memories of that time in my life flip back into my mind again and again like an echo in a cave. There was a young Zambian man in the early Nineties who was one of our community patients, not mine, but we would often speak in the waiting room while he waited for his appointments. He was a Chewa from the Machinga Hills in the east who told me that he thought he was bewitched. He said his father was a Nyau dancer, and that he also had danced from the age of ten. The Nyau was a secret ceremony performed by masked dancers who enact a part-satire, part-drama-therapy performance that's intended to help flush away bad witchcraft from the tribe. You could get killed if you were caught spying on the Nyau.

The young man told me he was being harassed by the spirits of the dead who inhabited the inner city council housing tower block where he lived. He reckoned this was happening because his own ancestors were angry with him for no longer remembering them in the Nyau dance. He couldn't discuss the issue with his psychiatric nurse as she only wanted to talk about delusions and medication. I sympathised and suggested that maybe he should send some money back to his village to get them to dance the Nyau dance for him and make a new mask to symbolise his plight. He liked that idea but added that his mind was full of lonely anger over being cut off from the world in which he was raised. I knew just what he meant but I have no idea what happened to him in the end.

Other memories from that time are the sort that do not forget you, even though you forget them. Street fights and fraught stand-offs. I always hated bullies and never fought anyone without a good reason, unlike the English around me. Maybe I attracted trouble because, at some level, I desired it. I never thought to involve the police. My childhood had taught me to settle your own quarrels. It was all good training for working with 'dangerous offenders' in maximum security units where I often found psychologists and the like puzzling over the motivations of sadistic killers. To me, that seemed a form of *bien-pensant* naivety. Prison doctors and forensic clinicians were so desperate to find all sorts of explanations and excuses for their clients' behaviour. It was clear to me though that those guys did cruel things because they liked it. It was something they enjoyed doing because it was in their nature to do it and they'd do it again given half a chance. Cruelty might originally stem from some weakness at heart as Seneca, the Emperor Nero's former tutor observed, but it is basically an appetite like any other. My time with Spear had taught me that.

Those were the days when I rode motorbikes, cultivated risky companions and fell into amphetamine and heroin use. I functioned for years as a working professional while addicted to a daily dose of brown skag. I eventually became sick enough of my dependence on the stuff that I quit by going cold turkey. It used to amuse me in clinics later on to hear junkies moaning about the terrors of detox. To my mind, they were simply soft people who couldn't bear much discomfort and hated to be left alone with their essential selves.

Another aspect of this same approach to life was that I liked to laugh at misfortune. I used to deal with fear by laughing out loud, the same way I used to chuckle or scream inside my helmet whenever I had a scare on the bike. Like the time I encountered two Alsatians loping towards me in the fast lane of a motorway when I was leaning flat on the tank of a 750cc Triumph Trident while doing over a ton. The dogs didn't survive the encounter and I nearly crashed. I chortled manically to cope with it. It was likewise my habit to smile and chuckle during street fights. That certainly used to unnerve my opponents. I'd become hard to hurt physically or psychologically, and was set on laughing uproariously at any execution party that I might have to face in future, thereby putting a Rhodie hex on my persecutors.

In my forties, I took to keeping and breeding horses. I had a particular fondness for temperamental Arabs. The beasts helped me keep in touch with nature while my salaried job trapped me indoors. They were hard work and drained me of money at a time when my finances were already rocky but they rewarded me with lonely transcendent moments like riding alone at night after work, especially when it snowed. Those times are imprinted on my mind: the muffled hoof beats, the squeak of leather and jingling of the bit as we passed over the phosphorescent snow. In those moments, in a world cast in frost, I seemed to be riding in the ghost tracks of a pale, long-vanished army of other lonely horsemen.

I once took my favourite mare, Sari, to be covered by a pedigree Arab stallion. The lengthy gestation that ensued could last from ten months to just over a year. In the later stages, I slept at night in the hay of Sari's stable. I loved listening to her soft breathing and quiet movements. At last, her foal was born one spring dawn. It came out bleating and blaring but I couldn't get it to stand up. Its back legs had become twisted up in the umbilicus and were malformed. I wrestled to free it while Sari moaned and threatened to strike me with her fore hooves. The newborn had a perfect, wet, miniature, dished face and its fawn body looked well-made but the wretched back legs remained twisted and inert. The vet came after several hours and told me it was paralyzed and would never recover. God only knows why, she injected the poor foal with poison without sedating it. It screamed for ten minutes before falling silent while Sari raged.

I'd buried Sari's foal in a field corner when, two days later, another breeder mentioned that he'd lost a mare but had a foal. We decided to try giving his foal to Sari to save it and to ease her distress. We brought the little orphan to her but she rejected the alien babe, kicking at it. I knew that she needed it to smell of her womb so I went back to the field, dug up her dead offspring, skinned it and tied its pelt over the new foal. At last, Sari accepted it, allowing it to suckle. A life was saved that day while, for me, a metaphor was born. I came to see myself as wearing the dead, alien pelt of English culture around me like a caul, the better to be accepted by my colleagues and friends. Later, when my books came out, if they took the trouble to read them, they expressed shock at the very different self that loomed forth.

*Riding Sari, 1995.*

My scars are my true 'madeleine', the touchstones of memory, a key to the rough times in Africa and after. There's the hole on my right jaw from the Van der Ruits' slug and the keratinised ridge on my right side ribs where a guy with a box cutter tried to unzip me after I confronted him on a night bus in Nottingham where he was harassing two girls. I didn't realise he'd cut me until after the fight was over and I noticed the blood sopping my shirt. There are the wealed ridges on my neck where Michelle, a mental health patient, attempted to hold me hostage, pressing a butcher's knife to my neck. Blood ran into my collar but I talked her out of it and she hugged me and wept afterwards.

And there are the white nodules on my chest from when Mum burnt me with her cigarette ends on bad days at Fort Roseberry. And there's the protruding knob of my sprung collar bone joint, an unusual injury from a motor bike crash.

A doctor at the time advised me to have surgery to relocate the bone back into the joint but I preferred to leave it as a reminder. At night, I sometimes draw my feet up and finger the toes on my left foot, splatted by a hoof in my horse-breeding days. That foot was further bent and splayed when my Triumph Trident slid over it in another high speed crash. I keep trying to straighten the gristly, pulped digits but, thirty years crooked, they spring back to their familiar mushed shape. How to count the heart's scars though? This body carries the half-acknowledged history of all the sins done both to and by me, everything I've sought to ignore and to disavow.

# PART THREE

# 28
# All the Christmases

*A life can be haunted by what it never was.*

*– Louis McNeice*

A hot and damp Christmas, Fort Roseberry, 1963: Susan and I crept up at dawn to look at our presents laid out in pillowcases on the rattan tables in the sitting room. The glass of sherry that had been left out for Father Christmas had been drunk and there were crumbs on his plate from Jonas' attempt at mince pies. We were sent back to bed with the threat that we would get nothing at all if we continued to be naughty. Later in the morning, we went for a stroll with Muso in attendance. He carried a panga in case we came across any untoward beasts. A shrilling noise from underfoot alerted us to scarlet, velvety mites in the rich, green spear grass that always appeared at this time. We called them 'Christmas Beetles'. Flame lilies glowed here and there in the grass, as well as puff-balls of the blood lily which the sunbirds liked to peck at for their nectar. Muso showed us where to find the flowers but I don't think they meant much to Africans. Those blossoms embodied a European idea of beauty.

Muso was keener on harvesting mangoes in the rain while I held a basket below. Same for the sticky pendant mulberries from our garden trees that would make up our Christmas pudding. Before harvesting, each tree had to be inspected for the green and black chevrons of the boomslang, a snake whose highly venomous bite would make you bleed from every orifice for five days before you died. Later, we gave out presents to the families of the nearby village, bright blue blankets and shiny galvanised buckets for the *mfazis,* the women with swaddled babes tied to their backs, tins of sweets for the kids, tobacco and cash for the men. All received their presents with a bow, softly clapping and murmuring thanks, "Natolelo sana", in Chi-Bemba. I'd reply politely and formally, "Eya mukwai", bowing and clapping in return. Instead of turkey for Christmas dinner, we'd have roast guinea fowl. Dad warned us not to crack our teeth on the lead shot they might contain.

I began writing full time at fifty-five after leaving salaried work early. I sold my house and lived off the money. My relationship with my parents had deteriorated badly over the previous decades. My life had been so chaotic it had caused them distress. At one point, a deranged, jealous lover of someone I'd been seeing had broken into my house one night and split my head open with a heavy metal torch while I lay in bed. I'd managed to disarm and overpower him and, after a fierce struggle, shoved him through a second story window.

The neighbours called the cops and my assailant was hospitalised and arrested. I had to have my scalp sutured. A court case ensued and the local newspapers got hold of it. My parents read the lurid story and were so upset by it that they cut contact with me for a year. Gradually, things improved. Christmas was always important to them. They were both orphans and set great store by seasonal family rituals. They invited me to visit one Christmas and that began to heal our rift. Over time, I became more and more involved in their lives and my role gradually shifted from that of delinquent son to trusted carer.

The high point of the festive meal was always Christmas pudding. Wreathed in blue flames from burning brandy, it was borne to the table by Mum with great ceremony. I think that moment was the one most prized by Dad. It must have been an occasion of great personal triumph for him, proof that he'd recreated the home life that had been snatched from him as a boy. He liked to hide silver coins wrapped in greaseproof paper that were seemingly cooked inside the dessert. We children and Mum would find our own smaller shillings and sixpences in there but Dad always managed to triumphantly produce a chunky half-crown from his portion. He kept up this Christmas coin trick to the end. I suspect he learned the custom from his own father, a Boer War and First World War veteran who became a publican in his home town of Lichfield, Staffordshire. He died at the age of fifty-six when Dad was twelve years old. My paternal grandmother followed her husband within a year; she died of grief, Dad always said.

There were further family Christmases to come as I spent more time with Dad and began to rebuild our relationship. I supported him when he had a heart-bypass operation. I think he appreciated that. He was not comfortable with too many intrusive questions but when I asked him what he most remembered of his father, he told me that he particularly recalled how he'd asked for his military medals to be brought to him when he was lying in his hospital bed at the end.

At the turn of the millennium, Dad informed me that he wanted to revisit the Second World War battlefields where he'd fought and lost good comrades. He asked me to accompany him. These were the longest periods of time we'd ever spent together. We revisited the Normandy landing grounds, where Dad had crash-landed in his assault glider. Then we went on to Belgium, where he'd witnessed the aftermath of the SS massacre of civilians at Bande, and to Haminkeln on the Rhine, where his best friend had burnt to death in front of him. While we travelled, we talked of the war and of Africa and found a way of being comfortable with each other. Year on year, there were fewer and fewer of Dad's fellow veterans at the remembrance ceremonies. We both knew that time was running short.

I think Dad instinctively understood my literary ambition. He was a romantic soul although life had tempered and hardened him. He used to make me pause to look at things when I was small: thundering waterfalls, or the black, rounded *kopjes* that jutted from the mopane scrub. He wanted me to drink up the wonder of Africa and was furious when I played the sulky, difficult son. Actually, I was taking it all in, just as he'd hoped. I was soaking up the incredible landscape around me, as well as the moonscape within me.

My first novel, a gritty crime thriller entitled *No Way To Say Goodbye,* sold decently and was well reviewed. I don't think Dad ever read it but he told others he was proud of me. Although he never said anything to me about it, it was as if he suddenly realised the direction I'd been heading in all my life and now he understood why I'd trodden such a rocky road. I like to think he appreciated my feeling of incredible, yea-saying luck to be so inhabited by a daemon of creativity. It has made many of the scars worthwhile and writing has been the only way I could confront my shame and sense of failing at life and love. My books have been a godsend but I still hunger for more. There's that Russian saying: *However much you feed a wolf, he is still looking to the forest.*

*2004 My father watching British airborne troops from his old unit doing a parachute drop at his own wartime landing ground at Ranville, Normandy on the 60ᵗʰ anniversary of D-Day.*

I went with Dad to the Ardennes to revisit the ground where his unit had fought. He told me that his best meal ever had been on Christmas Day, 1944. His unit had been thrown into the line to plug a gap in the front after the Germans had smashed through the American lines in their final offensive of the war, the Battle of the Bulge. Dad's unit had been hurriedly flown in as reinforcements from where they were recovering in camp in England after Normandy. He'd driven his jeep up to the front line from Dinant on Christmas Eve, past thousands of demoralised Americans pouring back in the opposite direction. He drew up his unit's anti-tank guns in the hamlet of Foy-Notre-Dame, a few miles from the Meuse bridges that were the ultimate objectives of the German thrust. He said it was freezing and the ground was snow-covered. His men had no winter kit. Some wrapped themselves in white bed sheets taken from empty houses for camouflage.

They heard the sinister squeaking and rattling of tracks and the gunning of engines as German armour began to filter through the icy woods to the east. It was to be the farthest point of the winter offensive led by *Zweite Panzer,* known as the Viennese Division. Dad's hidden guns fired seventeen-pounder sabot rounds that blew up a leading Panther tank and an armoured troop carrier and the heart went out of the German attack. The German vehicles burned at Foy crossroads as more Allied reinforcements rolled up. The next day, Christmas, Dad commandeered some bread from a bakery and somebody found a cow killed by artillery fire and kept fresh by the cold. They butchered it and grilled the meat in the open over an ammo-box fire. They all ate a glorious meal in the snow, watching the battle raging ever further off as the defeated Germans retreated.

Dad's unit does not feature in the historical accounts of this last clash close to the banks of the Meuse. Other units are credited with blunting the German attack but Dad knew what happened, as did the men who were with them that day. We carry our world within us and, if we are lucky, we pass on some of our memories to someone else. I'm not sure whether Dad fully trusted that I'd understood everything he imparted to me. Maybe that's why he used to greet me by saying, "Still here!", when he opened the front door to me each Christmas Day after our *rapprochement*. There were a few more Christmases to come but not many.

# 29
# Chitambo's Village

*I stood on the knoll and looked northwards across the wide water-logged valley. Below me, the tall, rank grass swept down to a wall of rushes at the water's edge. There, the green and yellows of the flooded land gave way to the grey of the encroaching waters. Time had little changed this scene and it was here, one-hundred years ago that David Livingstone crossed his last river, the Lulimala, at the end of his last journey. Here he took up his diary for the final time, grasped an old worn stump of pencil and wrote in a feeble hand, "Knocked up quite, and remain – recover..." These were the last words Livingstone ever wrote. When they went to fetch him from his hut to make his crossing of the river, he was too weak to stand...The party went very slowly on to the next village. It was called Chitambo...*

From "In The Last Steps of Livingstone" (1973) by J.E. Madocks.

I began to see my parents more clearly once our roles started to shift. We spoke about important things more readily and they opened up their lives to my help. Yet, I still realised that I'd never really know the full truth about them.

*My indomitable father. Serenje, Northern Rhodesia, 1956.*

They must have been hopeful dreamers as young people, eager to improve the lot of 'the African', taking their wives and children along to live in the bush, firm in the faith, like so many idealistic Imperial civil servants of the late colonial period, that the authority of the Pax Britannica would somehow protect them. I only realise now what an ordered life we all led in Northern Rhodesia, the formality of the whole system. I have a carton full of all sorts of household bits and pieces: cutlery, letter openers, ashtrays and the like, all bearing the Northern Rhodesian Government stamp; as if the British wanted to impress a level of control onto the smallest objects as a counter to the innate chaos of Africa and its inhabitants.

Dad was at the top of the N.R.G. tree. As a Provincial Commissioner, he was one down from the Governor. Below him were the District Commissioners and their subordinates. Then came the police and soldiers, then the Public Works Department and the Fisheries and Game officers, and so on down through the civilian ranks, or sidewise to the African chiefs and the new politicos. As a leader, Dad needed to be always measured and on the watch. Only at home could he relax. The Boma drums would go *boom–boom–boompa–boom,* marking an end to the working day and we'd see him coming home from work, parking the government Chevrolet, with its Union Jack on the hood, and marching up our gravelled drive in Fort Roseberry. He was usually dressed in a khaki bush shirt and shorts, with a yellow cravat around his neck. An outfit like that worn by the actor, Stewart Granger, in the 1950 film *King Solomon's Mines.* Dad's face, knees and forearms were tanned to mahogany but elsewhere his skin was abruptly pale. He was military looking — tall, big-shouldered, with a clipped moustache and neat wavy hair, although closer up you could see there was a somehow feminine curve to his lips.

I can visualise him now, his large, intelligent brown eyes are encompassing us. Mum rushes around, seemingly anxious, yet secretly pleased that he has arrived, but for some reason, hiding her feelings from us, as usual. She begins supervising Jonas in the kitchen. You can tell by the set of the old cook's shoulders that he'd prefer to work on his own. Dogs mill about, beating our legs with their wagging tails. Dad sits down with a Castle lager from the paraffin fridge. Mum asks about his day.

He tells us all an amusing story of how one of his officer cadets, fresh out from England and fearful of African wildlife, had gone gingerly for a visit to the outdoor, thatched outhouse or PK. The young man had erupted from the lavatory with his trousers around his ankles and clasping his backside. He screamed and threshed about and cried out that he was dying from snakebite. He was promptly held down and injected by Dad with anti-venom from an intimidating-looking glass syringe. The wounded cadet was laid down to rest and an assault party armed with clubs and hoes was mustered to get the offending snake. Next, the PK door was levered open with a broom handle, when out fluttered an aggrieved Rhode Island Red hen in lieu of a serpent. The boma kept chickens to contribute eggs for meals and they liked to catch spiders in the cool shadowy recesses of the PK pit. One of them must have spied the cadet's pale rump perched on the seat above her and given it a good peck.

We all laugh heartily. Dad is such a good anecdotist, at ease there before us, fondling Buster's ears with one hand as the dog leans up to him, a metal flash on his collar to indicate that he has been inoculated against rabies. In his other hand, Dad holds his lager. He does not embrace us when he comes home but we know he loves us. We accept this unspokenness between us. We children are free to settle in the background now. The house has been waiting for Dad to come home and fill it up.

Supper follows, always held at more or less the same time. There is some formality to the occasion. We are washed and our hair combed. Dad has put on a fresh shirt and Mum, a shawl. The brass pressure lamps have been primed with vigorous pumping and are fizzing away. Moths blunder against their luminous glass hoods. Our faces are lit by the warm, yellow light as our parents talk. Susan and I are happy simply to listen. A bat comes in from an open window in the kitchen and whisks around the room. Jonas begins flapping at it with a tea towel. That failing, he gets a larger towel, which he flaps more vigorously. We find it hilarious. Then there is a second bat and Dad says, "Leave it, Jonas. You seem to be breeding them in there, old friend." More laughter. The normally impassive Jonas laughs too. We are happy in the moment. We know this is *our* way of doing things.

Was this the life they imagined for themselves, after meeting when both were still in barracks and then marrying in June 1945? Dad wrote Mum from active duty in Palestine, *My darling wife of six months. Someday we will look upon this separation and laugh.* Or, on the troopship, R.M.S Maloja, going out to Africa, lifeboats permanently at the ready in case of mines left over from the war, what had they imagined for themselves over the horizon as they peered out through those hawsers and cables?

*Mum on the troopship Maloja, passing Suez, August 1946.*

Both my parents started with very little. They'd been orphaned by circumstance and by choice, and busied themselves creating their own new reality— a family — held tight together, but then dissolving, like the country where it was conceived. Was it enough to have all been together there, but soon after, no more? All that remains of them now is love remembered, and in these pages, a few images of their faces and last traces of their shades.

Dad had a genial, steady nature, though one of his university colleagues told me he could be very "steely". He was formidably clever and always seemed a step ahead of me, forbearing to show me up. He was always wanting to be a-doing and making advancements. Even when he was quite ill in hospital during the last year of his life, I found him clad in a red paisley dressing gown, with his signature yellow cravat and Moroccan leather slippers, restlessly pacing the corridors, studying the noticeboard in the hospital corridor, scrutinising it for what valuable information he might glean from it.

He was a likeable, capable, soldierly man. Mum called him 'Prince' and the nickname suited his regal, assured nature. Difficult to push over physically or otherwise, he played rugby at club level and at university. One finger on his large, handsome hands was permanently curled, broken in a scrimmage. He also played cricket for the army in Gaza. A wartime newspaper report said of him at a divisional athletics match: *No-one could beat the Major.* Dad thought winning was important and my indifference to sport, and unwillingness to compete, must have grievously disappointed him. However capable he was though, he knew he was better when he had Mum by his side. *The two of us,* he wrote on the pages of his photo album when it first began to feature shots of her. She was his focus, whatever other ambitions gripped his imagination. She gave him the base he needed to achieve his dreams.

Dad felt one should seize opportunity and thought diffidence a crime. I've already told you how, as a child, I would be sulking in the back of our Vauxhall Velox as we pummelled along a dirt road in the Luangwa valley, when a herd of Cape buffalo might thunder up and mass on a bluff close to the road, their moiling shapes limned by the violent orange of the setting sun. Dad liked to stop the car to observe them. In such situations, if I continued to sulk and avert my gaze, he'd grab my head and turn it to face the buffalo saying "Look! Look! Do not waste this chance." He was right to make me pay attention at all those magnificent sights. I must've been a trial to him at times with my withdrawn secretive ways. Still, despite my irritating rejection of his world, he showed immense forbearance and generosity towards me and, in the main, left me in peace to follow my own path.

Late in life, travelling with him by train to London where he was about to undergo a triple heart-bypass, I saw that Dad was looking pensively out the train window. I asked him if he had any regrets. It was a bumptious question but I was trying to connect with him. He looked surprised at the question and replied after a pause, "No, no regrets, son." It was not Dad's style to have regrets. He was irrepressibly optimistic. He told me he'd recently received a copy of a medical letter that described him as *this old gentleman of eighty-four.* He was indignant about the doctor's label and assured me he never considered himself "an old gentleman, nor indeed an old anything". At the close of his life, he never acknowledged the coming end, but instead maintained a forthright hope that his condition would improve.

"I've survived the army surgeons and I'll survive this," he used to mutter as the doctors kept trying new treatments to no avail. He fought my sister and me on his deathbed, having not eaten solid food for two months already. We were only trying to make him more comfortable but he kept flailing about. I suspect he was trying to get up so he could resume looking after Mum.

We brought priests to both Dad's and Mum's bedsides at the end but I'm still not sure about their religious beliefs. Both had been churchgoers, but stopped attending once a female vicar appeared and *The Book of Common Prayer* was phased out. I know they believed in their own story, the two of them together, although I think that Dad was more loving than loved. Mum was always at the centre of our world even though she was such an enigma. Together, both our parents were a paradoxical combination: they were rational, empirical, yet also repressed, dreamers. They shared a wry humour and a love of language, of books and stories. They also shared a sense of the romance of life and a belief you could transcend your lot and make a new world in the face of dissolution. It may have taken nearly three score years for them to become manifest, but all these attributes they passed to me, helping to make me a writer.

Dad had a number of somewhat surprising heroes, the foremost being: Richard the Third, Oliver Cromwell and David Livingstone. He wrote an accomplished article about Livingstone's nightmarish final journey to Chief Chitambo's village near Ilala in 1873. Ilala was close to the Bangweulu swamps in modern day Zambia, quite near where we'd once lived. Dad's article was much admired at the time, and was published in a historical magazine. I still have the manuscript. In it, he wrote about how Livingstone, crippled by malaria and dysentery, was attended by his two faithful servants, Susi and Chuma, to the very end. They nursed the explorer during his last illness, and unbidden, took on the herculean task of carrying his body a thousand miles back to the East African coast. They were never properly thanked. Dad clearly felt that Susi and Chuma were heroic men in their own right.

For me, Dad's article somehow presaged his own death, specifically the way he kept fighting to overcome illness for months, despite being unable to eat, yet still wanting to get up and help Mum. In this, he reminded me of Livingstone in his last journal entry, *knocked up quite and remain – recover...* There was a shared refusal to be beaten down by frailty and an indomitable will to keep going whatever befell them. At the end, we hired a night sitter from a care agency to help us nurse Dad. He turned out to be a quiet, young Malawian named Samuel. Dad accepted his help and seemed to like the way Sam attended him. Sam was a constant presence during those last weeks and I couldn't help thinking of Susi and Chuma when I watched him carrying Dad to the bathroom in his strong arms, or when he coaxed Dad to drink soup after he had refused to take any from us.

When I told Sam that Dad had died, he got down on his knees there and then and prayed for Dad's soul.

"So the big man has gone," he said, nodding sadly. It seemed to me in that moment as if I had been transported back to another place and time, Chief Chitambo's village maybe.

# 30
# Mum's Secret

*A still — Volcano — Life*

–Emily Dickinson

There is an African proverb, "Every scar tells a story". Mum's scars were hidden and hard to read. She served with the army during the war in shore batteries on the Immingham coast. She told me that she was promoted to being an officer as she was one of the few female soldiers who didn't faint when the fifteen inch coastal artillery guns thundered out. Mum could never bear to tell me anything about her life before the war, other than saying that her mother had died in childbirth when she was five years old, and that she hated her father. One night, near to the end of her life, she uncharacteristically asked me what I was interested in at that moment. I told her that I'd become fascinated by the treatment of wounded soldiers during the First World War. I'd begun to collect vintage photos of these British soldiers, and of the wounded *askaris* from the African Great War campaign against von Lettow-Vorbeck. The haunted eyes of the maimed and shell-shocked soldiers seemed to call to something in me.

I'd begun to research more into the subject and had amassed a collection of photograph albums that had belonged to military nurses. It's strange how obsessed I became with the hidden history of those tens of thousands of wounded men. I told Mum about my photos and watercolour sketches of soldiers in the uniform of the wounded. It was called 'hospital blues', a pyjama-like blue outfit with pale lapel facings and a red floppy tie. I wanted to write a book about the experiences of the men who wore that uniform and formed an idea that the meaning of 'a wound' changed during that time period to denote something psychological in addition to physical. I also wanted to explore the link between wounds and memory.

Mum looked very intent as she listened to me talking about the Great War wounded. She told me that she knew the hospital blues uniform very well because her father used to wear it. I asked her how that could be because she was born in June 1918 in the last year of the Great War. She said the uniform was worn by disabled soldiers for years afterward, and revealed that my grandfather, her father, had been "severely wounded" in the trenches, and that this had detrimentally affected his behaviour. He'd lost his wife and shuffled about Mum's childhood home in his hospital blues being a monster to her. I asked her what he had done that was so terrible but she only shook her head and her eyes filled with tears. She did once manage to tell me that she'd been given a dog to comfort her after her mum died, but that her father had shot it in front of her on a whim.

This was one of the very few times Mum ever mentioned what her life was like before meeting Dad. I was amazed to find out about that sequential path, which had led me to studying the First World War wounded, whilst I unknowingly bore the epigenetic emblemata of that war. My grandfather had received his wound, probably a head injury, and had, in turn, taken out his trauma on my mother, who had, in turn again, been unable to prevent herself from lashing out and passing on her terror to me.

Later on, I was introduced to recent research which suggested that this inheritance might be rooted not only in nurture, but also in nature, not merely psychological, but rather biological. Transgenerational epigenetics is a newcomer rival to Darwinian orthodoxy, which developed in light of evidence that being reared under radically different conditions — primarily ones of extreme stress, as opposed to relative tranquillity and contentment — leads human children, or juvenile great apes and monkeys for that matter, to develop an alternate neurochemistry, which both results from and leads to changes in the expression of genes integral to brain development that may then be passed on to offspring. Mounting evidence for this process has breathed new life into Lamarck's long-discredited theory of the inheritance of acquired characteristics, at least in relation to neurological, and hence behavioural, traits as an adaptive, or maybe it would be more accurate to write 'maladaptive', force.

Evidence of this surprising mechanism, whereby genes may be switched on or off due to environmental factors was initially noted by researchers working with the children of Holocaust survivors who suffered from a wider range of psychological disorders than could be explained by the effects of simply having highly traumatised parents. Researchers have dubbed this focussing of damaged phenotypes *canalisations*. I've often wondered, since having been made aware of this, whether my neurochemical, and thus behavioural, phenotypes were partly the result of Mum and Dad's respective life wounds, and those of their battle-scarred progenitors. I find myself relieved, in this respect anyway, that I have had no children to whom I might have passed on the damage. On the other hand, I do sometimes wonder whether my books bear the expression of those behavioural phenotypes, canalising for good or ill in the minds of those who read them with care.

# 31
# Shalineepo, Mum

*Tell me your attitude to pain and I will tell you who you are!*

– Ernst Jünger

Mum lived on in the old family house for two years after Dad died. I recruited carers to help her in the day and called in each night to assist her with getting to bed. She didn't often speak about Dad and seemed happiest when distracted by the TV. Gradually, her mind dimmed, past and present became muddled and her legs weakened. I took her once to see Dad's gravesite and she seemed shocked and frightened. I regretted doing it. Sometimes she'd say to me as I tucked her up in bed, "Pray that I slip off. You'll do that won't you?"

A succession of falls at home led to long nights in Casualty explaining her health problems to young doctors. I moved back into the family home after a gap of forty years. Despite my increased presence, infections came visiting, with mini-strokes and diagnoses that sounded like death sentences

— vascular dementia, ischaemic heart disease. I couldn't properly look after Mum at home although I struggled to keep going. She didn't seem to mind when I lifted her onto the commode and even used to laugh at the thunder of her droppings landing in the resonant plastic receptacle. She'd always say it was like the noise that the coalmen used to make unloading their sacks down the coal chute in pre-war houses.

More infections, fevers and hospital stays. Someone dropped her onto the floor in hospital, resulting in a terrifying leg wound where you could see the bone beneath. I never could find out who'd actually allowed that to happen. This accretion of disability, pain and humiliation led, in the end, to the doors of a care home closing behind her. Like uncounted legions of her generation, she had entered the abode of the lost.

I visited twice a day, morning and evening. I felt I couldn't leave her for long as my extensive experience of British state healthcare gave me little trust in the home's staff. Bacilli came and went, trying to claim her. The hospital-acquired wound festered and pneumonia visited, yet still she fought to live. I think Mum actually believed that she was in some sort of second-rate hotel run by barely adequate staff. Sometimes, she would question me about her situation. "Where has Dad gone?" she'd demand.

I'd look across the room at the photo of him on her windowsill. The one in a silver frame where he was wearing a white colonial uniform and a plumed sun helmet, taken at Fort Roseberry in 1964 as he was preparing to meet a tribal dignitary. "Dad's at home, having a lie down," I'd reply.

At other times, I'd find her fast asleep, her hair tucked behind her ears. So strange to see her ears, they looked beautiful, like pressed rose petals found in an old book. They'd always been hidden by her hair earlier in her life, one of her many secrets. Peculiar also to look upon the ruin of my last organic link to the world, my pith and marrow. Africans say that towards the end of their lives old people temporarily leave their bodies in order to visit the spirit world and have a preliminary look around, before returning for a while longer to the realm of the living. I wondered whether she'd been doing that. Sometimes, at night, the kitchen cupboards of the old house gave out a rapping sound and I'd wonder if it was Mum visiting.

At Christmas, I found her bent, half-asleep, over a plastic tumbler of cheap wine with a paper hat set wonkily on her head. Her wheelchair was parked at a long table of residents that reminded me of the Mad Hatter's tea party. I made her apologies and steered her back to her room. She seemed untroubled. Her eyes lingered on my face for a moment, then slid away to look at the telly, as if nothing much mattered to her any more. New Year, new fevers, new lung infections, new clots and cellulitis. She groaned and screamed whenever she was touched or moved.

"Leave me, dear. Leave me," she'd gasp when I tried to make her more comfortable. The torture of it, a fly always seemed to be buzzing at her window trying to get out. There was a Zimbabwean nursing assistant from Harare called Mavis for whom I had more time than the rest of the hard-faced English night staff. At least she wished the residents 'God bless you' at lights out. Mavis always giggled when I said, *"Hamba gashle"* to her, a Shona salutation that means, 'Take it easy'.

The care home made much of seasonal festivals, maybe because so many of the residents were unmoored in time. Not only was Christmas celebrated, but also Easter, when they had the women patients wear humiliating flowered bonnets. At Halloween, there was a display of illuminated skulls and skeletons in the dining room that struck me as macabre given its setting. I wondered what Mavis made of Halloween? Africans are more respectful of the spirits of the dead than we are. She was too polite to express her true feelings on the matter. When I asked her about it, she only held her hand up to her face and gave out an embarrassed, "Ki, ki, ki," the African version of 'Tee-hee-hee!'

Most nights, I tucked Mum up in bed the way she used to do for me sometimes when I was small. It was a strange reversal whenever I did that, like backing into the mirror of the past. It reminded me of the times when Mum and Dad used to attend social occasions at remote African outstations. They'd dress up in evening wear and travel miles down lonely night roads, their headlights illuminating the reflective eyes of numerous wild beasts, to enjoy formal dinner parties with their friends.

Usually, on those African evenings out, Mum would come into my room in an evening dress complete with stole and pearls, while Dad would be in a dinner jacket, his hair smoothed back with pomade and links twinkling at his cuffs. They'd come to check on me before leaving, often carrying a Tilley light in our electricity-less house. The lamp would cast a soft glow on Mum's earrings and pearls. She'd lean over me, redolent of the sweet and sour scent of Guerlaine's Shalimar, and remind me not to trouble Wilson, the house servant, and to keep Buster in my bedroom. No creature, human or animal would get past Buster. We knew that.

By the time she'd clocked a year and a half at the care home, Mum tended to already be deeply asleep when I returned there in the evening. I knew it was likely she'd slept right through the day, unaware of the wind-tossed trees and the wet, bustling skies. Now it was only the telly going and the inflatable, anti-bedsore mattress sighing as it perpetually adjusted. I'd steal up to her, wondering whether she was still there. Then I'd see that her eyes were moving beneath their lids. What was she dreaming about? Maybe being mobile again, escaping from the lonely care home and running through the blighted council estate outside. Or was she returning to the past, walking through the tall African grass?

I asked her once during those final years what she remembered most vividly from my childhood. She answered that she remained haunted by the times when I flew off from Lusaka airport on my way to boarding school in Southern Rhodesia. Mum said that after the Central African Airways Dakota had droned away to the south, taking my terrified eight year old self with it, she'd go walking in the bushlands on the outskirts of the city. She told me she would stumble along, blinded by tears and berating herself for sending me away.

After two years in the care home, Mum lay huddled in her bed, unarousable with a frail pulse tapping in her neck. It was always a sort of relief to see her folded into the safety of sleep. When I was a child in Africa, I used to sometimes creep into her room to watch her sleeping during the obligatory afternoon rest period when the heat of the day was at its worst. I risked her wrath if she awoke to find me intruding during those stolen moments but it seemed to fulfil a need in me to see her slumbering and at peace while, outside her window, frangipani leaves shivered and weaver birds swayed to and fro in their upside-down nests.

Again and again, I found Mum utterly still and unresponsive. Remains of food were often glued to her face. She frequently looked as if no one had come to check on her for the entire day and probably no one had. At other times she was awake but refused to look at me, her gaze remaining fixed on some TV news channel about more atrocities and disasters in the wider world, once even a jihadi going on about how much he and his fellow fanatics loved death. The old, angry Mum returned on occasion and she'd order me out of the room for not doing things "properly". At other times, when Mavis was in the room, she'd smilingly point me out and say, "My son."

In November, I mentioned that it was my birthday. "What *is* he saying?" She kept murmuring to herself in a puzzled way. She may well have wanted to forget my birth. It must have been a torment, with my having presented badly and being dragged out Caesar-like at the old provincial hospital in Broken Hill.

The unalterable music of the days and seasons passing played on to Mum's quiet, steady breathing and the harrowed calls from the demented souls locked up with her. There is an

African proverb, "Death does not knock on the door." Oh, but sometimes it does!

May arrived, the light like confetti and magpie nestlings squealing all day in the Lawson's cypresses outside Mum's windows. I found Mum curled over in bed with blebs of vomit down her front. The staff had been using medical grade maggots to cleanse the rotting hole in her leg. Her feet were spongy, purplish masses and her legs looked like thin bent railings distorted by great heat. Looking upon that flesh, charred by infections, I thought of those legs long ago, taking her away from the horrors at home to toddle alongside Grandfather Fergus, the travelling tinker, who she once told me was the only person who showed her affection in childhood. Those same legs, grown strong and lithe, in her Army gym classes in 1943, and later, carrying her over the dried grasses on Lusaka Common as she wandered and wept following the flights that droned me away to school.

Or much older, rubbing her legs when I accompanied her in the garden and complaining that the wet weather gave her arthritic pains that she named "the screws". Or again in Casualty, as a very old lady with a haematoma on one leg, brought on by the warfarin she had been prescribed to thin her blood against strokes, and the young doctor prodding the purple bulge until a jet of blood spurted out. Now her legs kept twitching and tremoring in spasm, as dogs' legs do when they dream. Perhaps they were returning to that time — which she divulged to me only late in her life — when she ran away from home as a child to escape the cruel hands of her war-damaged father. I prayed that those legs would help her to escape her bed of pain.

Often I'd watch as Mavis gently washed Mum's face, the expression on Mavis's own face so gentle as she did so. She had that characteristically button-like Shona face and the formal, rather serious ways of her people, though she used to burst into girlish laughter whenever I joshed with her.

"Have you brought us some *muti*?" I'd enquire when she'd enter the room. *Muti* was the universal word for medicine or cure-all in our part of Africa. It also meant witch doctor's potions of snakes' heads and such like. Only a witch doctor, I thought, could save Mum now. I sometimes wondered whether I should point out the photo of Dad in his colonial uniform on the window sill and tell Mavis that I remembered Harare from the days when it used to be called Salisbury. The city seemed so civilised and grand to me then with its dazzling white buildings and jacaranda-lined avenues. Salisbury was given the Shona nickname, *bamba zonke*, which meant 'grab-everything'. That would surely be the prevailing sentiment there today. It was a boom town when I knew it. It'd be far from that now. I didn't say anything to

Mavis in the end. I felt it might be unfair to remind her about the past.

Mum developed a scary, bubbling cough that made her gasp for breath. She looked untroubled by her peril, unlike the time when we were driving through a township in the Vauxhall Velox and a crowd of locals began stoning us. I can still picture her look of terror then, as she ground the gears in her haste to reverse while the crowd clamoured towards us and rocks bounced off the bonnet, only to reveal, moments later as we zig-zagged backwards at speed, a small green snake in the road that was the actual object of the crowd's pursuit.

With this cough, Mum seemed to be drastically slowing. Sometimes she held my hand and stared at me with blank, milky eyes. I sensed a shift and called my sister to come from her Italian home. Once Susan arrived, we took turns sitting up, watching over Mum.

Long, eerie nights, sometimes I'd hear Mavis processing down the corridor, the light sensitive switches feeling her warm presence and flicking on by themselves. "Urare zvakanaka. Goodnight and God bless," she'd say to each resident. Sometimes there'd be a muttered reply, or I'd hear her chivvying tardy ones, "Fred, Fred, not now," and the sound of plastic pill capsules popping open. I prayed at those times that I'd die quickly myself and not end up in one of these god-awful places at the end. If I weren't so lucky, at least there'd be no children who'd feel compelled to sit with me through the dark, ghost-making hours.

Mum groaned and expelled froth from her lungs, her mouth gummy. Her moaning noises might almost have been screams, if she'd had the strength for that. All she knew now was to keep on breathing for a little while longer. I found it odd how the nape nerves, the great trapezoid muscles on the back of the neck, remained strong to the end. Dad had kept raising his head, telling me to pull him up. The agonies of the body struggling violently to keep going. Mum's gaze was solely inward now though sometimes she made mumblings and plucked at the covers.

Once, I put my hand near hers and she grasped it, touching Dad's signet ring which I'd worn since his death. She opened her eyes then and I showed her the photo of her and Dad on their wedding day. Dad had left behind a slip of paper upon which he had written, late in life, "Love survives everything – even death." I was thinking of it when I showed her their wedding picture. She looked at the photo, then stared up at me intently. The stare was broken by a shuddering choking fit that swept over her before she slowly subsided into sleep. Her body had been such a frail engine for years but what murder it was to finally put a stop to it.

*Mum smiling, crossing the Kafue, 1948*

The other Zimbabwean night care staff scurried around me, plump girls with braided hair who giggled softly whenever I talked to them. They did not refer to Mum's being in extremis. It is not the African way to be explicit. They would say instead "The she-elephant is falling," or that the *vadzimu,* the ancestral spirits, were gathering. I went home after sitting up with Mum all night before Susan arrived and took over. Mum now had a shunt fixed into her veins that dispensed morphine and sedatives. She seemed to be in a coma-like state although once she opened her eyes and gestured toward the window.

I slept after being overwhelmed by a wave of insupportable tiredness. I dreamt I was fishing in the Mansa River again at Fort Roseberry. I was running in the 1960's African sunlight to show my parents the tiger fish I'd caught. Mum and Dad were stretched out on the other bank with a picnic basket and Buster was with them. Mum's hair glinted red in the light and they both waved, beckoning to me. I woke up feeling gloriously happy. Such an unfamiliar feeling, I'd not felt anything like it for years. Then my phone sounded. It was my sister texting, "She's gone."

# 32
# Katundu

*For mortals, mortal things. And all things leave us. Or if they do not, we leave them.*

– Lucian

The June earth in the garden of my parents' home felt warm as blood after Mum died and the black stalking shapes of dragonfly larvae gripped the flag iris stalks in their garden pond, ready to pupate and ascend in their winged forms to procreate. I posted thank you cards to people who'd helped Mum over the years and sent cash to four of the best of her carers at the home. I also sent a hefty sum to a Zambian charity. Mum would have wanted me to do that. She had left a note asking that her two gardeners from years before be remembered so I sent them each a cash present.

In addition, I cleared out Mum's *katundu* from the care home. In Africa, we used that word to describe one's 'stuff' or 'kit'. "Load the katundu!" was a frequently heard command to the house servants when my parents were about to go off on a trip. It was a serviceable word but, when used by black Africans, it also implied a sort of disapproval. In Africa, it was best not to be weighed down by too much *katundu*. Historically, tribal people only owned what they could carry.

On my first run to the tip, I took my parents' suitcases, filled with clothes and bric-a-brac. They were old-fashioned, heavy leather and plastic things covered in bright stickers from 1980s holidays. I hurled what had been their *katundu* into the shipping container-sized skips alongside everyone else's discarded crap. When I looked back briefly, I was sorry, and somehow sickened, to see the bin men rooting through the bags I'd chucked to check if I'd left any valuable pickings. Later, the TV news showed heaps of tangled metal and lingering trails of oily smoke from a passenger jet shot down by Russian separatists over Ukraine. In those fertile Ukrainian fields, camouflaged militia men were likewise stooping over and rooting through the suitcases of the dead, picking out clothes and children's toys to sell, or give away, or take home. I suppose somebody will go rifling through all our *katundu* in due course.

Clearing out a storage cupboard in my parents' old house, I found a now antique cardboard box full of objects of sentimental value from our life in Northern Rhodesia: brass light switches, a portable spirit stove with folding legs, letter openers and ashtrays with NRG stamped on them, and heaps of old keys from all of the African houses where we'd once lived. It was incredible that the box had survived all of our African moves, followed by a sea journey and several English house changes. The box carried the legend: *Blue Death Aerosol: OK Bazaar, Cecil Avenue, Ndola.* Ndola was the regional capital of the Copperbelt mining area of Northern Rhodesia, the nearest major settlement to our home two hundred miles away in Fort Roseberry. That avenue's name was likely a reference to Cecil Rhodes, whom the post-colonial revisionists now wish to delete from history.

I wonder whether Dad picked up the box of Blue Death at the OK Bazaar while I was having my tonsils out in Ndola in November of 1964? It must have been vicious stuff to have protected that fragile cardboard for sixty years. I suppose it contained a good dose of DDT to combat the tsetse flies, *pootsi* flies, *serowe* and white ants, along with all the other destructive bugs that threatened to invade our African homes. What we didn't realise then was that Blue Death, which is to say eradication and oblivion, are the true order of the ever-flowing world, and that the whole African life our family had lived was soon to be enfolded in it.

Memory is a salve against dissolution: remembering the firm jouncing seats of the Vauxhall Velox, or rolling with the pillowy suspension of the Chevy Impala, or holding onto the hand straps in the jarring, rattling Landy, over dust roads, dirt routes, laterite cut-throughs, rutted, ribbed, gouged from red African earth, morphing and bending in the heat-haze, on macadamised strips laid over gravel, or through porridgy mud, through smoke from bush fires and *chitemene* blazes, slowing for lions or buffaloes, bumping over suicidal village chickens, thudding into a warthog that took out the Vauxhall's nearside headlight, with bats, birds and butterflies stuck on the radiator grills, hair cauled by fine sand, taste of the road in our mouths, eyes narrowed against the westering sun, dropping like an orange balloon into a sudden, inky twilight, or by night, the semaphore of silvery acacias and the eyes of the bush creatures, phosphorescent in our headlights, grinding in low gear, or speeding so the vibrations smoothed out, dust plume behind, sweating canvas water bags, hooked to the roof rack swaying at the windows, Dad's hands steady on the wheel, our faces, our family, freighted with so many hopes and fears, as we looked towards the shimmering future awaiting us at the end of the track.

*Mum and the Velox, Zambesi Valley 1964*

# 33
# Appointment with a Cobra

*The desire to have a death of one's own is becoming more and more rare.*

*In a short time it will be as rare as a life of one's own.*

– Rainier Maria Rilke

I had a great fear of death as a young man but this is much diminished since watching over my parents as they ebbed away. I seem to be returning to the accepting African way of looking at the world, and to have rediscovered my unrelenting Rhodie nature. I find myself baffled by the saccharine sentimentality that has increasingly dogged Britain ever since the whole 'Death of Princess Diana' melodrama. I don't cry watching poignant films, or at TV programs about international and family tragedies. Rather, I assume that all human life is tragic, and am surprised when it's not. African tribal beliefs gave me the notion that when you were a baby your guiding ancestor spirits linked up with your immanent self in a great meeting-house of the spirit world and the two joined forces to set up your life direction, your destiny, for want of a better word.

According to the Bemba, nothing could really change that destiny. I once saw a man in a village lying on a truckle bed. A claw hand covered his face and his wasted form looked like a twisted piece of *msasa* wood. Jonas told me he would die in the month that the rains came because a witch doctor had seen it in his fate. And so it proved to happen. There was a nonchalance about the Bemba when faced with non-being. Musondo once scared me when he let me ride on the crossbar of his bicycle and proceeded to swiftly traverse a wobbly plank crossing over the Mansa River. We weaved about so much I cried out, "You're going to kill us!" He shrugged and chuckled, "*Natufwe fye,*" which meant, "Well, then let us die." That philosophy was so different from Dad's rather English constitutional one in which nothing was written. To him, you made your fate by striving. When Susan and I kept singing Doris Day's hit song "Que sera, sera. Whatever will be, will be," over and over in the back of the car as we drummed over endless dirt roads, Dad was always the first to snap and order us to stop it. I think the song's sentiments irritated him. Even now, I still like to sing it to myself.

Mum planted a eucalyptus tree in the garden of our English house. Maybe she wanted to be reminded of the massed groves of whispering eucalyptus in African plantations. It was dangerous to walk in the springy resinous litter of their dry bark and leaves which accreted beneath them. Those places were all too frequently the abode of snakes. As a careless boy, I was running along in a eucalyptus plantation wrapped up in a hide-and-seek game. I dashed through the leaf litter and ran right over a cobra who lay coiled in the dry chippings. I can still see its intent bead-like eyes, the fulvous sheen of the scales on its erect hood as it began to rise up whilst I leaped over it.

I was expecting the cobra to strike upwards through my thin canvas *takkies* and into my bare feet but, incredibly, nothing happened. I bounded onwards until I got to a clearing and saw some adults. I gave out the warning cry for snakes — "Njoka!" and they came with sticks and thrashed around looking for the serpent but it had vanished. I should have thanked the cobra for sparing my life by leaving him in peace, instead of bringing destroyers to seek him. I think now that maybe he was Death and did not bite me because he was surprised to see me then and knew he'd meet me later somewhere else.

Sometimes I dream that I am, once again, in a leaky canoe on Lake Mweru. It was more like a recovered traumatic memory because I actually did go out once in an outboard-powered dug-out on the shallow reaches of that lake in the

1960s. Dad took me there because he said he wanted to view a leper colony located in an isolated bay on the lake. The lake was supposed to be tranquil; *mweru* means 'muddy' in Chi-Bemba. It always struck me as a brooding place, rimmed as it was by the blue shadows of the Congo mountains to the west. A storm blew up out of nowhere and the narrow, crude boat got rolled around by violent waves.

I remember the District Officer's terrier swilling about from one end of the craft to the other in a welter of petrol-tinged water while the helmsman fought for control. Dad adopted a look of mild concern and put his arm around my shoulder even though the game ranger guards with us seemed utterly petrified. When, at last, we weathered the storm and arrived at the leper colony, Dad explained that the lepers earned their living by making fishing nets and taking fish from the lake. He said the medical officer had told him it was almost impossible to catch leprosy from ordinary physical contact. When the headman proffered me an arm to shake, instead of a hand, he had a congealed lump and a few abraded sticks for fingers.

"Shake it," Dad ordered, "And look like you mean it."

I think now he said that not only because he wanted to teach me to deal with any challenge in a courageous forthright way but also that I should not delude myself into thinking the leper headman was any the lesser man for his disability.

It was due to moments like these that I took to wearing Dad's Rolex Oyster after he died. I wanted to feel its reassuring weight on my wrist. He had bought it in Aden in 1962 when we were sailing back to Africa after our leave in England. I used to peer round from the back seat of our car and watch its heavy steel bracelet glinting on Dad's wrist as he held the steering wheel of the Velox while we barrelled down African roads. That watch seemed to exemplify Dad's solid, comforting presence. He always wore it with the face turned to his inner wrist, a habit from the war because a sniper might see the flash of a watch face in the sun. He specifically left me the watch in his will. Maybe his greatest wish for me was time. He saw I was a latecomer and needed more time to accomplish the things I wanted to do.

When I look around me, in the aftermath of my parents' deaths, Britain's population appears to be half made-up of the aged. How different that was from my boyhood in Rhodesia, where there were relatively few old people. Jonas was the oldest human I'd come across by far although some villages did contain a respected grey-beard who'd lean on a long stick and pass judgements on the doings of the young. Everyone respected such men and called the old fellows — *mzee,* a title that implies wisdom. I felt I'd become a *mzee* by default once my parents were dead. But it being contemporary Britain, the young mostly brushed past me impatiently. I didn't let this trouble me though as I lived in a condition of internal exile. As the Mweru lepers likely knew well, exile was not something to be whined or moaned about, nor was it a condition that dried you to a wizened husk. No, it was more like a state of sacred reclusion that freed you.

So it was that I stayed on in my parents' place after they had gone. I seemed to work well at my writing in Dad's old study and the house rustled and creaked with friendly spirits. I also laboured contentedly in Mum's garden, where I was frequently joined by a sparrowhawk who'd come scything down the hedge line and make all the other birds hide. The hawk was the empress of the garden. I thought I should get to know her and hear what she had to say. I hoped that she'd become my mentor and teach me how to be truly free. I knew too that the hawk had been — still was — the symbol of old Rhodesia, like the soapstone hawk found amid the vanished civilisation of the Great Zimbabwe ruins.

Time and again, the sparrowhawk piled straight out of a westering sun, the little birds peeting in terror as her shadow passed over. I decided to call the hawk *Bukaka,* from the uncompromising Chi-Bemba word for hardness, brazenness, and being stiff of mouth. Unlike me, Bukaka was certain of who and what she was. I watched once as she scorched over the roof-line and plucked a blackbird from the feeder. My drop-winged angel of death mantled over her victim on the lawn, then flew up onto the head of a bronze statue that stood a few feet from me. She stayed there a while with her victim caught in one foot. I could see it still moving feebly. The talons of Bukaka's other yellow foot ground onto the head of the statue as she kept her balance and glared at me with her orange eyes. I went over to the sculpture after she'd gone and ran my fingers over the deep scratches she'd left in the verdigris.

Her cruciform shape followed me for two summers after Mum died. Her head was always down, scanning and checking her domain. I longed for her to encompass me in her long-ranging vision. She beheld us humans in her gem-like gaze and knew that we were base creatures to be avoided at all cost. Each day must have passed like an aeon in the lens of her crystalline mind, an infinite succession of evanescent moments. She knew only how to rend skin, meat and bone. There was no passion in her though she lived an ecstatic life of the now. If she could have, she would have thought men insane in their purposeless movement and energy. How I loved her brutal simplicities during those early elder orphan years.

Working in my parents' old garden helped me to look at everything through my African eyes once again. The boy I was fifty years before came back to help me, especially during bouts of illness brought on by old injuries and thyroid problems, maybe caused by that Chernobyl dust. The sounds in the garden often used to trigger memories like the chuckling of next door's bantams, which brought back to me the days in Fort Jameson when I had a pet chicken called Henny Penny. Every Sunday I'd see Jonas dispatching a fowl for roast dinner. He'd stand on their wings with his large bare feet, clamping them firmly to the ground while he carefully raised his panga to lop off their heads like a golfer taking a tricky shot. Henny Penny would come to me, twisting her head upwards to peer at me trustfully, as if to say, "I know you'll look after me, won't you?"

I used to beg Mum, "Jonas won't kill Henny Penny, will he? Not Henny Penny?"

She'd assure me that Henny Penny was safe and, indeed, Jonas did not kill her. It was the caracal she-cat that got her, the one I'd caught that night in the beam of my Vesta Spacelight after the noise of her breaking into the coop had awakened me. She stood poised and soundless in my unsteady torch beam, winged-eared and glowing-eyed. Henny Penny was hanging limp in her nib face and there was a drizzle of feathers in the dust. Maybe I'd have taken the caracal as my muse had I still lived in Africa but instead I had sharp-shinned Bukaka. The bird carried her own nature effortlessly and taught me that I must learn to carry mine so. I was in Bukaka's debt even though I know you must seek nothing and expect nothing back from a wild creature. That's the only way to stay safe and sound in your respective worlds.

# 34
# The Leap

*All journeys have secret destinations of which the traveller is unaware.*

– Martin Buber

It took a long time for me to fully realise that I no longer needed to be on duty, that I'd get no more telephone calls in the night to attend to a parent in extremis. I spent a lot of time looking over old snapshots of my family in the Rhodesian days and some instinct began to tell me that only by understanding my African self could I find a track that would lead me out to the wider world again. I began to recognise that my African childhood was going to be my antidote against the menace of a spidery and stultified old age.

I found an old school diary that held my childish entry for 9th July, 1963: "*Rhodes and Founders Camp: Babijahns,*" This is a reference to Rhodes and Founders Day, the national holiday that celebrated the original white settlers. At Ruzawi School, thirty of us were driven many miles to participate in a two day scout camp at Albert Hall, a horseshoe-shaped cluster of granite kopjes that jutted from the surrounding flat bushland. I wonder now if it was called Albert Hall because of its acoustic characteristics. For us it served as a rocky amphitheatre where our shouts and calls echoed and mingled with the yipping screeches of rock hyraxes that we called *dassies* and the legions of barking baboons that inhabited the higher ledges. Our supervising masters left us to run wild half the night and gangs of us clambered up the rounded, smooth rock to challenge the *babijahns*, leaping from boulder to boulder beneath the light of the moon. I think that I was the least afraid I'd ever been as I stood on the crest of Albert Hall with my Rhodie chums and howled back at the *babijahns*.

There was a similarly memorable moment of fear confronted waiting for me at Parrot's Bill Kopje, an eighty foot outcrop on a ridge overlooking the school. I went up there with three other boys at the end of my last term. Tradition held that each boy had to leap across a cleft in the rock as a test of bravery. The approach to the jump was the most intimidating part of the adventure. You had to scale the dark slippery shoulder of rock with few handholds while observing the flat-topped acacias trees far below that would spear you on their thorns if you fell. The Shona of long before had buried their dead in these rocks and the gaping mouths of their tombs lent a further frisson of fear as we inched our way upward. The leap, when it came, was a moment of exultant terror and release, and we indulged in a little victory dance together afterwards, telling each other that it was all very *mushi*, the Rhodesian equivalent of 'cool'. We came back down the hill singing our victory song, "Skinny malinky, long legs vrot banana feet, Went to the bioscope and couldn't find a seat. He sat on a lady and out popped a baby, skinny malinky long legs vrot banana feet!"

It was at about this same time that I made a related leap that was yet more exhilarating, albeit in another sense, when a Russian ballerina came to stay with us for a week. It must have been part of some sort of cultural exchange with the Soviets, whereby members of a touring dance troupe were put up by the families of British officials. Government staff in Africa could be surprisingly well-acquainted with their Soviet opposite numbers on account of the new Great Game being played out between Russia and the West in that period. Dad once somehow arranged for me to go to the Soviet embassy in Lusaka. I walked the half mile from our home escorted by Jonas. The ambassador received me in his office with bodyguards, and presented me with some Russian stamps featuring Sputnik and cosmonauts. I have them still. The ambassador asked me what I wanted to be when I grew up and I declared, "Soldier." He nodded in mock seriousness, then said something to his guards and they all laughed.

Anyway, the striking Slavic dancer who came to stay with us for a week was named Galina, with the stress on the second syllable. She spent a while getting me to say it right while staring deeply into my eyes. She had no English and blithely took over Mum's dressing table, strewing it with heaps of powder puffs and bottles of exotic unguents. She seemed happy for me to hang around as she did her make-up and put pins into her braided hair, chattering to me all the while in Russian, sometimes angling the mirror so she could watch my reactions. One time, I came into the room while she was changing. I did it deliberately, drawn by a ten year old's curiosity that I could barely understand. She knew I was there but let her dressing gown fall to reveal the wonderful incurving *ensellure* of her sleek and supple bare back. Galina certainly knew what she was doing as, when she came back from her ballet performances, I'd rush to light her cigarette from Dad's big, silvered Dunhill table lighter.

"Spasibo, moi malish" — "Thanks, my little man", she'd say and she'd pat the chair next to her so I could come close to her and stare up entranced at her mask-like face, still dusted with stage make-up, watching her bright carmine-painted lips purse as she exhaled coils of cigarette smoke. Galina was my first real encounter with a woman and maybe it was she who started me on the wrong path of romantic passion, with her strong whiff of glamour and danger. Maybe I have her to thank also for my later love of the Russian language and literature. A strange emptiness came over me after she'd gone. I started playing my parents' Decca LP of the soundtrack from *My Fair Lady*, especially the song, *On the Street Where you Live*, that foundational song for all stalkers. I still think it's the first song that taught me about love's bitter-sweetness: *For there is nowhere else on earth I'd rather be...but on the street where you live.*

I was taken from Africa before love could make a home in my heart but there were intimations of it other than Galina, like the young secretaries at Dad's Lusaka office with their bouffant hairstyles, clotted mascara and shiny lipstick who'd fuss over me and laugh when I entertained them with my version of *Ag Pleez Deddy*; or sweet Sarah Andrew who kissed me in her family tree house in Chalimbana, or the unknown school girl who sat next to me as we both flew on our own from Africa to our respective English schools. We spoke together about all sorts of private things during that long, intimate flight. I'll always remember her curved eyelashes and the feline outline of her cheekbone in profile as she stared out the plane window while we descended over a grey, spooky London, her cool fingers shyly extending to hold my hand.

# 35
# Demons

*Between me and thee / what difference?*

– Percy Bysshe Shelley

Prior to my fateful encounter with Galina, I liked to climb the tall tamarind tree at the bottom of our garden in Lusaka. Peeping through the branches, I found that it overlooked an open showering area for the African servants. I spent hours watching the gleaming ebony figures holding large, brick-like bars of yellow Lifebuoy soap. They laughed and sang and sometimes they twined around each other. Those people seemed happy in their skins in a way I'd never imagined before, and which I'd never witnessed among whites.

Mum told me the first time that she saw a black person was in Edinburgh during the war. She said it was a tremendous shock to her to be confronted by the fact of different races of people in the world. In Africa, Mum enjoyed spoiling the black kids. She sometimes gave me jars of sticky sweets and instructed me to dispense them to the children I encountered. In really remote areas tribespeople practised a form of eugenics, under which any newborn who was the slightest bit sickly or disabled was left out to die in the bush. Mum got the District Messengers to collect up these weakling babies. She kept them in shoe boxes and even warmed them in the bread-making compartments of our wood-fired oven on occasion. She'd feed them up with baby formula for a time before passing them to Jonas to return to their families.

I think the locals almost invariably killed off the restored babies anyway because, when I asked Jonas about it, he shook his head and told me that the infants were *lowa*, meaning a spell had been put on them. According to the tribespeople, the weak newborns had been bewitched and were doomed. I accepted that this was the way of things in those remote places and, in general, tended to take the indigenous side in matters of ethical ambivalence. To my child's mind, the villagers had a kind of divine authority given to them by their indissoluble links to their land, while Mum held to the straightforward, modern western view that weakling black babies should be given as much of a chance at life as white ones were.

I eventually had the opportunity to experience what that unknown black person whom Mum had glimpsed in 1940s Edinburgh might have felt like. I was about ten and Dad took me in a motorised yacht called the *Masue* to tour hundreds of miles of remote swamps on Lake Bangweulu in far off Luapula Province. The word *bangweulu* means 'where the water meets the sky'. The Africans there lived secret lives as fishermen on island communities hidden among the endless whispering reed beds.

Those people lived without electricity, money or any of the usual trappings of modern life brought by the Protectorate. When I tried a spot of fishing with my brand new, red fibreglass spinning rod, they approached and wanted to inspect the rod with its centre-pin reel and tried to barter eggs from scrawny bantams in exchange for one of my glittering spinning lures. Young and old seemed to find me fascinating and pulled at my hair or touched my skin before running off squealing and giggling. Sometimes when we landed our boat, a big crowd would gather to stare at us. I began to resent the intrusion of those collective gazes and would hide in the hold in my bunk sulking.

Dad once went out in a skiff to meet a crowd of villagers and kept calling me to come out on deck to join him. In a horrible moment, the entire crowd took up his cry with a thunderous shout of "Rodoney! Rodoney!" When I did appear there was a great gasp of astonishment and swaddled babies with fly-tracked, snotty faces were held up to stare at me. Dad said they'd not seen many white people and certainly not a child. I heard the crowd muttering the word *ngulu*. Jonas told me later that it meant 'ghost' though I think 'demon' might have been a more accurate translation. Jonas said that never having seen a white child before, those lake dwellers thought I came from 'the spirit world'. Jonas was often diplomatic. We whites were usually referred to as *muzungu*, or in the plural, *wazungu*, I don't think anyone using it realised its old meaning that white people were 'spinning or wandering around', as if confused or bewildered. Although I've had the word chanted at me in a goading way, black Africans have always assured me that it has no derogatory import, but rather only denotes 'alienness', as was the case so extremely that day on Lake Bangweulu.

There were creation stories of every sort in Africa. It seemed to me that every time the long grass whispered in the night breeze, I would encounter a new one. Africans told those stories in their huts after dark, including the one about how Kamba, the tortoise, moved so slowly because he carried the world on his back, and how the world was created by an entity whose name could not be mentioned. He had no ancestors, no past or future. He couldn't be propitiated by gifts or sacrifices, and was at once inscrutable and all powerful.

According to the Africans I knew, this deity had vomited the sun, the stars and the sky and his tears formed the rain. He also voided out black soil, clay and white sand. The soil he moulded into black people, from clay he created brown people and from sand he made white people. All people were not quite the same to the tribesmen who explained all this to me. To them, races of people were distinct and each had their own propensities, in the same way that the physical world had its nature and laws, and the spiritual world had different ones — and all this was as it should be.

Nowadays, black Zambians and Zimbabweans often call whites 'colonisers'. Owing to all that this implies in wider geographical context, especially in relation to historic atrocities which occurred to the north in what is now Congo, or to the East and West in what are now Angola and Mozambique, this term is almost a form of short-hand hate speech. The late President Mugabe remains very popular in the memory of the African *demos* all over that continent. To them, he remains the heroic leader who had the temerity to thoroughly get rid of the Whites. That same expropriation process has been tried in other African countries, for example the *Ujamaa* in Tanzania in the 1960s. Not that England is always much more understanding. My parents came back from their life in Africa to a country that soon disavowed their work, and viewed them as personified reminders of a misguided epoch.

The reality was that my father and most other senior colonial administrators of the period, were idealistic, dedicated individuals intensely involved with the people they *served*. They were careful to orient themselves to African tribal life and prided themselves on the roads, hospitals and agricultural improvements they made to render the lives of local people better. Most important of all, they were completely incorrupt, unlike those who followed them in government. In Northern Rhodesia, pretty much all of them accepted that African people should govern themselves and they worked willingly to hand over power to the new nationalist leaders.

I have already mentioned my father's high estimation of Simon Kapwepwe, Zambia's first Minister of Home, then of Foreign Affairs, and the new nation's Vice-President. I remember Dad telling me that he once asked Simon how the British would be remembered. Kapwepwe replied, "You have done nothing of which you should be ashamed." That answer could have meant that the British conducted themselves in a way that fitted African realities and produced effective governance. It could also have meant that while the British had refrained from the depredations that characterised the Belgians or Portuguese, they had not done anything particularly positive either. Kapwepwe was a clever politician and liked to hedge his bets. Sadly, he was not wily enough to avoid later falling foul of his friend and rival, President Kenneth Kaunda, and was imprisoned before being virtually deleted from Zambian history for decades, until his reputation was rightly restored in recent times.

# 36
# Post-Colonial

*...makings of himself,*

*Were no less makings of the sun.*

*It was not important that they survive.*

*What mattered was that they should bear*

*Some lineament of character...some affluence*

*Of the planet of which they were a part.*

*– Wallace Stevens*

The old African photos I went rummaging through in clearing out my parents' *katundu* were a last analogue remnant of our African life, my final touchstones to a lost world. They reminded me that we often drove out from Lusaka in the Velox for weekend walks in the bush. Blue-black shadows of pedestrians were strung along the road amidst clouds of red dust. Women carried heavy loads balanced on their heads and hefted swaddled babies humped on their backs. Men wheeled dilapidated bicycles and goats wandered among the dust-shrouded figures. At a turn-off, thin, ragged children stood by the side of the road to watch us go by, their large eyes staring blankly. I was troubled by the way they didn't even bother to brush away the flies crawling all over their faces. I gazed back at them and wondered what they thought of us. Mum and Dad seemed to simply take in black Africans as part of the landscape but I was perplexed and troubled by their harsh life. It seemed to me, they would never think to go for a walk for the pleasure of it. Their existence was too bounded by poverty and toil.

Such thoughts used to fall away though once we left the car and set out on our walk. Buster would run ahead, questing through the dry season grass, while blackjacks itched my ankles. I used to tease Susan, nudging and prodding at her with a stick and whispering a rude song when Mum and Dad were out of earshot, *What's the time, half past nine. Time to hang your broekies on the line.*

*A family stroll, Lusaka Commons, 1965*

As a child, I gradually realised that there were yawning disparities, even fateful and cruel laws that disenfranchised and disadvantaged the Africans I encountered. My parents maintained a different attitude. They had an ideal of the broad sweep of history and saw themselves as being at the vanguard of helping black people out of a benighted state of ignorance and poverty. They were well aware of the critique of colonialism that had been gathering force since the war years. They saw the colonial system as flawed but necessary for the time being, a temporary scaffold to climb, yet dismantle once it was no longer needed. By their day, there was no sense of draining colonial countries of their natural sources for the benefit of the imperial homeland, but rather of a reverse process, whereby the mother nation expended energy and material resources on raising up the aspiring independent states.

Of course, this rearing could be tough. Dissent was interpreted as misbehaviour and promptly slapped down. Hitler had admired the 'efficient' way the British ruled vast areas with little manpower. Dad knew to the hour what was happening during the Lenshina revolt via a highly developed network of informants and the machinery of control was swiftly reactivated on the very eve of independence in 1964. Nowadays, it seems any official announcement from Britain to African Commonwealth countries routinely includes an apology for colonialism, while every failing of those nations, all of them independent for more than five decades now, is ultimately blamed on the original sin of their having been colonised.

Do ordinary Africans sincerely believe this official party line? Hard to say. In the media you have loud voices blaming the Continent's dire economic woes exclusively on the depredations of colonialism but, in private, you will find many who readily admit that rank corruption rooted in the pursuit of wealth and power, primarily for family and friends, secondarily for political party and ethnic group, is the cornerstone of their nations' post-colonial failure to experience adequate socio-economic development half a century after the end of European imperialism. I see the politically-correct obsession with post-colonial guilt and shame as mainly the revenge of the present on the past, a grand sophistry born of wounded *amour propre*. But I should leave such speculation to others more inclined to it. As a novelist and memoirist, I have little interest in the mass movements of society but rather the struggle of the individual in face of all the rags and the ghostly raiment of this strange old world.

I believe I drew my own concept of self largely from reading Kipling's *The Jungle Book* during the enforced afternoon rest periods that we had to take at Ruzawi School.

I found the two volume, red-leather covered 1908 edition in the school library and was enchanted by it. I read and reread the tales and pored over the illustrations, while my peers drowsed in silent rows on lumpy kapok mattresses. I've already told you that my favourite story was *The King's Ankus,* in which Kipling describes the remains of a ruined city where a giant, blind, white cobra sits guarding ancient treasures, killing any men that came to rob them. Mowgli is immune to the snake's lethal power because he has been raised by wild animals and, as such, is of the jungle.

I think an idea sprang into my head when I read that, my very own self-creation myth that I could tap Mowgli's strength and invulnerability by being unified with nature. The book contrasted the febrile world of human vanity against the brute facticity of nature and reified the idea that only through the act of imaginative engagement with the living physical world could you really be free. I still enjoy imagining what our cities will look like once we humans have vanished in the wake of disasters yet to come.

When is a dream a memory or vice versa? Where was it? At Kafue or Luangwa that Dad woke me in our tented camp on the game reserve? A charcoal African dawn, tinted faint apricot in the east. Loading the Landy, trying to be quiet about it so as not to wake the camp. Only Dad, me and a game guard. Clunk and rattle of a locking chain as the tailgate shut.

Further off, folk coughing over the first fires of a chill morning. July was the coldest season; the camp guard dog had beads of dew along his back. Churning rattle of the diesel engine propelling us along a sandy track that ribboned through thick scrub. Into a clearing flanking a slow, wide river. The pale twists of game trails leading down and conjoining at a drinking spot by the water. Parked up, we sat on the cabin roof, feet resting on the warm bonnet. I was glad of my wool school jersey. The engine ticked as it cooled. Everything showed in tones of grey. Nothing was moving, not even the puff adders that liked to sleep in the warm sand on the tracks.

It gradually lightened and the first insect and bird sounds started up, at first faint then getting louder, like musicians warming up in an orchestra. I asked the game guard if I could see his rifle. He let me hold it after Dad nodded that it was alright. I grasped the weapon to me, taking in its almondy, gun-oil scent, caressing the scape of the stock and prying open the secret butt plate trap with its oil bottle and pull-through string. My forefinger briefly explored the business end of the muzzle. It was an Enfield P14 .303, surplus from World War One, issued to the Game Department. The power and purposeful beauty of it. You could do anything with a gun like that. The ranger lifted a reproving finger when I tried to work the bolt. Dad opened a flask of tea made with Klim powdered milk. Then he produced a jam sandwich and a strip of tangy biltong.

I handed some biltong to the game guard. "Wena funa?" Did he want some? Again, he looked at my father before taking it. We waited and watched the tree line. Something was about to manifest. Our eyes strained, trying to read movement. The hubbling and bubbling of a guinea fowl flock, a cluster of dappled dots moving rapidly beneath the bushes. They were running away from something. Yes, there were moving shapes out there, barely distinguishable in the grey tangle of scrub. The game guard took back his rifle from me. Something, an apparition, in the smoky light was gliding towards us.

"Ndhlovu," the ranger whispered, pointing with his chin. He'd seen them long before we did. Drifting, miragy, a string of them, indistinct at first. Then there they were — three cow elephants ushering a young one out into the open. The ambling rubber-legged stride of the giants, their nodding massy heads. A big bull followed behind and stood facing us, guarding his family and trying to sense our purpose. White egrets rose and fell around him. He watched us for a minute, an immense black shape. The egrets flickering around him, his ears fanning back and forth in challenge and interrogation. It seemed an eternity that he stood there before he swung round and disappeared into the *miombo* again. The sun rose and its light touched our faces. Dad put his hand on my shoulder. He looked as happy as I'd ever seen him. He loved the romance of Africa. I was happy also in that amazing dawn and it felt then as if everything was possible.

*Me looking for elephant, Zambesi Valley, 1964*

# 37
# My Murderous Self

*Hate exists before love.*

– Sigmund Freud

Five years had passed since I'd buried Mum, ten since Dad's death, and still I lived on in their old house. I took time out from my writing to start growing gloriosa lilies again, the symbol of old Rhodesia. The tubers sulked for months in their pots, then shot up during the hottest days of the year. The leaves looked tough and leathery and the stems had barbs like fish hooks even though the flowers had a tremulous delicacy. The tubers are so poisonous that that they are a favoured means of suicide in some countries and the sap from the stems and leaves is an irritant. In Africa, tribespeople used them to cure skin ailments and rubbed a paste from the ground leaves onto the abdomens of mothers who were late in delivery, thus rendering it a flower of death and rebirth.

I also planted Zantedeschia, the lily of the Nile, or white arum. Africans used to eat the plant in days gone by. Its roots are toxic and you had to boil them twice to render them edible. The Shona around Chipinga used to recount how their ancestral enemies, the Matabele, once raided the villages of the region and ate all the arum they found in the cooking pots. It was the first boiling though and the raiders perished in convulsions. Much laughter used to accompany the telling of that one.

I think *Schadenfreude* must be an African invention. Maybe it's a joke that reaches back to the earliest epoch of human time. Musondo, or Muso for short, he of the dangerous cycling habits, our gardener and my mentor, once exemplified this to me. His name was a good one for a gardener as the *musondo* were goetic forest spirits that helped bring forth fruits, mushrooms and delicious caterpillars to eat. Those sprites weren't protective of human lives though and, one day, Muso accidentally sliced off two toes off his bare foot with a *badza* and screamed, "Aina! Aina!" All his fellow workers threw down their tools and rolled about laughing. They thought that Muso's misfortune was completely hilarious as he was always cutting and uprooting various veggies and had now done the same to his toes. Dad drove him fifty miles to a mission hospital and he returned smiling to the continued laughter of his friends. To laugh like that in the face of the random cruelty of the world is the African way.

It was early December and Britain, along with the rest of the western world, was readying itself yet again for the consumer-fest of Christmas. Of course, I knew it was Shangani Day, the holiday dedicated to commemorating Major Wilson's last stand against the Matabele. I was working in Dad's old study, where a novel I was writing was giving me some trouble. The dialogue and transitions were not reading right and I'd printed off a chunk of it to see if I could figure out on the page how to get it to read any better.

I was busy sorting through the sheaf when the doorbell rang. I ignored it and it rang again so I glanced through a gap in my study curtains to see who was troubling me. He was dressed head-to-toe in the obligatory black. The hood on his sweatshirt was thrown back and he had a beanie hat on that covered his hair. A young, white guy, with a flat pugilist's face and a bony brow ridge sheltering sloping, deep-set eyes. He stood in my driveway for a moment, looking up at the house as if considering something, then moved on. I watched his head passing along the laurel hedge that bordered the front garden until he went out of sight.

I sank back into my work and twenty minutes passed. Then the doorbell rang once more. I stood up and peered over my desk out the window to see if I could glimpse the caller. The drive looked empty. I ignored the bell. I'd made some progress with the manuscript and wanted to stay in the zone. Then, there it was again, that insistent, loud doorbell. Once more, I briefly wrestled with the distraction. I did have the idea that it might be the man in black I'd seen earlier. I wondered what he could be wanting. He couldn't be a door-to-door seller because he didn't have a bag. Maybe he was wanting to tarmac the drive, or to sign me up for senior taekwondo classes, as some other canvassers had previously sought to do. Whoever he might be, I decided to ignore him.

Five minutes more went by as the text of the problematic novel twirled before my eyes. All of a sudden, there was a dull but distinct thump from downstairs. I raised my head and puzzled briefly over the sound. I reasoned that it was probably one of the wood pigeons flumping down onto the ground floor windowsill. They often did that as they clambered in the ivy. I could hear the radio burbling away downstairs. I'd got into the habit of leaving it on after years of living alone. I liked to hear the human voice sounding distantly somewhere. Another distinct clunk sounded. I listened but there was nothing more, only the radio. I told myself it was nothing and continued leafing through my papers — but actually there was something. I sensed it at that moment. Yep, there was definitely something unusual happening. My mind started to rev and a prickle of alertness spread through me. The hairs on my forearms rose and my nape nerves tingled with an expectant buzz. I had the intuition that it was time to gird myself.

I'd read or heard plenty of accounts of home invasions on old schoolmates from Ruzawi, or friends of Mum and Dad who'd remained in Africa so I was ready. I swung my office chair round and reached for the shagreen-covered handle of the samurai sword leaning against one of my bookcases. It was a full sword in a japanned scabbard, and well sharpened, the real deal. I'd been given it by a friend a few years back, who'd understood my propensities and gifted it to me in return for helping him with a difficult task. Sometimes I'd take the weapon out and swish it about when trying to fix on *le mot juste*.

Now I gripped the wide, solid handle as I quietly revolved the chair to look through a crack in the half-open study door towards the broad, oak panelled staircase, where I saw a figure stealthily ascending towards me. Already he was very close, maybe six feet away. His hood was up now and a scarf covered his face to the eyes. It was the same man I'd seen earlier. I didn't think he'd spotted me yet in the shadowy study. As I silently unsheathed the *katana*, I had all sorts of scampering thoughts but the chief one was the Rhodie commandment from way back that if you were going to fight, then *attack at once and go at it like you mean it*. I saw that he was now maybe four feet off and was turned away from me as he looked into another room. I knew that it was no use pretending with the weapon. He was forty years my junior and if he took it off me, it was likely to be *Good Night Irene* for me.

I lurched forward with a clatter. He was damned quick, already pumped with adrenaline I suppose. He lashed out with a karate kick that slammed the study door back onto me and remained standing there as if willing to take me on. I brought the sword to the 'at the ready position' and told him, "I'm going to fuckin' kill you now." I could hardly believe my hissing voice. I could see his eyes widen in response to my threat but he still remained face on. He had something in his hand, a long screwdriver maybe. You don't focus well in combat. Vision comes in bursts. I saw that his body moved in a sort of jerk and at once I took a step and brought the sword up, ready to slash downward onto his head. But the long blade hit the old ceiling and a cloud of plaster chips and dust fell over both of us.

This must've surprised him as much as it did me and he turned and fled down the stairs. I stumbled after him, extending the sword downward behind me so as not to skewer myself if I fell. I heard booming sounds I couldn't identify. My ground floor hall had five heavy doors but all were shut. *Where had the bastard gone?* There was a crash from the sitting room. I entered cautiously, blade first, to find he'd leapt through the antique leaded windows and was outside somewhere. I pelted to the front door to confront him. *Where were the keys?* They'd disappeared from their place in the hall. He must have them. Seconds passed as I scrabbled for a spare. At last I got the door open. At this point, I ditched the sword thinking: *It won't look good for you if you run him through on the driveway while he's trying to escape.* Instead, I picked up a heavy, steel-cased Maglite torch I kept by the door.

*2005, shortly after the sword and burglar incident.*

I pounded outside to hear my car starting and only then realised that the shit had stolen *all* of my keys. A kind of fury overtook me when I saw my trusty old car beginning to move. I ran forward and chucked the Maglite straight at the windscreen but it missed and ricocheted off the bonnet. It must have unnerved him because his reversing became erratic and he careened into the side of a sandstone rockery that lined the drive, where he became jammed. I picked up the Maglite again and approached the driver's side to bash the window in but he steered the car at me trying to run me over. After further frenzied bumping and banging, accompanied by some fierce sandstone block throwing from me, he finally freed the car from the drive and went screaming away.

The police came surprisingly quickly for contemporary Britain. One of my neighbours had witnessed some of the melee and had rung them. Two meaty immediate response-type officers in body armour came running up within a couple of minutes. They told me that my car licence number had been patched into the local speed cams and would soon be automatically spotted. They sped away and I took the opportunity to hide the samurai sword behind a curtain.

Shortly afterward, two police women turned up. One with a narrow doleful face like a whippet and the other, plump, with dreadlocks tumbling from her cap. They soon wanted to start writing details down but I found it hard to speak. A fight gives you an awesomely dry mouth. I swigged some milk from the fridge. I was damned if I was going to make them any tea. Something fell upstairs, perhaps dislodged in the first scuffle and one P.C.W. whimpered, "What's that? I'm scared!" I had to reassure them that the invader had gone. When they asked what the burglar looked like, I gave a full, novelist's description.

"What's a snub nose?" asked Dreadlocks.

"Not a pointy nose." I clarified.

"Can we write that?" asked Whippet Face, "It's not racist, is it?"

"It isn't racist," I explained, "It's simply a fact and besides, your suspect is white."

They wrote it all down and gave me a crime number for the insurance. Naturally, I gave them a bowdlerised katana-free account of my own conduct. They took a look around the scene of the crime, but didn't notice the hole the sword had made in the ceiling. Then they asked me my occupation.

"Writer," I answered.

Whippet Face pointed at the study and asked, "Did you write all them books in there?" There were hundreds of volumes on the shelves.

"A few," I said, "Writing a book takes a long time. The others are just ones I've read."

They gave me the standard advice to seek medical help in case the shock of my experience had affected me. I showed them to the door, poured myself a scotch and smiled an African smile at the chaos of the world. I'd managed to pull it off. I'd summoned the honey badger back from the past.

# 38
# I Am a Rhodesian

*Tell me what you think you are and I will tell you what you are not.*

– Henri-Frédéric Amiel

The hedonistic world-changers of my boomer generation implanted in our culture a naive notion, which has since become an orthodoxy, that the broad sunlit currents of progress are sweeping us inexorably towards a world with no countries and no borders, where the intrinsic goodness of humanity will fully express itself and everyone will share the same liberal, humanist values. To my mind, this is a post-Christian, heaven-on-earth fantasy, as foolish as the discredited Marxist one that following the dictatorship of the proletariat will come the stateless society in which each will give their best according to their abilities and take only according to their basic needs. I'd learned in Africa that the natural world could hook or stab you like the devil thorns that poked through thick shoe leather, or the soldier ants that ran up your leg to attack you with their fiery bites, as well as that there are plenty of people who resemble the malignant *tokoloshe* demons who would invade your house unless you took a firm and wary stand.

There was a flurry of activity after the burglar and sword business. I needed to do a lot of phoning. My front door locks had to be changed and a glazier came and painstakingly reinserted all of the diamond-shaped panes in the leaded window that the intruder broke on his way into and out of the house. I reflected upon how the police who'd come after the incident in which I was attacked by a jealous lover fifteen years before were totally uninterested in my plight as a victim, and indeed questioned me unsympathetically at the time, yet did make an arrest; while in this more recent experience it seemed that the police were solely concerned to offer me succour as a victim, rather than showing much interest in actually catching the perpetrator.

Meanwhile, shadows made me jump. I sorted through my weapons and whenever the old house creaked in the darkness I put my fingers out to touch the handle of the bowie knife with its saw blade that I had tucked under the mattress. I harboured a fierce determination to hurt anyone else who might make the mistake of assessing my character wrongly. I ruminated upon the truth that most writers are like the mole snakes we used to find in the thorn scrub and *kopjes* in Southern Rhodesia. They were powerful blunt-headed snakes, usually an ominous black or dark-brown colour. They were preternaturally aggressive and struck out wildly whenever you went near them. But they were not in the slightest bit venomous. It was all bluff. If you picked them up, they'd coil around your arm and lash wildly but you'd come to no harm at all. I now aimed to become the molesnake who is the exception, the one that bites and holds. Moral for burglars — don't break into houses where old Rhodies live.

The police found my old car dumped only half a mile away. It seemed that my uninvited guest had nicked the vehicle primarily to get away from me. A Forensics Officer called and dusted the outside windows. His work revealed a sinister, floury imprint of the man's face pressed to my living room window glass with two hands cupped around it where, after breaking into the rear garden, the burglar had shaded his eyes while peering into the house as I worked upstairs. A 'support officer' turned up later that afternoon. She kept twitching at her body armour as if it was constricting her while she doled out conciliatory leaflets and a free sample window lock. She warned me, however, not to put razor wire up as I had 'a duty of care' even to intruders. Maybe she sensed something different about me because she commented, "You seem a self-possessed sort of man, not like my usual punters."

A week or so later, a Detective Sergeant arrived, a sleek, besuited professional. He introduced himself by asking, "So, you're the Maglite chap?" I thought I detected a note of approval. He took a quick look around and told me that the police did not show photographs of potential offenders to witnesses any more, despite my telling him that I'd had a good look at my intruder's pug face. He said they relied on forensics instead as witnesses were unreliable. He also confirmed my suspicion that the burglar had taken my low-value car because he wanted to get away from me. According to him, my man in black was 'a doorbell burglar', looking for houses with no one in. If someone answered, he'd surely have had some fake story ready about looking for someone who used to live in the neighbourhood.

The D.S. also urged me to seek counselling for trauma. He looked discomfited when I guffawed outright at that. He rang me a few days later to tell me that the forensic tests had yielded no results. The case of the attempted burglary at my home was therefore closed. He added that crime was a rare event. I asked if he believed in his own statistics, which appeared to show that crime was steadily decreasing. He laughed but gave no answer. A man from a gate company arrived and took measurements and we discussed the aesthetics of proposed gates. I told him that as long as it had spikes along the top I didn't mind what it looked like.

I slammed in additional fence posts along weak spots in the garden boundary and garlanded them with the most vicious barbed wire I could find. As I worked, I reflected that it was not property that I feared losing from a burglar. I had little that a thief would covet. No, what I feared and resented was another person imposing his will on me. I'd learned lessons like that dealing with the likes of Viljoen at Ruzawi, at Blundells and on the streets in Paris. I inwardly thanked the Rhodie boys who'd taught me early that a bully won't come back once you gave him a *maningi snot-klaap*; that meant 'a big punch on the nose'.

The tides of adrenaline slowly ebbed over the months after the burglary incident. When I got up in the night, I sometimes thought I saw a man's shape in the shadows of the room and any untoward noise made me whip round, coiled for action. Still, I could not say I was badly affected by the incident. In the long run, I saw it as a reminder that had left me better prepared. I'd done the right thing according to my lights but I was not sure that I had gone about it in the right way. It had been hard to contemplate thrusting the sword into Burglar Bill. Somehow, it had seemed too visceral an act so I'd chosen to slash at him instead. I wondered what would have happened had I connected with that blade. Given the present state of British justice, I tended to doubt that I'd still be gardening and working on my next book in the old-fashioned comfort of my familial manse. The prospect of prison held no great dread for one such as me so I have no idea why my unconsciousness made me fluff the blow.

What I did know was that I was still determined to revenge myself on anyone who tried to harm me physically. It's the Rhodie way. Maybe it was the rage of the weak that made me plot to try and use my old work connections to find out where Burglar Bill lived, set fire to whatever rat-hole he inhabited and skewer its inhabitants as they came fleeing out. Yes, I am forced to admit that I was thinking along such lines.

# 39
# Gudubai Meri I Am Going Falaway

*Although my pieces of home are scattered, I will always find a way to them*

– Nina Powles

I ventured into my parents' former bedroom today and lay there in the cleared space where their beds once stood. Eleven years empty, I usually avoided the room and it was a new experience to allow myself to remain there. At first, I stared at Mum and Dad's empty clothes cupboards looming above me. The room seemed to be holding its breath. My gaze travelled over the dusty dado rails, the striped liner paper, with its damp patches and the leaky leaded windows where the breeze rippled the curtains. I'd tended to view the room as a place of injury and sickness and had avoided it but this time I gradually relaxed. My fingers began to stroke the thin old carpet where Mum and Dad had shuffled to and fro for so many years. It began to seem peaceful there, with the curtains stirring and the leaf shadows moving over the bare walls.

There is a small round occasional table in the room, a copy of an English table made by an unknown Rhodesian craftsman out of *mukwa* wood. It is battered, water-stained and not a handsome piece of furniture. Yet, it has something indefinably African about it despite its borrowed style. I have kept it on the premise that it holds a sound memory within its crevices like an old vinyl record, echoes of Mum and Dad talking, the thump of a Castle Beer bottle being put down on it, the sound of bare feet whispering over the surrounding parquet, a hoopoe calling somewhere outdoors. I've begun to see at last how tightly bound up with my parents I've always been. I over-emphasized the gap between us when I was a young man.

There were dozens of African languages in Northern and Southern Rhodesia. They rubbed up against English and all manner of loan words and borrowings took place. The English language itself is, of course, already full of borrowings. As a family, we had a tenderness for these African loan words. They made us smile and we used them as a sort of secret language long after we left southern Africa. It is bittersweet to hear them again because they somehow show that there can be an interfusion, a cross-cultural blending, in words at least if not between peoples: Words like *bafwa* for bath, or *bekete* for bucket and *kafwafwa* for a kerfuffle.

*Sekeleti* for chocolate was Mum's favourite. She'd still ask for a *sekeleti* biscuit in the care home.

There was a popular song in Northern Rhodesia called *Gudubai Meri I Am Going Falaway* (Goodbye Mary, I Am Going Faraway). The title was the chorus from a Serenje song of lament. Its African composer must've heard English folk songs like "Over the Hills and Faraway" and created a syncretic version. That song still pulls at my heartstrings, combining, as it does, English elegiac and African fatalism, a blending that I can observe at my own core. It is autumn in England now, as it also is for me. Autumn is a time of ghosts. They like to come to visit as the light dwindles.

A conker fell from the misty air onto my car bonnet with a loud *donk*. Where it came from I've no idea. The nearest horse chestnut tree is three gardens away. I took it that it was someone knocking, attempting to communicate through the diaphane. Were those ghosts trying to release in me memories of myself and the Van de Ruit brothers collecting matamba fruit on the high veldt? We used to call them 'kaffir oranges'. They were the size of cricket balls and came encased in a similarly hard shell. We used to strike the shells on a rock until they split to reveal the citrusy, sweet-sour pith inside. That falling conker brought me back to those cold, clear mornings sixty years ago, the horses clinking their head collars as they browsed.

In Mum's wardrobe I found an old photo that showed me lying on the anchor chains at the bow of the government launch, Masue, on Lake Bangweulu in the remote northwest of what is now Zambia. I had just eaten the blanched, slimy fingers of some tinned asparagus. It was unknown as a vegetable in Africa at that time and I'd never eaten it before. My parents must have bought, or been given, it as an exotic treat. I let the empty can drop overboard as we sailed across the enormous lake, peering down as it descended into the pellucid depths, remaining visible for a long time, swaying to and fro.

I spent long, contented hours gazing into those tantalising waters as we sailed through rifts of Bangweulu papyrus. The lake was thick with fish: there were clouds of tiny sardine-like *kapenta,* bustling through which came red-breasted tilapia with humped backs and their banded aquamarine and bronze cousins, green-headed tilapia, which Africans called *pale.* Those shoals would suddenly explode when saw-toothed tiger fish zipped through them. Sometimes I'd see aquatic monitor lizards called *leguaans* swimming in a net of silvery bubbles like miniature amphibious dragons. I always wanted to catch a glimpse of the fabled giant catfish, the *vundu,* but they always eluded my searching gaze.

Gliding over Lake Bangweulu like that was the ultimate magic carpet ride. I was entranced by the vivid nowness of the natural world as it regressed infinitely below me. We are forever moving into a future which does not yet exist, from a past that has already ceased to do so. All that persists is a trace of beauty, which is eternal. This photo is a *memento mori* of an instant in time. When I look at it, I am again making the search I began in boyhood, still staring down into the depths below the surface trying to scry out a hidden world.

*Me at my observation post, M.V. Masue, Lake Bangweulu, 1965*

Night has settled in my parents' old bedroom. A tawny owl hoo-hooing somewhere. The moon entangled in tree branches. Awareness of my heart thudding, full of yearning all of a sudden, as if I were young again and brimming with misty passions. I was always taking risks in those days, and thought the world would get better and better. How came I to such a bare place now? No, not bare, simply real, a shedding of illusions. You feel naked if you throw off so much that once swaddled you. I'm going back to the way I learned to see the world in Africa as a boy. Like that learning moment at Ruzawi when I rescued a cape dove riddled with shot.

I was ten and had found it on a walk in the bush. It had lost half its feathers in the blast. I wrapped it in my shirt, talked to it and trekked back to school, full of plans about how I'd rehab it and make a pet of it. I showed the battered bird to Mr. Steyn, the school groundsman, a grizzled character with a growly voice roughened to a buzz-saw by brandy and rolling tobacco.

Steyn said, "Sorry, boy but it's kaput. Nix. Beste om did dood te maak."

That meant 'Best make an end of the critter'. He told me to wring its neck. I cried, resisted, thought for a while that I could still save it as it looked up at me blinking its pale, velvety eyelids. In the end, I took it behind some sheds and struck its wounded head with a rock. I covered it with eucalyptus leaves and dried my tears with my shirt. Steyn was waiting for me. He put a hand on my shoulder and consoled me, "Leef sterk or glad nie leef. Do you unnerstand, boy? For man en animal." That meant "Better live strongly or don't live at all."

I went out into the garden at midnight among the drunk leaning shadows. I wanted to feel the tugging of the earth and lay down on the grass. It was harsh like a loofah on my cheek.

Long orange slugs traversed the sward looking for where the dead sleep. Those who tried to understand the world used to turn to the uncanny, the esoteric, the back door light that shone on the truth. Freud and Jung, Heidegger and Wittgenstein all did that. Mysticism is as good as dead these days. We are armoured in raw digital knowledge about how all sorts of things work across the proportional scale from charmed quarks to event horizons but they don't tell us everything about the world. Time to go back indoors, resolved to let the dead rest. Who am I to disturb them? Rain came a few hours later, tinkling in the gutters. It woke me and I looked out and watched it veil the stars. A single cry sounded in the woods a mile away. Human or fox, owl or hawk, ghost or *tokoloshe* I knew not. It sounded *in extremis,* whatever it was, it made my nape hairs stand up on end. My breath sounded hoarsely deep in my throat,

"I am truly alive now," I said to myself and this at least was true in that moment.

# 40
# Scatterlings

*And we are the scatterlings of Africa*

*Both you and I*

*We are on the road to Phelamanga*

*Beneath a copper sky*

– J. Clegg

The years rip, O my Rhodesians, my fellow scatterlings, white and black. We are like the migration I saw when I was travelling with my father near Choma on the Livingstone road. It was late in the day, the sun a fast-dropping, blood orange. I heard Dad exclaim and we came to a halt. We were confronted by hundreds of tortoises crossing the road all plodding in one direction. Cars and the occasional truck were ploughing through them but they kept on going. I begged Dad to try and rescue them and we ran along the sides of the road collecting the creatures and setting them down again in the long grass safely away from the road. Some wary *kambas* retracted themselves when lifted but most kept on rowing with their sturdy legs as if they couldn't wait to get where they were going.

As soon as we put them down again they'd go waddling onwards and westward into the gloaming. I gathered up a few of them in the footwells of the car but they moiled around so desperately, hating their confinement, that we soon stopped and let them go to join their friends. Why so many of the creatures were crowding through the bush and across the road like that, we had no notion. Perhaps they sensed some great peril was on the way. I watched them go with an inexplicable ache in my heart, their handsome chequered shells bobbing obstinately as they dispersed. Those torties were so determined to make their way in the world, toiling ever onwards to fulfil their mysterious destiny.

I find it *maningi* strange how all these recollections of Africa have washed back into my mind of late, so many years after Mum and Dad have gone. It's as if I'm carrying something ancient within myself. It makes me think of the time I went with some other Ruzawi boys to look at cave art made by the Khoi-San, the primaeval Bushmen people, in a rock shelter in Macheke, Southern Rhodesia. I stood hypnotised by the panoply painted onto the rock. Scores of tiny ochre human figures running, conversing, holding spears and bows aloft among painted herds of eland, long-horned cattle and giraffe of millennia ago. The vastness of time in Africa first became obvious to me then. It came home that our Federation of Rhodesia and Nyasaland was a fly-speck in the sempiternal chronicle of the continent.

There was a period during my time at Ruzawi when we took to raiding the kopjes where the ancient Shona had buried their dead. We climbed the treacherous cliffs, braved the snakes that lodged there and hunted for treasure. We found only bones, heavy metal chains and penannular rings. We showed some of these mysterious metal hoops to our history master, Mr McLaren, back at school. He said they were *manillas*, copies of slave collars that were commonly used as currency in sixteenth to nineteenth century Africa since they could be melted down and recast as tools and weapons.

Those centuries old torc-like rings were yet more evidence that dominance of one over the other was the true currency of man. Long before whites came, Africans took each other as slaves in vast numbers, just as Europeans had in Europe. It is reliably estimated that four million were taken from the area of my birth country, now called Zambia, and dragged off to Arabia and India by way of Oman. I remember being shown 'the slave tree' at Ndola, a pod mahogany known as the *mupapa,* planted by East African Arab slavers and used as a marker for a slave assembly place where a stronger tribe would muster the doomed captives they had taken from weaker ones.

Yes, Africans made slaves of each other and paid no attention to whether their fellow Africans ended up in Jeddah or Jamaica, the Ottoman Empire or the Spanish and Portuguese ones. That's why I reject the contemporary liberal obsession with exclusively white guilt over slavery. Slavery is as old as civilization itself. We might as well demand reparations from Tunisia or Turkey for the two and quarter million white Europeans the Barbary pirates took as slaves. Yes, Europeans initially enlarged African slavery beyond anything it had been before but it was also they, or Britain at least, which first sought to uniformly extirpate it.

One of my more hard-boiled schoolmates brought a skull back from among the rock graves and hung it on his cast-iron bed post in our dormitory. The moon shone onto the dread object in the night and its eye pits seemed to glare at us with fury at being so disrespectfully used. We begged him to go back to the *kopje* and return the skull to its resting place. That Rhodesian farm boy who was so careless with the African dead was likely in turn, burned out of his farm and later driven out during the Africanisation that followed. There have always been harrowings whereby one people subjugates, and often obliterates, another, whether in the Americas, Asia,

Africa, or indeed Europe. The Africans had a name for it —
the *mfecane* — the great scattering. The word came from the
scourging of the Shona when the Zulu chief Mzilikaze struck
north and shattered Shona civilization in the 1840s.

There's no end to the cycle of *mfecane*. The African story
and that of the wider world is one of recurrent dispossession
and destruction. In times immemorial modern humans like
the Khoisan Bushmen and Hottentots outhunted and
outbred their and our hominid ancestors, like the rugged
Kabwe man whose skull was found near my birthplace.
Eventually, the Bantu thrust out the Bushmen after their long
dominion, leaving them scattered desert-dwelling survivors
who left ancient cave paintings all over Southern and Central
Africa. Then there were the sixteenth and seventeenth
century Portuguese explorers and settlers who were, in their
turn, pushed back by the Manyika, the Mashona and Rozwi
kingdoms of stone builders in the lands that came to be
known as Rhodesia. The word *rozwi* means 'destroyer' in
Matabele. Next came the Zulu bulldozer and its offshoots,
the Matabele and the Ngoni.

They could not imagine it would happen but, sure
enough, the Rhodie farmers soon followed in the same
endless process of *mfecane*, bullied and burned out by
Mugabe. Some remnant settler Rhodesians who scorn Britain
for abandoning them to their ineluctable fate now find it

funny that the former colonialists are in turn moaning about the social splintering accelerated by their own influx of recent subjects from other tribes. *Ki ki ki ki,* the Africans are laughing and they are right to do so.

Throughout my adolescence and adulthood I always considered myself homeless but as I entered old age, it dawned on me that I did have a homeland once, although it has quite gone and its name is abjured by the high-minded hypocrites who rule western intellectual life nowadays. Yes, I was once, and still remain, a Rhodesian, even though to proclaim myself one is to be declared a pariah. I had confidence enough in boyhood to leap across the *kopje* boulders at Parrot's Beak. My Rhodie school fellows had to keep on taking that leap.

What days followed for them under the imperturbable African skies, Hondo days, shot in their bakkies, chopped by pangas, dragged by nooses behind their trailers, legs removed by landmines, mortared in the streets of Bulawayo. They slugged it out as reservist troopies, sweated in home-made armoured pickups and turreted Mazda trucks on convoys to and from Beit Bridge, and cleared up the civilian dead from downed Comet airliners. Yet the whole white population of Rhodesia numbered not much more than that of an average English provincial city. Then again, patriotic Rhodesians were far from solely white. There were many more black soldiers than white ones in the Rhodesian army. They had not been dragooned into it. Many Africans distrusted the savage revolutionary nationalism of Zanla and Zipra, and have been proven right to have done so. Those black 'freedom fighters' suffered tremendously also, not only during the Bush War, but also in vendettas once it was over. Thousands of them were lost, along with tens of thousands of utterly apolitical villagers, innocents caught in the crossfire.

# 41
# My Teeth

*Searching nature, I taste self but at one tankard, that of my own being.*

– Gerard Manley Hopkins

Someday, if there is a human future, maybe some anthropologists will dig me up and find my teeth full of south-central African minerals and isotopes. They might hypothesise upon how the skeleton of this modern day analogue of Homo Rhodesiensis had come to lie in Middle English soil. My teeth could then become further evidence for some social historian to pontificate about Britain's radically increased diversity from the late Twentieth Century onward. But my bones would be telling a much more subtle tale.

Just before the start of 'the lockdown years', I agreed to a rare teaching session in a creative writing class at an English university. It was an experience not to be repeated. I read them a draft of an experiential piece about the British in Africa that dared them to think differently from what I knew they'd been taught in secondary school history lessons. As I read on, I watched their childish faces glaring ever more truculently back at me. The few who were articulate enough to speak extemporaneously spouted the usual belligerent post-colonial clichés, while the tutor, who had, no doubt, helped to inculcate these, looked on approvingly. Their thoughts seemed as if minted by a group mind, and dropped ready-made into their individual ones. Their ability and willingness to question had been smothered by the dogmatic orthodoxies of the horrendous educational system that had landed them there.

The only history they appeared to have been exposed to was the rise of fascism leading up to the Second World War and the dissolution of the erstwhile equal evil of imperialism following it. One girl from the group stopped me afterwards, spying around to make sure her peers were all out of sight and earshot before divulging the secret that her mum was a Rhodie-Zimbabwean exile living in England. She said her Mum often spoke of her lost Africa and about how no one understood, nor wanted to understand, the complex four century long history of the interaction and admixture of races in southern Africa. She thanked me for writing about my birthplace, for bringing lost Shona and Afrikaans words back to mind, and for remembering the lives of forgotten people who loved Africa, and who, like me, dreamt of their mother country, which had turned its back on them, and despaired of their adoptive nation, which wished to forget their existence.

African history runs closer to that of Europe than many people realise. I was surprised and pleased to find out recently that my sister and I were not the only Madockses to be born in Africa. In the mid-nineteenth century, John F. Madocks, brewer, of Somerset, England took his family to South Africa. It is recorded that one of his sons, my great-grandfather, John E. Madocks, was duly born in Durban in 1876. I have never discovered what the family were doing in Durban. Perhaps they were plying the family trade, making cheap beer for migrant workers in the diamond fields, or for the military on the eve of the Zulu War. Perhaps John F. even helped to supply Chelmsford's army with its six-hundred wagons of goods moving through Natal in 1879. He could have seen the survivors of the Natal Native Horse come galloping back to Durban to tell of the shattering British defeat at the hands of the Zulus at Isandlwana and of the subsequent siege of Rorke's Drift. Maybe the Zulu War drove the Madocks clan away or maybe they were naturally restless. Whatever the case, the 1881 census shows them back in England running a brewery in the West Country.

Then, there was the African sojourn of my grandfather, Sidney Madocks, later to become a publican in Lichfield. He took a troopship to Africa in 1901 as a teenager, riding with the Imperial Yeomanry light cavalry, wearing a slouch hat and bandolier. His letters home reveal a high-spirited teenager's enthusiasm for a "hot skirmish". He also sent expended Boer Mauser cartridge cases home as souvenirs. He was back in Africa in the Army in 1917 in Egypt and Mesopotamia, arriving in time for the recapture of Baghdad and the breaking of the Ottoman armies. There'll be no more Madocks in Africa now, that's for sure. Equally certain, I think, is that my pessimism and awareness of the ambiguous nature of reality derive from my African childhood and perhaps from my ancestors' experience of it. This understanding sets me apart from the preponderance of deracinated English people who often seem naïve to me in this regard.

As a boy, listening to the ceaseless buzzing of the insects in the African bush, I first got an inkling of the immense, mysterious vacuum at the heart of life. I realised instinctively then that we humans could never understand the meaning of our existence and the only way to cope with this was to tell ourselves, or be told, stories that would help us deal with peering into that terrifying abyss. I turned out to be one such tale-teller. It's been a benediction and a torture. To record something is to change and reorder it. I see this work, which follows the African thread in my life, as the making of a map that can guide my first steps out into a new world. It is acting like Buster's leash that drew me along as a lost boy and has given me a newfound ability to look unflinchingly at the doomed self, and find a new track.

In the latter years since my mother's death, my little family has shrunk further through illness and time's gnawings. I'm just about the last one left. Freed thus from all familial bonds, what have I got left? Only the self and the potential to love. What do I seek in that situation? A numinous nowness, as sensual life ebbs out of me. I recognise now there is an occult creativity in my family legacy of repression and screwed-up genes that keeps on feeding me as an artist. I think my ancestor spirits or the DNA are telling me I may be inhabiting a different sort of self than the one I've always imagined.

*2020, aged 68, accompanied by my cat familiar.*

I think I've found the ur-memory that illustrates the formation of my paradoxical questing nature. It has its origins in those amazing mornings in Fort Roseberry when I was on holiday from boarding school and left to my own devices. The bulbuls would be making wolf-whistle calls from their hang-out in the backyard mulberry tree, the sound coming through the open veranda doors as I breakfasted on pawpaw and lemon slices, followed by bread that Jonas had baked in the wood-fired oven, spread with honey from our hives and fresh milk from the boma herd that grazed the golf course. The boma drums had thudded much earlier calling Dad to work, and Mum to market or to chat with other government wives. Our servants usually took it easy once *Bwana* and *Dona* were out. They trusted me, as I did them, and knew I'd never tell.

Other servants would arrive with notes from other government officials, bearing written invitations to dinners, requests to borrow household items and such and they'd all gossip together sitting on the red-polished front steps. Their conversation would be joined by wandering tribesmen who'd turn up selling tortoises, animal skins, bantam eggs, monkey bread tree pods with their delicious creamy pith, and all sorts of fabulous things. Sometimes I'd leave their conversations to wander into our sitting room and re-tune the radio from the World Service to LM Radio, broadcasting from Lourenço

Marques, which played current hits like *Ag Pleez Deddy*, Jody Wayne songs and American early rock'n'roll stuff like Bill Haley. I'd practice jiving and twisting on our highly-polished parquet floor for a while before heading outdoors, still barefoot.

The *nkoya-nkoya* call of the fish eagle over the nearby Mansa river would often accompany me as I walked under the cassia trees with their yellow flower racemes. The trunks of those trees were wrapped around with earthed-up termites' nests that were in the process of consuming the tree from the bottom up. Blueskop agama lizards bobbed on Mum's rockery and sunbirds flickered in the honeysuckle and roses — English plants that Mum grew. Going down the sandy track to Ndewenu's vegetable garden, I'd pause to inspect the pug marks a leopard had left in the night. The tracks would still be crisp and sharp and, if I got on my knees to sniff the impress, I'd catch the musky foetor of big cat. That wild reek made my nape hairs rise with a delicious terror. My senses would prickle with alertness and I'd notice everything those glorious African mornings had to offer. Those days were such gifts and, wonder of wonders, I still get that feeling that the everyday world is waiting to give up its remarkable secrets to me.

# 42
# The Last

*No more for us the knowledge...*

*No more for us the meeting place.*

– Ezra Pound

You'd sometimes find abandoned gardens and homesteads out in the bush, places where the land had been too sour or dry to prosper, or where rinderpest had wiped out the cattle and ruined the ranchers. Now, I expect, there are many more. Our own old African gardens must all be deserted and gone. All those footpaths, rondavels and rose arches Mum created have long since crumbled away, eaten by termites, or covered over by new shanty towns and new developments. And all those farms down south in Zimbabwe, on land taken from the Shona and Matabele and, in turn, removed from their white proprietors, are now disassembled, their metal and stone scavenged, falling back to the wild to end up like Changa-Changa's house, which I saw that time crumbling away out in the Luano.

Often you can discover on these abandoned farm sites a remnant old fig tree, the obliterating runners of the bitter gourd or karela, or the orange flame of marigolds gone feral among the grasses. Insects still buzz and blue skop lizards flicker like shadows over the remnant heaps of stone. To me, those flickering lizards are the ghosts of lives lost or unled, despoiled lives both black and white. All the lost are becoming *tokoloshe* spirits that inhabit those ruined waste places. The buzz of the insects in the long grass amidst them is the everlasting sound of emptiness, one of the signs that the earth is not really interested in humans and will get on very well without us. My parents' English garden, now mine, will also be lost in due course, an abandonment that is a natural occurrence in the shape of things. It's alright. I accept it, and all relinquishment, as a sacral rite. I, the lifelong exile, am expecting that everything will eventually end up covered by the bitter karela, like the radioactive city of Pripyat near Chernobyl in Ukraine.

I saw once in my school days a pangolin imprisoned in a makeshift cage. They were rare creatures even then and it was a most unusual thing when a villager at Marandellas caught one and kept it in a thorn kraal for the amusement of visitors. I watched as the humped shape of the scaly anteater was prodded with a stick to make it skitter about its little enclosure. It hobbled on bent legs on the points of its strong digging claws designed to grub out termite nests. It was a sorry sight. Some scales were hanging off its back. Its tiny bewildered eyes were blinking and its pink rubbery tongue flicked around its long mournful snout. It curled itself up whenever its captor went near it, trying to protect itself with its armoured scales. Though these might have helped against predators in the bush they were no good against humans.

It was strange, even sacrilegious, to me that this Shona villager treated the pangolin so badly. Among the Bemba they were revered as messengers from spiritual realms. They were totem animals for spirit mediums or rain-makers, and featured in the initiation rites of young men. Often, pangolins appeared in dreams and tales to warn humans of some impending calamity. I paid the villager sixpence to stop tormenting it and begged him to let it go, saying I would pay him much more money to free it. He simply shook his head at me, the foolish *muzungu* child. I doubt the poor creature lived much longer.

Now, I read that there are hardly any pangolins left in this dark world and wide. Apparently, the Chinese eat them for medicinal purposes. Their flesh is supposed to improve the circulation, and their ground-up scales to impart magical protection. I comfort myself with the thought that the pangolins, in both Asia and Africa, will have their revenge somehow. Maybe they themselves will become the disaster that African myths say they predict. I pray that they will incubate some noxious, new virus in their innards that will produce a pandemic far worse than the recent one, which will sicken and kill off the heedless species that is exterminating them. And I take comfort from the notion that there are abyssal secrets lurking in the natural world, entities yet unknown to, and I hope, beyond the reach of the scientific mind and its technologically-enhanced senses. Perhaps these will become known to me when my soul is finally loosed from its cage.

As a young man, I was drawn to the Hindu, Buddhist, Jain and Druze ideas of samsara, the great circle of life, the idea of metempsychosis and being born to many lives. The Africans I knew tended to believe in inhabiting ancestor spirits, rather than reincarnation as such but a few tribes did have such notions. The Ila of what is now Zambia were one rare example. Fittingly, their name meant "the set-apart people". They were a cattle-herding tribe who had submitted to the authority of 'Changa-Changa' for a while. They lived along the Kafue river basin and were traditionally distinguished from other tribes by their exceptionally tall height and the way they pulled their hair up into cone-like shapes to make them look even taller. The old hairstyles were almost gone by the late 1950s but I saw one sported by an Ila chief who'd become a nationalist leader and who occasionally came to our house and to Dad's Boma office.

This chief also carried a carved stick and had long claw-like nails, a sign of wealth and privilege among the Ila. His hair was teased up in a conical, loaf-like shape and held in place by a tarry pomade that also trapped all of the bugs that happened to come into contact with it. Mum said he looked absolutely revolting but I was fascinated with him and often hung around him. Sometimes he'd smile and gesture to me to come closer by crooking his long yellow-nailed forefinger. Jonas didn't much like him either and told me the Ila were possessed by ghosts. Only later, did I find out the reason for Jonas's claim. Although many tribes believe that shadows are really 'soul-entities' that follow us, but which can also travel on their own accord, the Ila hold that something called their *musedi chingubule,* their 'shadow-double', accompanied them everywhere. This was a tutelary spirit from a former life. I have long been enamoured of this idea and sometimes, in quiet moments I seem to sense my own protective shadow-double following me.

The last time we saw Jonas was in June of 1965 but he has reappeared to me since in waking dreams as vividly as the molten primal colours of the Cine Super-8 home movies that Dad used to make.

We are packing up our home in Lusaka in preparation for leaving Africa and going to our new life in England. Dad has arranged for a departmental lorry to take Jonas and his wives and still-at-home younger children back to his tribal home territory of Chinsali in the Northern Province. We have given him all of our left-over furniture and household goods, along with a handsome cash stipend to last him the rest of his life. Dad has also gifted Jonas his old Birmingham University Cricket Club blazer, its fabric a pattern of multi-coloured vertical stripes and adorned with colourful appliqued chevrons. Jonas is especially delighted with it and keeps turning around, urging his family to admire it.

I have known and loved Jonas my whole life and it seems inconceivable that I may never look upon his wise and benevolent features again. My heart is a stone crushed to powder and I cannot not reply when he takes my hand in his and gently says not *'Shalineepo'* which means 'Goodbye forever', but *'Twalamonana'*, which signifies, 'See you later'.

"Go well and remember us," these are his last words to me, called out as the Boma truck bumps slowly away, heaped with our tables and chairs and Jonas' blazered arm waving. That truck seemed to me to be taking away everything I had known up to that point. It is so difficult to say goodbye to the past. I have returned throughout my life to the image of that arm waving in the African sunlight. Let there be no finitude and that arm go on waving in memory forever.

*2022, Lying on the empty grave plot my parents bought for me to rest next to them.*

*Gudubai, I am going falaway.*

# <u>Acknowledgements, Notes & Sources:</u>

Every effort has been made to trace copyright holders and obtain their permission to use copyright material. The publisher apologises for any errors or omissions and would be grateful to be notified of any corrections that will be incorporated into future editions of this work.

All photographs are copyright of the author apart from Kirby English's Hawkhurst photograph and the image of Ruzawi School boys - I've been unable to locate the copyright holder for that one. This book teems with a mass of direct and indirect quotations from so many sources. Apologies in advance to the inadvertently uncited, your words have formed compost for new growth. All translations are mainly my own unless otherwise noted. Thanks to Bettell Hone, Bro G Phils, Moh M. and members of the NRZ Facebook Group as well as The Last of the Rhodesians group on MeWe particularly Patti North. I'm indebted to Patti for reminding me of Jonny Clegg's song "Scatterlings of Africa". Thankyou also to Jonathan Kruger of Kitwe, Zambia, curator of 'The Forgotten Heroes' Museum, for checking on my Bemba. I've donated all my parents' African memorabilia to that museum. I've also been influenced by a set of remarkable memoirs about Africa, most prominently among them: Alexandra Fuller, Scribbling the Cat, 2013, Judy Rawlinson, Finding a Flame Lily, 2015, Ian Hassall, Hamba Gashle, 2012, Carolyn Slaughter, Before The Knife, 2002, Peter Godwin, Mukiwa, 1996 and Jonathan Lawley Beyond the Malachite Hills, 2010. Thanks too to Will Straw for taking my cemetery photo. I'm greatly indebted to my editor, James Bloom, for wrestling my knotted text into shape. I've changed a few names here and there in the text to avoid hurting the living or distressing the dead.

Rod Madocks

# Chapter Notes & Acknowledgements

1 Lost

'Bwana mkubwa' – a big man, big boss.

'my kinders' – my children (Afrikaans)

2 Muzungu Chronicles

Modern history concentrates on Rhodes' misdeeds however if the curious reader wants to learn more about the struggle to crush the Arab Eastern slavers then you will find information online in 'The Northern Rhodesia Journal'. Robert Codrington of B.S.A.C. played a prominent role and Fort Jameson, where we once lived, was thought to be the site of the last slaver's column to be destroyed in 1896.

3 Ek Se

"You, who never arrived..." A free translation of an unpublished fragment by R.M. Rilke.

8 Nights

"You, darkness from whom I came", a free translation of R.M. Rilke's 1916 poem 'The Night'.

17 My Generation.

"Why don't you all f - fade away" from . 'My Generation' by 'The Who'. Copyright U.M.G., all rights reserved.

18 No Cause At All

"How steep the stairs in stranger's houses, how bitter-salt the bread of exile" is a version of the well-known lines from Canto XVII of Dante's *Paradiso*.

19 Toujours Rhodésien.

"The cracked speakers are dead..." from Sidney Keyes', 'The Message', 1941.

21 La Golondrina

Ovid, "It's a kindness" comes from one of Ovid's poems of exile.

22 The Comanche Trace

"The depth and dream of my desire,/The bitter paths wherein I stray..." is from Kipling's
Poem, "My New-Cut Ashlar" 1922.

23. On The Other Shore.

The chapter title alludes to Vladimir Nabokov's Russian version of his autobiography, 'Drugie Berega', the other shore which is the shore of exile, It is also the 'Ex Ponto' of Ovid. Goethe and Pushkin also wrote about 'the other shore'.

"We are given rivers so we know..." is from a poem called 'Timber Frame' by the talented contemporary West Montana poet, Emily Walter. My thanks to her for kind permission to quote.

25 In Search of My Kochanka

"Kochanka" (Polish) – a lover, a mistress, someone to whom you are not married. "Bold lover..." comes from John Keats' "Ode On a Grecian Urn".

"Jodina " : Iodine tincture (Polish).

"Which arrow flies forever? The arrow that has hit its mark" is from the short story 'A Russian Beauty' by Vladimir Nabokov, copyright The Nabokov Estate.

26 All Aboard for 'The Ship of Fools"

The chapter title alludes to a short story collection I wrote about my mental health career. The notion of the wounded healer became a staple of psychotherapeutic theory in the 1960s and 70s. Jung explored the concept in many of his writings.

27 The Caul

The Yeats epigraph comes from his poem 'Under Ben Bulben'. A self-penned epitaph. Those words are to be found on his tombstone.

28 All the Christmases

"A life can be haunted..." from Louis McNeice 'Selva Oscura' 1961

29 Blue Death

The purpose of life is to be defeated by greater and greater things is a loose translation of R.M. Rilke's poem 'Der Schauende'.

30 Mum's Secret

"A still- Volcano- life.." is an 1863 poem by Emily Dickinson.

31 Shalineepo, Mum

"Tell me your attitude to pain..." from Ernst Jünger 'On Pain (1934)

32 Katundu

"For mortals, mortal things..." from the Greek by Lucian in 'Dialogues of the Dead', (about 175 A.D.) I've not been able to find who made this translation although it's been in my head for years.

33 Appointment with a Cobra

"The desire to have a death of one's own..." a free translation from R.M. Rilke's only novel, 'The Notebooks of Malte Laurids Brigge'.

34 The Leap

"All journeys have a secret destination..." Martin Buber. 'The Legend of the Baal-Shem' 1955.

35 Demons

"Between me and thee.." appears in P.B. Shelley's song 'Rarely, rarely comest thou.' The whole stanza in which it appears is relevant to this piece.

36 Post-Colonial

The epigraph stanza by Wallace Stevens appears in his late poem: 'The Planet On The Table' (1957).

37 My Murderous Self

S. Freud's "Hate exists before love" is an Englishing of a concept he mentions numerous times in his 1915 paper 'Instincts and their Vicissitudes'.

38 I Am a Rhodesian

"Tell me who you think you are..." Henri F. Amiel was a Swiss 19th Century philosopher. I wrote this quote down in a notebook years ago and have lost the source!

39 Gudubai Meri I am Going Falaway

Although my pieces of home are scattered, I will always find a way to them"

Nina Powles from 'Small Book of Water', 2021, by permission of Canongate Press.

40 Scatterlings

"Scatterlings of Africa" derives from the lyrics of a song by Johnny Clegg & Savuka. 1987, I've not been able to locate a current copyright holder.

41 My Teeth.

The Gerard Manley Hopkins epigraph is from his notes on 'The Spiritual Exercises' of St Loyola (published in 1937).

42 The Last

Ezra Pound's, "No More for us the knowledge" is from his early poem 'Threnos', (1909), a poem of farewell.

# <u>Glossary</u>

Agh or Ag: expression of dismay, disgust, protest or resignation as in the Rhodie saying, "Agh shame!" or the song title *Ag (or Oh) Pleez Deddy*

Aikona: no, not, no way, absolutely not (Zulu, I think).

Aina or Eina: Ouch, sore! (Chilapalapa)

Babijahn: Afrikaans for baboon

Badza: soil-tilling implement

Bakkie: open-backed pick-up, utility vehicle.

Basop: beware, from the Afrikaans 'Pas op!'- look out!

Biltong: strips of tangy dried buck meat, usually left hanging on the stoep so you can pull off a piece while contemplating the day.

Bliksem: An Afrikaans word originally an exclamation of surprise and shock but it morphed into a curse-word meaning 'bastard' or 'arse-hole' and sometimes tacked onto any phrase for vulgar emphasis.

Boma: administrative offices for provincial government. The seat of local power and control in the colonial era. The word originally meant a thorny stockade for protecting livestock.

Boerewors: spicy sausages that came in distinctive spirals, usually cooked on the braefleis or brae, the wood-fired outdoor pit BBQ.

Boomslang: A green venomous snake that likes to coil in the branches of trees.

Borrachos: Spanish for drunks.

Broekies: undies. Afrikaans in origin.

Bundu: the wilderness bush.

Capitau: boss, usually a leader of a work gang, (from the Portuguese).

Chimurenga: Shona for uprising. The First Chimurenga was the 1890 Matabele insurrection against the early settlers. The Second Chimurenga was the 1964-1980 Rhodesian Civil War.

Chitemene: slash and burn agriculture.

Chitenge: Distinctive African cloth patterns.

Chongo: shut up (Rhodie slang).

Chongololo: curly-wurly, massive centipedes that come out in the wet season.

Dagga: cannabis. Usually smoked by the rural poor in my time. Acrid home-grown stuff, maybe blended with other herbs to give a distinctive reek and glassy stare to its users.

Dambo: low-lying areas, quickly flooding in the wet season.

Dankie: thanks in Afrikaans.

Dona: polite African term for white married woman, often paired with Bwana.

Donga: a ditch, ravine or gulley, (from Nguni and thence to Afrikaans).

Donner: from the Afrikaans word donder for thunder, to beat, bash, as in "We're going to donner up the okies next door" from Jeremy Taylor's hit song, "Ag Pleez Deddy".

Eish: expression of disgust or negation as in, "Eish wena", 'No man!'.

Ek se: literally 'I say', a popular, slangy, meaningless interjection attached to the end of sentences to make the speaker sound tough.

Ewe: Hey you. Chilapala word. Quite often used rudely.

Flatties or Flatdogs: crocodiles

Gummadoolahs: fantasy land, Shangri-La, the place you can never quite reach.

Hamba Gashle: take it easy, go carefully, walk like a chameleon, a greeting and a farewell.

Hondo: war, from Shona. Sobriquet for the Rhodesian Civil War of 1964-79.

Kia: house, as in PK, pikkies' house, or kid's house, the lavatory.

Katundu: gear, kit, equipment, or just stuff.

Kleilat: Afrikaaner childrens' game where you throw clumps of mud wrapped around sticks.

Kopje: rounded heaps of granitic boulders that jutted out from the acacia and mopane scrub , the abode of guerrilla fighters, leopards, baboons and dassies.

Lekker: Afrikaans, delicious, tasty, nice. A universal term for pleasant things as in the kids' bedtime chant of: "Lekker, lekker shakanaka", meaning , 'good, good, goodnight'.

Maningi: adverb, meaning much or many or strongly.

Muti: medicine, usually but not always of the witchdoctory kind.

Mfazi: A woman of marriageable and childbearing age.

Mfecane: Shona word meaning a scattering, a fugitive people.

Mkubwa: from Swahili I think, big, important, as in bwana mkubwa.

Miombo: thicket, scrubland, low forest.

Mooer: verb , to murder in the figurative sense, to beat up see also donner, I've always assumed, rightly or not, that it was linked to the Afrikaans word moerin meaning a hellish upset.

Mooshie or Mushi: nice, good

Muzungu: A wanderer. Prevalent term for white person right through central and southern Africa. Plural is mazungu, probably first used to describe Portuguese explorers.

Mzee: Swahili word but commonly used throughout Southern Africa, an older man, a grey beard, could be a wise oldie or an old fool, depends on the benignity of your interlocutor. Used interchangeably with Mdala, a Chilapalapa word with the same meaning.

Nyama: meat, usually game.

Nyoka: a snake, a universal warning shout.

Okies or uggies, deriving, I suppose from Afrikaans, outjies : guys, fellers, friends and enemies.

Rondavel: a small round hut with a conical roof in the style of African traditional huts.

Piccies, Pikkies: a Chilapalapa term for kids, applied to white and black. The word has a derogatory association nowadays but back then and there it had a neutral connotation. The PK was the universal Rhodesian term for a lavatory. It stood for *Pikkie's Kaya*, the euphemistic 'little boy's room' or 'kid's room'.

Schelm: pronounced skellum, Afrikaans for rascal , rogue, often addressed to kids, as in a little scamp, but also to criminals of the adult variety.

Shamba: field, a Swahili word.

Siama: Bemba for a natural healer, also known as *sangomas*, they dispensed remedies, pills and potions. Distinct from the malign sinister *indoshi* who laid out curses, spells and all manner of bad voodoo.

Sis or Sus: expression of disgust.

Sjambok: a whip bound in rhino or hippo hide, formerly used for driving oxen, could be a noun or verb, a threat to naughty boys and to any recalcitrant creatures.

Soutie: a potent, insulting Afrikaaner term for white Africans of English ancestry. Literally means 'salty dick', implying that the Anglicised whites keep one foot in Africa and one foot in England with their privates dangling in the oceans between.

Spruit: a water course, a welcome find in the dry veldt.

Sterek: very

Takkies: canvas tennis shoes usually bought from Batas.

Tickey: silver threepenny bit.

Tokoloshe: prevailing evil spirits, sometimes connected to water, primordial goetic entities which retain a power to frighten and to annoy.

Tot siens: farewell in Afrikaans.

Ulendo: A regular two week walkabout in the remote bush areas conducted by colonial district officers. During these journeys villages would be assessed for tax, a census taken, minor disputes would be settled, sick and injured people would get first aid, agricultural advice would be dispensed and rogue wild animals shot. A man wearing a toilet seat worn around his neck had a prized job of running ahead of the party to seek out the next night's camp ground and construct a new toilet base and screen out of branches and woven grass!

U.N.I.P. : United National Independence Party, a nationalist political party that won the 1964 elections and formed the government of Zambia. It became a one-party state until 1991 when its hold over the elections process was at last broken.

Muzungu

Utumbuna & Utuybele: tokoloshe-like spirits which inhabit rocky outcrops in the bush.

Veldschoen: vellies, desert-boot like shoes usually worn with no socks, young Rhodie style.

Voetsak: get lost, F.U.

Vrot: Afrikaans, rotten, putrid.

Whenwes: Jocose South African description of exiled Rhodesians always going on about, "When we lived in Rhodesia…"

Zareba: An improvised stockade for protecting people or enclosing domestic animal, usually made of thorny sticks.

Printed in Great Britain
by Amazon

20165718R00210